COURTFIELD AND THE VAUGHANS

An English Catholic Inheritance

COURTFIELD AND THE VAUGHANS

An English Catholic Inheritance

MARY VAUGHAN

QUILLER PRESS
London

FOR MY CHILDREN

Love ever gives, forgives, outlives,
And ever stands with open hands
And as it lives, it gives,
For this is love's prerogative
To give and give and give.

Anon.

First published 1989 by Quiller Press Ltd
46 Lillie Road, London SW6 1TN

Text copyright © 1989 Mary Vaughan

ISBN 0 870948 35 1

Printed and bound in Great Britain by
Butler & Tanner Ltd, Frome and London

Contents

Foreword

Shortly before the publication of *Courtfield and the Vaughans*, Mary Vaughan died – as she had wished at her much loved home, Glen Wye, Courtfield, Herefordshire – on 13 August 1989.

She had worked long and hard in researching, writing and preparing this family history, and therefore my brothers and I feel it most fitting that this book be considered a continuing tribute to a remarkable woman, who – amongst a number of other not inconsiderable achievements – can probably most significantly be credited with having held the Vaughan family together during her generation. This she accomplished through a mixture of tenacious faith (coupled with the practice of regular prayer), great strength of character and a strong sense of family.

In an effort to keep this family history up-to-date to the time of publication, an epilogue has been included that endeavours to bring in brief mention of today's generation of young Vaughan sons and daughters, all of whom – with one exception – are the late author's grandchildren.

Thomas Vaughan
September 1989

Prologue

'You break your neck getting there, but break your heart leaving,' they used to say of Courtfield in the remote parish of Welsh Bicknor, the home of the Vaughan family since 1563.

Originally called Greenfield, it was changed to Courtfield in the fourteenth century when King Henry V was nursed here after his birth in Monmouth Castle on 9 August 1387. At that time the manor of Welsh Bicknor belonged to Lady Margaret Montague, daughter-in-law of the Earl of Salisbury and mother of the future Earl John de Montague who was beheaded at Cirencester in 1400. Lady Margaret was kinswoman to the royal infant, both being descended from Edward I, and as the baby was delicate (probably what is now known as a 'blue baby'), it was no doubt considered that Welsh Bicknor would be a healthier place than Monmouth to rear him. It is not known how long Henry was at Courtfield but Lady Margaret died in 1395 so probably he would have left there when he was seven or eight – old enough to be able to remember an early childhood among the lovely woods and grounds of this most beautiful peninsula, and his good nurse Joanna Waring to whom he later left an annuity of £20.

In the small Welsh Bicknor parish church there is a recumbent stone effigy of a lady in fourteenth-century dress, with neither a coat-of-arms nor inscription, which must almost certainly be Lady Margaret. Her son, Sir John de Montague, inherited the manor of Welsh Bicknor and later, on the death of his uncle without issue, succeeded to the earldom of Salisbury. He became implicated in a plot to reinstate King Richard II on the throne and was beheaded in 1400. Since he was attainted his property was confiscated by the Crown, but later returned to his descendants and for the next hundred years the family's circumstances fluctuated according to the various treasonable activities of the Montagues.

The last person of this illustrious race mentioned by Dugdale as possessing Welsh Bicknor was Margaret, daughter of the Duke of Clarence and wife of Sir Richard Pole, Lord Montague. After witnessing the imprisonment and execution of her brother the Earl of

Warwick and of her son Henry, Lord Montague, she herself suffered the most brutal beheading in 1539 when she was sixty-nine years old. This was in revenge for the opposition offered to King Henry VIII's religious and matrimonial proceedings by his kinsman, Reginald Cardinal Pole, her youngest son, who had escaped to the Continent. Stoutly maintaining she was no traitor and that the sentence was unjust, she refused to lay her head on the block. She was then manhandled and dragged by her hair while the executioner inflicted horrible wounds until she was finally decapitated. She was the last of the Plantagenets and courageous to the end. Her manor of Welsh Bicknor became forfeited for high treason. In 1540 it was leased to George Bayneham at a yearly rent of £7 7s. 8d. and again leased in 1547 to Thomas Reve and George Cotton, London gentleman, with various other leases to London speculators until, in 1562, it was sold for £800 to John Gwillym of Gillow, Herefordshire, who became the Lord of the Manor of Welsh Bicknor.

This John Gwillym had a lovely daughter and heiress called Sybil who married in 1563 James Vaughan from Llangattock-veibron-Avel. Perhaps they met when James came riding over to buy cattle or on some other agricultural business, spied the fair Sybil and decided that marriage and Welsh Bicknor would suit him. Thus the Vaughans came to Courtfield where through varying fortunes they have remained ever since. James was the eldest son of Thomas and Anne Vaughan of Llanrothal, a family of ancient Welsh lineage who trace their ancestry back to Sir Caradoc (a Knight of the Round Table), Lord of Ferlix, prince of the Country between Severn and Wyne. His wife was Tagay-ap-Vron, daughter of King Palinor, Prince of South Wales, and it is about them that the 'Ballad of the Magic Mantle' relates: the female court of King Arthur being accused of want of chastity and Caradoc's wife implicated in the censure, he felt his honour wounded by the charge. To put her virtue to the test a boy is made to enter the room where the company are assembled and to produce a mantle which cannot be worn, except by a woman of the strictest virtue. Naturally the Queen tries it first, with disastrous results, and so on until it comes to Tegay-ap-Vron's turn.

Ballad of the Magic Mantle

The Queen:
When she had taken the Mantle,
And all was in it cladde,

2

From top to toe it shivered down,
As tho with shears beshradde.

One while it was too long,
Another while too short,
And wrinkled on her shoulders,
In most unseemly sort.

Then it is offered to Sir Kay's wife:
When she had taken the Mantle,
With purpose for to wear,
It shrunk up to her shoulders,
And left her backside bare.

Most embarrassing! Other ladies tried it but
with similar unfortunate results until it
came to Tegay-ap-Vron:
Sir Caradoc called his Lady,
And bade her to come near,
'Come win this Mantle, Lady
And do me credit here'.

The garment fitted her beautifully except
for the tiniest wrinkle about the hem.
Alarmed she hurriedly confessed:
Once I kissed Sir Caradoc
Beneathe the Greenwood tree,
Once I kissed Sir Caradoc's mouth
Before he married me.

· 1 ·

The Fourteenth and Fifteenth Centuries

HARRY OF Monmouth, born 1387, is remembered and regarded in this part of the country as our great national hero. Part of his education was gained at the court of his cousin King Richard II who, according to a contemporary historian (Thomas de Elmham), was greatly impressed with his spirit and understanding, frequently pointed him out and prophetically observed, 'We have heard that our England will produce a prince called Henry, who will be renowned for dignity of manners, splendour of action and military skill, and we conclude infallibly that this is the Henry thus predicted'. Perhaps this assessment was made during his time at Oxford where he studied and impressed great and learned men. He is described as excelling in learning, being fond of songs and musical instruments. Tall, slender and good looking, with small bones but 'of marvellous great strength and swift in running, in so much that he with two other of his lords, without hounds, bow, or other engine, would take a wild bucke or doe in a large parke'.

Henry was well trained in the use of arms and before he was sixteen had distinguished himself by his bravery in the battle of Shrewsbury, and later by his sorties against Owen Glendower whom he defeated in various encounters, and in raids against the Scots from which he returned to London loaded with booty. All this made him popular with the people but his father was not a little jealous and disapproving of stories of his wild escapades with some of his more dissolute companions. However, on the King's death he underwent a most dramatic change with fasting and vigil for three days and nights and fervent prayers for divine assistance in the government of his kingdom.

After his coronation, says Stowe, 'he called unto him all those young lords and gentlemen that were the followers of his young acts, to everyone of whom he gave rich and bounteous gifts, and then commanded that as many as would change their manners as

4

he intended to do, should abide with him in his court, and to all that would persevere in their former light conversation, he gave express commandment upon pain of their heads, never after that day to come into his presence'.

These sudden conversions are not always lasting but in King Henry V's case it is too well authenticated to admit of the smallest doubt. Shakespeare's description sums it up:

> The courses of his youth promis'd it not:
> The breath no sooner left his father's body,
> But that his wildness, mortified in him,
> Seem'd to die too: yea, at that very moment,
> Consideration like an angel came,
> And whipp'd the offending Adam out of him,
> Leaving his body as a paradise,
> To envelop and contain celestial spirits.
> Never was such a sudden scholar made;
> Never came reformation in a flood,
> With such a heady current, scouring faults;
> Nor ever Hydra-headed wilfulness
> So soon did lose his seat and all at once
> As in this King.

It is not generally known that Henry was remarkable for his qualities of justice and humanity and every day after dinner used to spend an hour listening to the petitions of the oppressed which he tried to redress. He condemned the imprisonment of Richard and treated all concerned in his murder as traitors and as an atonement for his father's crimes he ordered his corpse to be magnificently interred in Westminster Abbey among his royal ancestors and himself attended the funeral, declaring 'that he mourned him as freely as if he had been his natural father'.

Henry's military victories against the French and the never-to-be-forgotten battle of Agincourt on 25 October 1415 was the occasion when ancestors of the Vaughan family, Roger Vaughan and his father-in-law David Gam, seeing the King's life in peril, placed themselves between him and the attacking foe thereby saving his life with the loss of their own. In gratitude Henry conferred the honour of knighthood on these brave men as they lay dying on the battlefield.

On 2 June 1420 Henry married Catherine, daughter of Charles King of France, and soon after made a triumphal entry into Paris where he and his lovely Queen Catherine held court at the palace of the Louvre in their coronation robes with their crowns on their heads.

5

But alas, he was not to live long. Taken ill of a fever in the midst of his victorious career in France, he died on 31 August 1422, aged thirty-five, having reigned for ten years with enormous advantage to his country. His son, an infant, became Henry VI under the regency of his uncle the Duke of Gloucester.

Henry was a king loved and respected by his people, his death was mourned by the whole nation, who brought his body home and gave him a magnificent funeral in Westminster Abbey.*

* We take a justifiable pride in the fact that King Henry V was raised here at Courtfield, where he took his first toddler's steps – no doubt with the aid of his good nurse Joanna Waring – and as a little boy played in the lovely grounds and woods of this Welsh manor house and perhaps learnt to ride his pony in the deer park where, 400 years later, Herbert Vaughan (later Cardinal) also rode. We have a charming nineteenth-century oil painting by Dunn of Worcestershire of Herbert as a small boy in the park at Courtfield firmly astride his stout Welsh pony engaged in a contretemps with one of his father's large white chargers. He has lost his hat, but with raised whip is energetically seeing off the unwelcome aggressor. This is a picture I am very fond of and it now hangs in the hall at Glen Wye.

The Sixteenth Century

JAMES AND Sybil were the first Vaughans to live at Courtfield on the lovely Welsh Bicknor Peninsular, in the marches of Wales included in Monmouthshire until it was transferred to Herefordshire by Act of Parliament in 1845. After the conquest of Gwent Welsh Bicknor formed part of the lordship of Monmouth and was held in dower as of the Castle of Monmouth. The name is Saxon for 'a Welsh place' and there seems to have been a church here from very early times (in 1150 the list of churches belonging to St Mary of Monmouth includes the Church of Bickenoure).

The present church of St Margaret's was rebuilt on the ancient site in 1858, with the medieval effigy of Margaret Montague being about the only part that was preserved. A number of old Vaughan tombstones were also removed and brought up to Courtfield where the Vaughans had built their own chapel about 1850. These are carved in stone with crests and coats of arms and can be seen in the crypt under the Courtfield church.

The approach is from the small village of Goodrich with its fine twelfth-century Border castle, up a little winding road on the left flank of Coppit Hill which provides increasingly spectacular views. The first turn gives a beautiful outlook of Kerne bridge with its five grey stone arches spanning the Wye directly above Swan island where these handsome birds optimistically lay their eggs in spite of often having their nests swept away when the river floods – as it can do very quickly from rain in the Welsh mountains. This bridge was not built till about 1840 though it looks older. An Act of Parliament dated 20 May 1825 refers to the benefits that the villagers of Walford and Goodrich and adjacent parishes would derive from the building of a bridge. Its first builder, in 1826, was a Richard Burton of Monmouth who later asked to be released from his contract saying that it would ruin him and his family. This was granted and a David Jones completed the work. Compensation was paid to the Goodrich ferry for loss of trade following the building of the bridge. A toll house was incorporated on the far side which was demolished in 1949.

Those allowed to pass without paying tolls were: royalty, all mails on foot or by coach, soldiers on duty, and anyone carrying stone for repair of the road. Tolls for others were as follows: stage coach, hearse, chariot, gig and whisky (a light gig), 9*d*; every horse or mule laden or unladen but not drawing a wagon, 2*d*; every ass laden or unladen, 1*d*; oxen and cattle, 10*d* a score; pigs, lambs and calves, 5*d* a score; for any person walking, 1*d*.

On this side of the bridge is the picturesque old Flaneford priory founded by the Augustinian Order in 1346 when Goodrich Castle was an important fortress and the ford was hereabouts. It was here at the Goodrich ferry in 1387 that Henry of Bolingbroke, Duke of Lancaster, on his way back to Monmouth, first got news of his son's birth from Joanna Waring the ferryman's daughter. So delighted was he that he straightaway granted Joanna and her family free rights to the ferry forever. What a wonderfully happy scene it must have been and one can imagine the Duke galloping on post-haste for Monmouth six miles away. He was devoted to his wife Mary, a good horsewoman, who often accompanied him on his expeditions. She was a daughter of Humphrey de Bohun, Earl of Hereford. Her sister Eleanor married Thomas of Woodstock, Duke of Gloucester, sixth son of King Edward III. He eventually obtained the earldom of Hereford and the castle of Caldecot.

Lady Margaret Montague was no doubt instrumental in having the baby Prince brought to Courtfield. She was a lady-in-waiting at the court in Monmouth and soon procured a post for Joanna Waring in the nursery where it was noticed how well she and this delicate infant got on. Her Manor at Welsh Bicknor, six miles away, became a little court with Lady Margaret in charge when the Duke and his lady were off on their frequent expeditions.

KING HENRY V's CRADLE

Paragraph from the *Daily Express*, London, Monday 17 February 1908:

> The valuable Braikenridge collection of medieval works of art which was formed early in the nineteenth century by Mr George Weare Braikenridge of Bristol, will be sold at Christie's at the end of this month.
>
> One of its most interesting features is the cradle of Henry V. A

little fourteenth-century carved oak cradle in which the baby Prince is said to have reposed while in the care of Lady Montague, the grand-daughter of Edward I, at Courtfield, near Monmouth. The history of this royal relic can be traced right back to the time when it held the royal baby.

In May 1911, the Right Reverend John S. Vaughan, DD, Bishop of Sebastopolis, wrote to his nephew, Charles:

> My dear Charles,
> I think this record of the famous cradle is worth putting into your box of family treasures. It is well to be able to trace an old relic like this,
>
> Your devoted uncle,
John S. Vaughan

The baby's cradle used to be at Courtfield. Country-made in oak in a somewhat box-like shape, it was slung between short strong posts surmounted by carved wood Falcon finials. It looks as if made by the local carpenter (perhaps from Courtfield oak?). Welsh legend has it that it was given to one of the Prince's nurses and Heath writes that he saw this cradle in the house of the Rev. Mr Ball, rector of Newland in the Forest of Dean about 1800, who said he had inherited it as an heirloom from an ancestor who had been employed as a rocker to the Prince. Subsequently bought by the King for 230 guineas, it is now in the museum at Kensington Palace. There has always been a room in the old part of Courtfield referred to as the Henry V bedroom. There is also a small stone figure of a youth in Tudor dress that used to be in the garden at Courtfield and always known as Henry V.*

In Heath's *Wye Tours* of 1799 he writes:

> Little if anything was before known of Courtfield even though it is immortalised for being the nursery of King Henry V. Who can tread such a spot without feeling their minds warmed from contemplation of the virtues of this magnanimous Prince? He, who with a handful of his countrymen subdued the whole Kingdom of France and forced the weak and pusillanimous Charles to yield him up his title of king and accept peace on such terms as he would deign to offer. A mansion like this should be kept in repair at the Public Expense as a testimony of the nation's gratitude to the memory of such an illustrious Sovereign.

James and Sybil, the first Vaughans to live at Courtfield, had three

---

* We brought this figure to Glen Wye when we came to live here in 1955 and it now stands facing the front door. He wears a flat Tudor hat and sometimes I place my hand on his head, endeavouring to draw courage from it.

sons: Richard, William and Charles. Richard, the eldest, married Eleanor, daughter of Walter Parker of Llanllowel, and their son William married Anne, daughter of Richard Mynors of Treiago, a most romantic old manor house near St Weonards still lived in by the Mynors. Charles, the youngest, is described as of Llanrhyddol and half the manor of Llanfihangel so perhaps he married a damsel down there. William, the second son, inherited Courtfield. He married Jane, the daughter of Richard Clarke of Wellington near Hereford, who eventually became heiress to her father. William seems to have been known as 'of Courtfield' and 'of Clifford Park' which he may have inherited through his wife who was probably a considerable heiress. Their marriage took place about 1570 and they had eight children – five sons and three daughters. William died in 1601 but Jane was still living as a widow at Welsh Bicknor in 1620. She was a member of another prominent Catholic family and is named in the Recusant Rolls from 1592 to 1619.

John, their eldest son, inherited Courtfield and Clifford Park. He was born in 1575. In the state papers he is described as a Royalist and Popish recusant and as such was liable to the confiscation of two-thirds of his property and a monthly fine of £20. In a letter to a friend he says he has had to sell a lot of his land for the sake of Church and king. Their second son is described as William of Wellington, presumably his mother's place. Then there is Richard, and Walter of Welsh Bicknor who must have had a house on the estate – his will is dated 13 January 1631 – and Charles. Of the three daughters, Margaret is the one we know most about, there being a fine carved stone memorial* to her on the wall in Mordiford Church with Vaughan and Brydges coats-of-arms and the following inscription:

> Here lyeth the body of Margaret, daughter of William Vaughan of Courtfield in the County of Monmouth, Gent and the late wife and widow of William Brydges of Upleadon in the Parish of Bosbury in the County of Hereford, Gent, who died at her prayers in the form in which you see her portratured in Langport Court, upon the 14th day of April 1655, aged 80.

It seems likely that Jane as a widow lived with her son Walter and his family either at Baynhams or The Green as they are both described as of Welsh Bicknor. We do not know who Walter married

---

* We have a small framed drawing of this memorial rescued from the attics at Courtfield showing Margaret kneeling on her *prie-dieu*. It now hangs in my bedroom at Glen Wye.

but he had three sons, the eldest being Richard Vaughan of Welsh Bicknor, whose son Walter born 1672 made his course of studies at Saint Omer and went to the English College in Rome on 25 October 1689, being admitted as one of the Pope's scholars. He was there ordained priest on 24 June 1696, but died in Paris in the ensuing October, aged twenty-four.

The severe trials sustained by this family through the course of two centuries, on account of their steadfast adherence to the faith and worship of their forefathers, are written in crimson on the pages of local history. The fines inflicted on them for non-attendance at the Protestant service amounted to many thousands of pounds, and confiscation deprived them of quite half their ancestral lands. For at least two centuries members of this family featured regularly in the lists of recusants, Popish malignants and convicts. Courtfield, by its situation in the remote parish of Welsh Bicknor, became a favourite hunting-ground for priests who were known to seek sanctuary in woods and quarries and disused lime kilns on the estate. Priest hunting* was probably regarded as a good weekend sport by the local Protestant mob. They once hunted a certain Father Richardson for several days through the woods along the Wye Valley but he escaped by hiding in a lime kiln for seven weeks, during which time he is believed to have carved with his penknife the beautiful figure of the hermit – a kneeling monk carved out of a solid block of wood. Allens Grove, a small wood halfway along the back road, was named after a Father Allen who frequently occupied a sandpit there. These priests were fed and succoured by the Vaughans who took them food in the dead of night at great risk to themselves.

The Vaughans stood firmly by their ancient Catholic faith, refusing the easy way out which the majority of old Catholic families accepted. It was enough if Papists stood in the porch of the Protestant church during the sermon, and understandably many Catholics conformed to this extent and this was accepted as a denial of their religion. The stauncher Catholics called this practice schismatic.

The Vaughans would have none of these things. They paid their fines and even suffered imprisonment for the Faith. John, during a term of imprisonment, on a trumped-up charge of treason, translated the whole of Horace's poems into English, preserving the metre of

---

* Priest Hunting. From a speech by J. F. Vaughan on papal aggression, 18 December 1850: 'Those happy times when wolves and priests alike were hunted as wild beasts, and five pounds was the price per head for bagging either live or dead.'

the original.* One of the few families in England who remained Catholic throughout this cruel Parliamentary oppression, they were often greatly helped by their neighbours and friends (not necessarily Catholics) leasing their land and acting for them, otherwise they could not have survived at all.

The Lingen Family Connection

John Vaughan's first wife and the mother of his children, Anne Lingen of Sutton Court, Hereford, came from another important Catholic family, the Lingens having been Sheriffs and MPs since the days of Edward IV. She thus reinforced the Royalist and Papist blood already flowing in the Vaughan veins.

A story of heroism shown by an earlier member of the Lingen family is worth relating. When Constantia Lingen's husband Grimbald was captured by the Moors at Tunis during the Crusades he could only be freed by a 'joint of his wife' as ransom. This valiant lady sent a message by carrier pigeon to the monks at Gloucester for a surgeon to come and amputate her hand which was preserved in salt and wine and shipped abroad to procure Grimbald's release.

The couple were buried together in the village church of Much Cowarne, Herefordshire, where their effigies lay side by side facing each other, and for some centuries pilgrims paid homage to the heroic Constantia until about 140 years ago when fire destroyed the building.

During the Civil War, Sir Henry Lingen of Sutton Court (he may have been a nephew of Anne's), kept a regiment of horse at his own expense and with great gallantry defended Goodrich Castle for the King. Colonel Birch, the Parliamentary leader, succeeded in burning the stables but was unable to capture the Castle until, in the hot summer of 1646, he managed to win the siege by cutting off the water supply. Sir Henry and his men marched out playing a tune known as the 'Lingen Air' which later became popular hereabouts. Brave Sir Henry escaped with his life but was fined £6,342 for his delinquency against Parliament. This must have been an enormous sum for him to find. He appears to have paid it in two lots. The receipt for his first payment is in the possession of Mr Unet of Sutton:-

Received by us Richard Waring and Michael Herring, Treasurers of the Monies to be paid into Goldsmiths Hall, of Sir Henry Lingen of Sutton

---

* We have this, and also his Pardon, a splendid document with the Royal Seal signed by King Charles I.

in this country of Hereford, Knt. the sum of Two Thousand Pounds in part of £6,342 for his first and second being in Warre against the Parliament, and so imposed on him by the Lords and Commons as a fine for his delinquency to the Parliament. We say received this 28th day of May 1649. In part. Richard Waring. Michael Herring.

Sir Henry Lingen hath secured by recognizance for payment of £4,342 being his last payment. Entered 13th November. T. Bayly MH.

Probably the Lingens had to sell all their property in order to pay, as from that time they do not seem to feature any more in the county, although previously they were an important family. In 1799, Heath wrote:

John Lingen, Knight, is mentioned as a Sheriff in the reign of Edward IV (1461) being the twelfth in succession, and other branches of the family have been appointed to the same Honourable office down to the time of Charles I (1625). In the latter situation John Lingen Esq is returned to the County of Hereford (as MP) first of May, ann. 1554. . . . In March 1643, the King being in extreme distress for want of money was lent £20 by Henry Lingen Esq, High Sheriff, as well as Plate: One guilt bowle with a cover, one guilt salte with a cover, one guilt trencher salte, one great silver salte, one caudle cup and cover, one little spoone, and one Tunne. No doubt this cleared out the Lingen silver cupboard and for a certainty was never returned.

3

The Seventeenth Century

THE GRAND OLD MAN OF COURTFIELD

RICHARD VAUGHAN of Courtfield (1600–97), eldest son of John Vaughan and his first wife, Anne, Lord of Welsh Bicknor (Clifford Park seems to have disappeared by 1600), undoubtedly had the longest innings and remained hale and hearty to the end. He well deserved his title of 'the grand old man of Courtfield'.

The muniments record him leasing lands in 1683, 1687 and 1694. We also have an old letter from Clare Wigmore, his sister-in-law, relating to borrowing £100 to which Richard has added a note on the last day of July 1673 in beautiful handwriting with a firm and clear signature. He was born at the end of the Elizabethan era and grew up during James I's reign and through the Carolian and Commonwealth days, sorely tried by the persecution of Catholics when his lands were confiscated and goods and livestock sold over his head. In 1651 Commissioners for Sequestration leased to Philip Nicholas Llansoy for £38. 8s a year 'the Manor of Welsh Bicknor with the mansion house of Courtfield, being the lands of Richard Vaughan, a Papist and Delinquent'. In 1654 Rudhall Gwillim of Whichurch Esq. sold to Charles Herbert of English Newton, Gent, all the goods, cattle and stock at Courtfield. All that was left to Richard was a nominal possession of the freehold, together with income of one-third of the lands.

On 3 October 1631 Richard had married Bridget, daughter of William Wigmore of Lucton, and they had two sons and three daughters. One of the daughters, Clare, entered the English Benedictine nunnery at Pointoise on 14 September 1657 at the age of nineteen. She died on 10 November 1687 and her mortuary notice says, 'Through the esteem the Community had for her solid virtues she was made Mistress of the Novices, whom she carefully trained in the true spirit of religion, leading them by example as well as advice.'

Two of Richard Vaughan's daughters seem to have become nuns: Clare, already mentioned, and in a letter to Teresa Vaughan from a nun at Cocken Hall, dated 14 February 1829, we have a description of Sister Mary of St Joseph, called in the world Miss Mary Vaughan. She was a native of Monmouth and daughter of Richard Vaughan Esq and his wife Bridget, the daughter of William Wigmore Esq:

> This dear sister made her holy Profession on 27th May in the year 1649. Being 17 years of age, she was the first nun professed in our Convent. The Convent was founded in the year 1648. Her religious parents perceiving the early inclination of their child to piety and devotion, endeavoured by a careful education to cherish those seeds of divine grace which in the course of her life would grow up into many fruitful plants of all Christian virtue and perfection.

Mary was a delicate child and her father did not want her to go to a convent but was eventually overcome by her importunities and sent her to the English Benedictines at Ghent where she arrived with two noble ladies, the Marquess of Worcester's daughters. But her heart was set on becoming a Carmelite and with her father's consent she went to Antwerp and joined the English Teresian Carmelites. She seems to have been a paragon of all the virtues and for thirty years presided over the choir. About six months before she died she developed a strong sweet smell, like musk but more agreeable. All her clothes and her choir stall had the same sweet smell. She died in the odour of sanctity on 3 March 1709 aged seventy-eight, after sixty-one years in religion. A niece of hers, Miss Teresa Griffin, also entered religion as a Carmelite and died on 12 October 1742 aged sixty-four.

Richard seems to have taken trouble over the education of his children and was continually paying fines. In 1637 a statement of 'Fines paid to the King for the Children's Worship with £24 charge to make the composition £528 6s 8d', a lot of money in those days.

His brother-in-law, John Jones of Dingestow, wrote in 1642 to warn Richard of a 'Commission come down from the Lord Keeper and Mr Pymme to the Sheriffs and Justices to enquire of the lands and goods of Recusants, which is to be executed on Tuesday next at Caerleon. The warrants are already out, all of which I thought good to give you notice of.' Such staunch friends must have been of inestimable value and in many cases Protestant neighbours would take over the lands of Catholics, thereby helping them to survive. Marshall Bridges of Tiberton, a relation, and Thomas Cocks of Castle Ditch, Eastnor, frequently rendered this invaluable service to the Vaughans of Courtfield during the seventeenth and eighteenth centuries.

On one occasion a priest-hunting mob broke into the house and tied old Richard to his bedpost while they ransacked and plundered the place and even drove the deer out of the park. They didn't find any priests, who were probably holed up in sand pits in the woods, but they must have angered Richard enormously. We have a good seventeenth-century oil painting of him in which he looks extremely tough – broad forehead, straight nose and just a hint of humour in his brown eyes; he must have needed it in the times in which he lived. There is a story of him visiting his son John who lived in Huntsham but, after many years of marriage, was still childless, and his father frequently railed him on the subject. Coming to a gate on their walk old Richard, then seventy-five, suggested they vault it. John attempted but did not succeed, whereupon Richard nimbly vaulted over, exclaiming, 'as I have cleared the gate for you, so I believe I must e'en provide you with an heir'. Soon after he married for the second time; his bride was Agatha Berrington of Little Malvern Court and the desired heir was born in 1676. This son, also called John, eventually inherited from his half-brother and so carried on the family.

There were also two daughters of this marriage – another Mary, and Theresa – so Richard really does seem to have been the Grand Old Man of Courtfield! He was buried at Welsh Bicknor and his tombstone reads, 'Here resteth ye body of Richard Vaughan esq, who departed this life the 17th of May, Anno Salutis 1697, Aged 97. Here also ye body of his youngest son, John Vaughan, who became his sole Heir. He died November 27th 1754 in ye 78th year of his age.'*

Richard, born in 1600, three years before the end of Elizabeth I's reign, would have been brought up in a Tudor house. Alas there are no pictures of what Courtfield looked like then, though Heath, writing in 1796, describes a somewhat dilapidated house approached through a short paved court, walled on each side and fronted with iron gates of considerable height above which was a rather broken Vaughan coat of arms. He had expected a much grander establishment and was disappointed, yet remarked that the garden,

> though in the fashion of former years and running into disorder, has claim to attention, for its beautiful situation and remnants of ancient grandeur. It is divided by and intersected with fine stone terraces,

* These tombstones and others were brought from Welsh Bicknor church when the present Catholic church was built at Courtfield about 1850 and are now in the vault.

shaded with yew hedges now in luxuriant wildness, the growth of ages past, but I suppose when attended to were cut into showy peacocks with spreading trains and other fanciful ornaments of that day. Flights of steps, tiresome for their numbers, conduct us to the upper and lower part of it, but the former is a mere wilderness. On the south side is a beautiful terrace, looking down to the Wye and over the works at Lydbrook, but the view is more pleasing than extensive.

At that time Lydbrook was a busy wharf, with horses and carts pulling in small vessels shipping coal to Hereford and other places. Heath continued:

On the North side of the house and on an eminence in the park, stands a high parapet wall, with gothic-shaped arches, which when viewed from the river has the appearance of a ruin. The effect was, till within these few years, considerably increased, by some lofty walnut trees which grew about it – but that kind of wood being valuable, the axe has deprived them of their honours. A small room adjoins behind called the Hermit's Cell, in which was placed the figure of an old man, with a flowing beard, kneeling, his hands in the attitude of prayer; but it has been removed from hence into the house where it remains.

Before I visited this place, I had filled my mind with ideas of its magnificence, similar to romance. On entering by a deep stone gateway, over which was placed the arms of England, with extensive passages and lofty walls, and conducted by wide and extensive oak stairs to bedrooms hung with ancient tapestry, whose figures represented subjects from Holy Writ; but if in this (as well as in other occurrences in life) I kept in mind the Poet's beatitude – Blessed is he that expects nothing, for he shall not be disappointed – I should not have been surprised on my arrival. For instead of the images my fancy had created, I found a neat, desirable mansion, which the property of the heir would easily improve to the comforts of modern life. All that is objectionable is the want of a good carriage road to it, which it would be difficult to form. I suppose Mr Vaughan's father or grandfather took down the ancient wainscot of the rooms and gave them their modern dress – white paint not being used for that purpose in Henry's time.

Heath's imagination was fired by the circumstances of Courtfield having been the nursery of King Henry V. He appears to have visited it by boat on his trip down the Wye. He writes, 'it occupies a commanding eminence on the right bank of the river (but the approach is of easy access), falling down in a fine slope to the water's edge'. He mentions that the ground floor has nothing of interest except some portraits of Mr Vaughan's family and of Mr Jones of Llanarth. He also mentions the chapel and the curious fact that in the passage leading to it are two full-length figures of dead religious 'which have

17

some merit though unpleasant subjects to look at'. Could they have been Richard's two nun daughters?

'The Chapel is in good order and is used by neighbouring Catholics when Mass is said there.' This is really the best account we have of the earlier house over 100 years after Richard, whose long life spanned six reigns and almost the entire Stuart period. Both his wives were fairly local and of good Catholic families. No doubt he kept as low a profile as possible and probably did not move much from Monmouthshire. Riding would have been his chief means of getting about and a boat on the Wye could have taken him to Huntsham when his son John was living there, perhaps on the occasion of the famous leap! The defence and eventual capture of Goodrich Castle about three miles distant would have been of great interest, as he was related to the Lingens through his mother, and of course stories of the appalling treatment of the Swift family of Goodrich by the Earl of Stamford in October 1642 must have shocked the parish.

His son John's marriage in 1659 (see page 21) must have been a happy occasion for Richard as it united two of Herefordshire's oldest families and much increased the property. Another important landmark would have been his second marriage and siring a son and heir at the ripe old age of seventy-six. As he died in 1697 he just missed this son's first marriage to Catherine, daughter of Sir John Curzon, in 1698.

As well as many family affairs to attend to during his long life, and the everlasting Recusant fines and conflicts he had to cope with, Richard would have had problems of a different nature relating to farming, the weather, and the inaccessibility of Courtfield. Through long dark winters keeping his house and family warm was a preoccupation and they would have made their own candles and had games and singing in the evenings. Religion being the dominating influence of their lives, almost certainly they would have spent a great deal of time in prayer and very likely Richard gathered the entire household together at least once a day for worship. From the family muniments it is evident that he had much business relating to leasing and selling of farms and outlying properties, probably to circumvent the penal laws.

The fact that Richard and his brother Thomas had their portraits painted places them as fashionable members of society; they probably hunted and shot and maybe Richard was fond of fishing for salmon in the Wye which bounded his Welsh Bicknor estate. In 1641 he leased the Byfield and Osier bed to one Henry Morgan of Ruardean, basket-maker, for 'one covered white basket and two green baskets yearly'.

News of the stirring events in the outside world would have trickled through: the execution of his King, Charles I, in 1649 – Cromwell and the Protectorate – the Battle of Worcester and Charles II's defeat in 1651 – the Restoration in 1660 and the reign of the Merry Monarch when England again breathed more freely – the Dutch wars – the dreaded Plague during the hot summer of 1665 when thousands of Londoners died and the people fled into the country – then the Great Fire in 1666 which ended the plague but burnt half the town, including old St Paul's Cathedral and eighty-four churches, but had the merit of clearing a lot of slumland and making room for the superb architecture of Sir Christopher Wren.*

Catholics were treated with great ferocity during Richard's life-time. One extreme example was the appalling ordeal of Blessed John Kemble, a local priest, who, when old and ill, was forced to make the long journey to London strapped to his horse and facing backwards, and was finally executed on 22 August 1679 for the crime of professing 'the old Roman Catholic religion'. The year 1678 marked the Titus Oates plot in which my kinsman, Oliver Plunkett, Archbishop of Armagh, was falsely implicated, imprisoned in Newgate, and hung, drawn and quartered at Tyburn on 11 July 1681, thus becoming the last of the English martyrs. No doubt Richard, along with other Papists of his day, was saddened by this horrible murder of a great and good man, but he could not have foreseen that 300 years later Oliver Plunkett would be canonised in Rome by Pope Paul VI before a congregation of about 200,000 in St Peter's Square.**

Saint of the Severed Isle
(St Oliver Plunkett, canonised 1975)

> Betrayed was he,
> His own compatriots turned Iscariot! –
> Irish Iscariots who touched,
> With pointed fingers of untruth,

* It was his opportunity and he grasped it with both hands, enriching us with London's lovely city churches and his greatest work, the new St Paul's. Sir Christopher Wren said, 'I am going to dine with some men. If anybody calls, say I am designing St Paul's' – Edmund Clerihew Bentley.
** My son Oliver and I attended this memorable and beautiful ceremony on 12 October 1975.

That inexorable wheel of treachery,
To be hanged, drawn and quartered,
Fashion of his day.

Earlier had he been a scholar,
But a graduate first in love of God and Man,
Archbishop he, leader, guide – exemplary;
Yet a man so poor he'd seen,
Through the broken thatch of his shelter,
The stare of those island's cold stars,
A fugitive, the time of testing come,
No hireling he,
But a true son.

His own Gethsemane he found to be,
Shouldered by the Christ,
And calm was he,
As a cowled and cloistered monk,
Forgiveness his matins,
Tyburn his monastery:-
At final call,
'Deo Gratias' said he,
That particular ignominy
His entry into joy.

Fay Clayton (New Zealand)

Charles II died in 1685, then followed by the brief reign of James II and, in 1688, that of William and Mary. By then Richard had lived through six reigns and apparently was still hale and hearty. He may have been interested in James' defeat at the Battle of the Boyne in 1690 and the Massacre of Glencoe in 1692. Of course he would have heard of America, the Pilgrim Fathers and the founding of the New World, but this splendid old patriarch on the sidelines of life in Welsh Bicknor stuck to his Monmouthshire roots and was staunch and true to his Faith, his King – and Courtfield. After all, *Duw-a-Digon*, the family's Welsh motto, means 'God is enough'.

In 1627 Richard's younger brother Thomas* was ordained abroad by the famous Dr Giffard, Archbishop of Rheims and Primate of France. He was sent on the perilous English mission and is said to have died of ill usage on board ship at Cardiff in 1650. It seems that

---

* We owned a nice portrait of him, painted in the Lely manner, which shows a good-looking young man in a yellow coat and full-bottom wig. It unfortunately got left behind when we moved from Courtfield in 1950 and is now in the possession of the Mill Hill Fathers.

the Vaughans had a love of God and serving the Church from a long way back which reached its apogee in the nineteenth century with John and Eliza's amazing family (see Chapter 5).

JOHN VAUGHAN OF HUNTSHAM

We do not know why Richard's eldest son, also Richard, relinquished his inheritance to his brother John, born in 1633. Perhaps he fell out with his father, was considered unsuitable or simply didn't want the place. Whatever the circumstances, he seems to have been still living in 1675. Of the daughters, as we know, Clare became a Benedictine nun, Mary a Carmelite and Theresa married Joseph Griffin of Monmouthshire. John, described as John Vaughan of Huntsham, was presumably his father's heir for the time being but as he was childless Richard had to remedy this (see pages 16, 18).

John had married when he was twenty-six Mary Vaughan of Ruardean and Over Ross on 7 September 1659. She was of a different family, being descended from a twelfth-century chieftain Moreiddig Warwin and bore his arms, Sable, three Saxon's Heads proper. Her mother was a daughter of Sir William Pitt of Strathfieldsaye and had been twice widowed – first from John Rudhall of Herefordshire and secondly from Sir Alexander Cholke of Shalbourne, Wiltshire. Her third husband was John Vaughan of Ruardean and Over Ross, son of Vaughan of Cleiro and Kinnersley in North Herefordshire and of Dame Joan, daughter and sole heiress of Thomas Baynham. This marriage brought a lot of property into the family. Perhaps the 50,000 acres mentioned in Father Martinadale's life of Bernard Vaughan dates from then, but as there were no children it eventually passed to John's half-brother, also John, born in 1676.

John and Mary lived at Huntsham Court,* a strongly built old manor house about four miles from Courtfield. It has a beautiful columned seventeenth-century porch and an interesting old front door with a curious locking device. A flight of stone steps from the porch to a flagged path enclosed by walls topped with ancient urns which leads on through herbaceous borders to an iron gate between

---

* Where my son Richard now lives and farms. He and his wife Susan have done a lot of sympathetic restoration, taking down walls – discovering in the process an enormous open stone fireplace in the dining-hall behind a hideous modern grate – and generally putting this lovely old house back to what it may have been like when John and Mary lived there (with, I'm glad to say, the addition of good modern central heating!).

ball-capped pillars to a parapet above the road where one can enjoy a beautiful view of some of the finest land in Herefordshire. More steps lead down to the road which may have been used in old coaching days, perhaps when John and Mary set off on the steep way through the forest on a visit to their Ruardean relations. There was no bridge at Huntsham in those days, but various ferries would have enabled them to cross the Wye and they probably used the river for visits to the important town of Monmouth.

Huntsham formally belonged to the Drew family and was probably bought for John and Mary on their marriage. It lay on a bend of the river and comprised about 400 acres of nice flat land with the hill behind running up to the Forest of Dean and the world-famed beauty spot of Symonds Yat. Originally a township consisting of a large farm, an inn and a few cottages, the post box still there is no doubt a relic of this. In 1186 there was a chapel belonging to the Priory of Monmouth. The early spelling 'Honson' may have derived from Huns-ham, meaning the 'Hamlet of the foreigners', indicating that Teutonic invaders lived here with the conqueror Godric. The remains of a large Roman villa were uncovered by the Woolhope Club in 1960. A small skillet spoon found in a kitchen culvert dating from about the third century and some coins of that period are now in Hereford Museum.

Very much earlier is the gigantic 'Queen's stone' in a field near the river, standing 7 feet high with many deep manmade grooves carved in the circumference (runnels for the victims' blood?). It is thought to be a sacrificial Druid stone dating from 4000–3000 BC, and bears some resemblance to the Stonehenge group. Mr Drew once tried with a team of horses to pull it out, without success. Apparently it is buried 8 feet in the ground and his workmen, probably superstitious, rightly considered it best left alone.

In his will of 1717 John left directions for his body to be carried by water and interred in the Church of Welsh Bicknor, in or near the grave of his late wife. Mary had died on 14 September 1717 and her tombstone is inscribed:

> Here lyeth ye Body of Mary Vaughan, eldest daughter to John Vaughan of Upper Ross of ye Vaughans of Ruardean, and of Lady Mary Cholke, his wife. She married John Vaughan of Huntsham eldest son of Richard Vaughan of Courtfield and dyed in ye 69th year of her age, full of good works. Ye second fit of ye Palsie oppressed her mild heart and carried hence to a better life, a soul entirely dear to God. 14th September Ano .D. 1717 Requiescat in Pace.

John's tombstone reads:

> Here lyes the body of John Vaughan Esq of Huntsham. Eldest son of
> Richard Vaughan of Courtfield. He dyed ye 27 of March in ye year of
> Grace 1721 and 88 year of his age. Full of years and hopes of a future
> Resurrection. Requiescat in Pace.

What a dear pair they sound. Perhaps, like many childless couples,
they were devoted to each other, and fulfilled, Mary pursuing her
good works and John happily farming.

The Baynham Family Connection

Mary Vaughan's paternal grandmother, Dame Joan, appears to
have been a most redoubtable character. She was the daughter
and heiress of Thomas Baynham who was lord of the manors of
Ruardean, Mitchel Dean, Clowerwall, Abenhall, Noxon and Hatheways Court all in Gloucestershire. He was also High Sheriff from
1582 to 1602, so he was a man of considerable substance. Thomas
married Mary Winter of Lydney from another ardent Catholic and
Royalist family, related to the Worcestershire Winters (Robert and
Thomas of the Gunpowder Plot), and also to the Throckmortons.
He died on 12 October 1611. Joan's grandfather, Sir William Winter,
was Vice-Admiral of the Fleet which played a large part in the defeat
of the Spanish Armada by an intrepid attack off Dunkirk. He built
a more splendid mansion which he called White Cross House – an
allusion to his post as Admiral of the White. His grandson burnt it to
the ground rather than let it fall into the hands of Cromwell's troops.
The Winter estates were forfeited in 1645.

Thomas Baynham's mother, Dame Joan's grandmother, was Cecily
Gage of the Gage family* of Firle, also a notable recusant family. The
Baynhams had interests in the Forest of Dean and ironworks in the
area. On both sides therefore Joan came from staunch and prominent
recusant and Catholic families.

Joan, who was baptized in 1585, married John Vaughan of Cleiro
and Kinnersley, son of Roger Vaughan of Radnor and North Herefordshire, but he died young in 1619 and left her to survive him for
more than sixty years. She figures regularly in the Recusant Rolls
from 1619 to 1681. The acquittances for her fines during this long

---

* About 200 years later William Michael Vaughan married as his second wife
the widow of Sir Thomas Gage. These Gages were the propagators of the
greengage, which the botanist Sir William Gage (1777–1864) brought from
France.

period are preserved among the Courtfield muniments. An illustration is 'the Acquittance in 1631 of the Sheriffs of Gloucestershire and Herefordshire for £66. 13s 4d, one year's farm of the manors of Abenhall, Ruardean, Hatheways, Netherley, Blideslow, Nash, Mitchel Dean, Little Dean, etc. in County Gloucestershire and divers lands in County Herefordshire, parcel of the lands of Dame Joan Vaughan, widow, a recusant; which lands are in the hands of Thomas Wigmore and Samuel Aubrey, esquires'.

In 1620 this valiant lady paid £300 in fines for her Cleiro estate alone and in 1625 they amounted to £326. 6s 8d for the year. The fines extracted from Catholics were a double land-tax and £20 a month for non-attendance at Protestant worship. Catholics had become the milch cows of the state. Owning so much property, Joan obviously needed a steward and at one time employed a Father John Broughton. For this she was imprisoned in 1641 in Gloucester gaol on a treasonable charge of harbouring a priest. Her pardon, signed by King Charles I, is preserved among the Courtfield muniments.

In 1643 the Recusant Roll for the Gloucester parish of Ruardean names Joan Vaughan, widow; Baynham Vaughan Esq. and his wife (Joan's eldest son who married Elizabeth, daughter of Sir Henry Guildford, Knt. of Hemstead, Kent); John Vaughan, Gent, Thomas Vaughan, Gent, and Roger Vaughan, Gent, with Anthony Greeninge, servant of the said Joan Vaughan.

Joan's third son, John, inherited her Ruardean and Over Ross property which his daughter Mary brought eventually on her marriage to John of Huntsham and later the Cleiro estates etc. came to the Vaughans of Courtfield.

The reason we had so many of Dame Joan's papers here (now in Aberystwyth National Library of Wales for safekeeping) may be that during her long widowhood she was happier among her Gloucestershire friends and neighbours – the Baynhams and Courtfield Vaughans must have always known each other – and she may have enjoyed staying with her granddaughter at Huntsham. Cleiro, forty miles away in Radnorshire, may not have been so friendly without her husband.

· 4 ·

The Eighteenth Century

WHEN Richard died in 1697 he was succeeded by the son of his old age, John Vaughan, born when he was seventy-six from his second marriage the previous year with Agatha, daughter of John Berrington Esq. of Cowarne (see the Recusant Rolls of 1679–83) and later of Little Malvern Court. This John was born on 24 April 1676 at 6.45am so would have just come of age before his father's death. He inherited all the Welsh Bicknor property, also the manors of Ruardean, Cleiro, etc. from his half-brother John of Huntsham. His first marriage in 1698 was to Catherine, daughter of Sir John Curzon of Waterperry, Oxfordshire. They had a daughter, Mary, born on 6 October 1699, who married Roland Bartlett of Hill End, Worcestershire on 23 November 1723 and died on 11 May 1727. John married secondly, on 24 July 1705, his kinswoman in the paternal line Elizabeth, daughter of Philip Jones (Herbert) of Llanarth Court, Monmouthshire. Both Catherine and Mary died in childbirth.

The charming pair of pastel portraits of John and Elizabeth that we have show them as a good-looking, elegant couple. She was twenty-four on their marriage and John nine years older. They had four sons and one daughter: John, born in 1707; Richard, 12 May 1708; Philip born on 11 November 1715 who died young in 1734; and William, born on 8 December 1716. Their only daughter, Theresa, born in 1713, married Edward Weld of Lulworth, Dorset on 15 October 1740 and started the fashion for marriage between Vaughans and Welds – hence the expression 'welded together'.

Catholic life at this time was not the perpetual martyrdom of the era of Titus Oates or the reign of William of Orange, for the very ferocity of the newest penal code had rendered its strict enforcement impracticable. It was now once more possible for a Catholic country gentleman to live in peace with his neighbours and call his soul his own. In 1712, following the custom of the larger landowners, Mr Vaughan obtained from the Chief Ranger a licence to hunt and shoot in the Forest of Dean (except red and fallow deer). These licences feature in the muniments of 1716, 1729 and 1741, 'to hunt, hawk, course, set, shoot and fish in the Forest of Dean with two or three persons in his company'. It must have been very pleasant for John and his sons to go on hunting and shooting expeditions in this lovely forest just across the valley from Courtfield and it seems he must have been popular. As evidence of this, we have a record of a remarkable grant made on 15 February 1731 by a Jury of Free Miners of Dean Forest to John Vaughan of Courtfield and his heirs and assigns for ever, of 'liberty to send for and carry away from the said mines, all such coals as he and they shall from time to time have occasion for, to be used at Courtfield aforesaid, any law, order or custom whatsoever to the contrary notwithstanding'.

This certainly was a handsome present and when the river was fordable in summer time the wagon and horses would go down Boat Lane and across the Wye at Lydbrook and up into the forest to bring the coal to Courtfield. This grant was rescinded only in 1938.

THE JACOBITE BROTHERS

From John and Elizabeth's union sprang two of the most romantic members of this quixotic family: Richard and William Vaughan, the fiercely Jacobite brothers who tried to persuade Prince Charles to march to London through the principality where they thought Celtic sympathisers would rally to his standard; but in this they were overruled by the Highland chiefs with the subsequent disaster at Culloden. Their father and their step-uncle John had both refused to take the oath to George I, which no doubt contributed to these spirited young men's resolve to back Bonnie Prince Charlie in his attempt to regain the throne.

Only a very few Welsh gentlemen went to join the Prince in Lancashire, but Richard and William were among them. The following story is told by Lord Elcho:

> Mr Morgan, [David Morgan of Coed-y-Goras] an English gentleman then came up to William Vaughan who was riding with the Life Guards and after saluting him said 'Damn me, Vaughan, they are going to Scotland'. Mr Vaughan replied 'Wherever they go, I am

determined now that I have joined them to go along with them', upon which Mr Morgan said 'I had rather be hanged than go to Scotland to starve'. Mr Morgan was hanged (on Kensington Common in 1746) and Mr Vaughan is an officer in Spain.

Richard became deeply involved in the Stuart cause and made frequent journeys between Madrid, Rome, and Paris where his brother William joined him prior to the 1745 rebellion. They must have become personal friends of Prince Charles who, after the disaster of Culloden, gave them his pistols on the field of battle – who knows, they may have saved his life as their valiant forebears had saved Henry V at Agincourt.

After the disaster of Culloden in 1746, where they fought in the Duke of Perth's division, both brothers were outlawed and their property seized; as a further disgrace, Richard and William were of the half-dozen Englishmen who had the distinction to be excluded from the general pardon of June 1747. They fled to Spain, to join the Army of his Most Catholic Majesty, Philip V – which seems to have suited them: Richard became a cavalry officer and William in particular rose to high rank (see pages 29–31). Before leaving the country Richard and William stopped at Lulworth, Dorset, to see their sister, Theresa Weld, and with her they left for safe keeping the beautiful pair of pistols given to them by Bonnie Prince Charlie.*

The Spanish Bride

Tradition has it that the Fords of Munster, exiled from Ireland after the Battle of the Boyne, had been well known to the Vaughans of Courtfield and in each succeeding generation one at least of the Courtfield sons had been over to Spain. The Fords too were powerful supporters of the Stuarts and pledged to help their cause. It was inevitable that both Jacobite families should become close due to their shared Spanish connections. In 1736–7, in fact, Richard, while staying with General Fuord (Ford) in Madrid, fell in love with his beautiful daughter, Doña Francisca Fuort y Magueire. They married and he brought her over to Courtfield in the autumn of 1736. As they approached Courtfield his wife exclaimed at the beauty of its

---

* Mary Noyes once showed them to me when I was visiting her in the Isle of Wight in 1950. She obviously regarded them as great treasures and mentioned that she had thoughts of giving them back to my husband. Her first husband was a Weld of Lulworth and she had them with the Weld property on his death.

surroundings: 'It is Paradise. Your description had not prepared me for such loveliness.' Richard answered, 'To me it is the fairest spot on earth: but when one loves a place as I do this, one is apt to overrate it.'

Richard's marriage had at first alarmed his parents, who feared his connection with the exiled Fords could do them no good – and it is quite possible that this was one reason for the brothers' exclusion from the general pardon of 1747. But the señora's grace and beauty and her cheerful, happy nature soon won their love, and made her a general favourite with tenants and cottagers on the estate. Her good influence on Courtfield was sadly missed when, for political reasons, they had to return to Spain in the spring of 1737.

This marriage of Richard's with his señora also brought interesting Irish blood into the family. In a letter written in Spanish, dated 13 May 1777, from Señora Vaughan to her son William and addressed, 'For Mr William Vaughan of Courtfield, Near Monmouth, England', she says that her health is bad and fears she will not see him again. Also his father is five leagues away with his regiment (probably the Dragones de Edinburgo) and his fortunes are not flourishing. She continues:

> In case God should call me, or should deprive me of the power to write to you, as I am the last surviving daughter and have lost all hope of ever seeing you, then, for my part if I die, and for yours if you have no wish, I desire, Billy of my heart, to tell you who your mother is, in case you should happen at any time wish to answer the question. Although I am unfortunate and poor, I desire you to know that your grandfather was from the county of Munster, his surname was Ford y MacMahon – distinguished people. Your grandmother was from Ulster; her surname was MacGuire y O'Neill, her Christian name Catherine, and your grandfather's William. Unfortunately for me they lost the papers (like everything else) in the wars of Philip the Fifth, but although I have no papers, I know as much as anybody can . . . And so, son of my heart, I beg you for the love of God, not to forget your poor sister and, if I die, to shelter and look after her like a brother, since she is without protection save God's and yours. She embraces you affectionately as also your wife feeling deeply her misfortune in having a brother whom she does not know. And so, my Billy, imparting to you my blessing, as also to your wife and all your generation, that Heaven may prosper you for many years; and commending myself to God, that He may give me what is best for my soul – which is the chief thing – whom I pray to give you prudence in all things, and grace to serve Him and love Him; and

embracing you from my heart, my blessing and God's be with you and yours.

What a touching and beautiful letter and what a truly religious, loving and valiant woman the Señora appears. But what of her husband? Was he perhaps not much help to his family? He was a soldier and she may have got used to him being away a lot. If she was still living when Francesca, the only surviving daughter, married the Irish Colonel Count Kilmallock, she must have been pleased.

The Irish ancestry Senora Vaughan gives – Ford, MacGuire, Mac-Mahon and O'Neill – includes the most illustrious families, who were probably officers in the army of King James II who on the final defeat of the Jacobite forces at the Battle of the Boyne in 1690 fled to Spain, where there appear to have been a number of Irishmen and Irish regiments – Regimento de Hibernia, Regimento de Ultonia (Ulster) etc. – the Wild Geese, in fact.

William Vaughan, on Prince Charles' recommendation, was admitted to the Hibernia regiment as Lieutenant Colonel and served with this for twenty-nine years. One of his first duties, early in 1747, was to accompany the Prince on his journey from Paris to Madrid.

In the family papers at Glen Wye, we have kept the following:

The Directors   24th June 1987
of the General Archives
of Simancas

John Mac-Crohon Esq

My dear sir of my distinguished consideration,
It is due to my long experience in these matters that has enabled me to find out for you the antecedants of William Vaughan, which I have the pleasure of forwarding to you.
   I have the honour to remain, My Dear Sir,
Your Obedient Servant,
Claudio Perez y Gredilla.

On the one side of the sheet have been noted all William's services and on the other side notice has been taken of the title of Field Marshal, and various minor details.

In the pages of the services of the year 1765 there is a note which states, concerning William Vaughan, 'He is an Official full of recommendation and worthy of honour from His Majesty'. This comes from War Ledger 2592.

In the General Administration of the Treasury, Inventory Ledger 18, there is an account of the sums which the Grand Treasury will pay him and it says, 'For the royal title of October 26th, 1777, His Majesty granted to William Vaughan, Colonel of the Hibernian regiment of Infantry the title of Field Marshall of the royal armies with a salary of 500 crowns (escudos) when on active service and 250 crowns monthly when in the barracks'. In the certificate of the paymaster of Andalusia of 1 December 1778, this pay ceases from that Treasury on 1 January 1779 for the expedition of Buenos Aires and that they will pay him until his embarkation at Cadiz. By Royal Command of 29 March 1780, he was ordered to serve in the troops under the command of Don Victorio de Navia.

In the Rewards of War, the Indies and Lands, Ledger 61 of the Direction of the Treasury – Inventory 2 – there is noted the title of Field Marshal as mentioned above in the account of the Grand Treasury. Here, in 1775, is 'Colonel William Vaughan, aged fifty-nine years, country England, position gentleman, health good', and his services according to the following particulars:

Dates of Entry in the various ranks				Times of service and the length of time in each rank			
Pos. in army	*Day*	*Month*	*Yr*	*Pos. in army*	*Yrs*	*Months*	*Days*
Lieut-Col	1	Mar	1747	Lieut-Col	15	2	20
Colonel	20	May	1762	Colonel		10	14
Lieut-Col	3	Apr	1763	Leiut-Col	7	–	8
Colonel	11	Apr	1770	Colonel	3	8	16
Brigadier	26	Dec	1773	Brigadier	2	6	4

Total until the end of June 1776: 29 years, 4 months.

Regiments in which he served

In addition to the above named as Lieutenant-Colonel in the Manchester regiment in Scotland and in the Army of Charles, Prince of Wales.

Campaigns and battles in which he took part

The whole of the last campaign in Portugal, in Scotland, those of '45 and '46, he took a part in all the battles of these wars. He accompanied His Majesty to the Court of Madrid, the King retained him in his service with the same rank. He fought in the battle of Argel, July 8th in which he was seriously wounded in the chest. Terence Fitzpatrick.

Information of the Inspector	*Notes on the Colonel*
This Brigadier is on account of his bravery, conduct and zeal recommended to the favour of the King, and worthy to be promoted.	Bravery: Application: Ability: Conduct: Condition:

General Archives of Simancas – Secretary of War, Ledger 2593.

It is thought that William died on the expedition to Buenos Aires in 1779. In fact, neither brother was to return to the home they loved so well: Richard died at Barcelona in 1795.

WILLIAM VAUGHAN INHERITS

Francesca's blessing (see her letter, page 28) seems to have bene-fited her son William and his family. He returned to Courtfield well before his father Richard's death in Spain, married an English Lady and retrieved his ancestral lands. How exciting his 'first' visit to Welsh Bicknor must have been – meeting his relations, Uncle John and Catherine, still living at Courtfield, the Joneses at Llanarth and all the Herefordshire neighbours, who must have been curious to meet this half-Spanish great-grandson of old Richard. William would then have been in his early twenties. We still have his little old vellum notebook written in Spanish and English. An entry dated 25 April 1763 reads: 'If it is God's will to call me to Himself before I am settled, I beg of my worthy Uncle being the last favour he ever shall do for me to pay sixty pounds to my cousin Billy Jones at Clytha for money that has been so good to get for me to supply my poor Mother when my Father was at the Havanah.' Dear William! He sounds so like his mother and was obviously a good and devoted son and was probably still learning to speak and write English! A number of entries have to do with engaging staff, lending and borrowing money: 'I had of Mr Webb of the Kings Head in Monmouth ten guineas at Hereford musick meeting this day being the 16th of September 1764. Paid.' There are records of the distance from Courtfield to London and the route travelled, and to various other places. Also recipes for sick dogs and humans and even one for Madame de Pompadour's tooth powder. 'One ounce of myrr, one ounce of Cole Almanac, one ounce of Dragon's Blood! The whole to be pulverised together in a mortar as fine as possible.'

William married, on 15 April 1767, Frances, daughter of John Turner Esquire of Hampstead, and obtained restoration of the main portion of his estates as heir to his Uncle John, who had not been involved in the Jacobite rebellion. He had married on 10 August 1749 Catherine, daughter of James Cornewall of Buckland, Hereford. They had no children, and probably lived quietly at Courtfield.

In 1764–5 John Vaughan contracted to supply 6,000 tons of limestone for the rebuilding of Bristol Bridge at 12 shillings a ton, the stone to be quarried and cut at Courtfield to the required dimensions and floated down the Wye when there was sufficient water in the river to carry 15 tons of stone in 20-ton barges. The trustees appointed by Parliament insisted on various guarantees, one of them being that,

> Mr Vaughan should employ constantly not less than twelve quarry-men and proportionable number of labourers to raise and square the stone under the direction of a surveyor to be appointed by the Bridge Trustees. Not less than seventy tons of stone to be delivered every fortnight, provided there is sufficient water in the Wye. One Thousand Pounds to be paid to Mr Vaughan on signing the contract. Fifteen hundred pounds when the Bridge shall be built ten feet high above the level of low water. One Thousand Pounds when the first twenty feet of cornice are set and the remaining moneys shall be due for stone thirty days after the Ballustrade and Ornaments of the Bridge shall be finished. Mr Vaughan to give security for the performance of this Contract to the amount of Fife Thousand Pounds.

I think this contract netted John Vaughan about £6,000 and took about three years to fulfil. I wonder if he made a profit out of it? John took the new oath of allegiance to King George III at Monmouth in 1778 and Frances his niece-in-law did the same. Both John and Catherine were buried at Welsh Bicknor:

> Here lieth the Body of Catherine, Wife of John Vaughan Junr., of Courtfield, who departed this life the 26th June 1778. Aged 50 years, R.I.P.

> Here lieth the Body of John Vaughan Junr. Esq, of Courtfield, who departed this life ye 21st January 1780. Aged 73 years. R.I.P.

In his will dated 1770 John says, 'I recommend my soul unto God, my body to the Earth and to be decently interred in ye Manner, more or less as my poor father and mother were before me.'

The family still have a delightful pair of portraits of William and Frances Vaughan painted in 1768 by I. Blackburn: William, debonair and dashing in his gold and red coat and cocked hat under his arm, and Frances elegant and rather haughty in pale blue silk with lace and pearls. He also had a very interesting hand-drawn map made of his estate in 1792 by Joseph Powell, a surveyor of Castle Street Bridgenorth.* From it one sees that most of the farms in Welsh Bicknor were let, but William kept the woods and a paddock near the house for himself so perhaps he was fond of shooting. They lived mostly at Cornwall House in the main street of Monmouth. Perhaps, coming from Madrid and Hampstead, they found Courtfield too remote and difficult of access in the winter and they preferred the comforts of their pleasant Georgian town house, set behind iron railings with fine gates and a lantern overthrow, and a paddock and a large garden at the back.

Heath in his Wye tour also mentions that in 1799 Courtfield was divided, the Vaughan part being looked after by an elderly domestic and the rest occupied by Mr John Jackson, a jolly farmer with a wife and twelve children who took their dinner off a magnificent refectory table in the kitchen. Jackson farmed a good deal of the estate and was also church warden at the Welsh Bicknor Protestant church.

William had one sister, who married Colonel Count Kilmallock of the Spanish Army, probably a great-grandson in the male line of Patrick Sarsfield, the heroic defender of Limerick.

There are entries in William's accounts for 1783: 'Paid John Lucas for appraising Goods in Chappel and Priests Room, Courtfield . . . Paid Mr George Knight a year's annuity £10 Knight was a Jesuit Chaplain . Expenses of Miss Vaughan's education at Lovain . . .' And in 1789, 'Pd Mr Watkins for serving Clirow £2. 2s.'

William and Frances had only two children, also called William and Frances, so the reference to Miss Vaughan's education at Louvain in 1783 indicates that Frances was their first-born and that they are having her educated abroad. She married Thomas Watkins Davies Esq., a major in the Royal Monmouthshire Militia and had one child, Cordilia Mary, who died unmarried in about 1867.

Their only son, William Michael, was born on 25 September 1781 after they had been married thirteen years (Frances had several miscarriages) and was only fifteen when his father died suddenly. In

* We found this in an attic, had it framed and it now hangs in the hall at Glen Wye.

his will, in 1790, William entrusted 'the whole care and management of his son, and his person, education, estate and fortune to Charles Bodenham of Rotherwas, Esq. and John Jones of Llanarth Court Esq. My wife and family to pay what they think proper in charitable donations for the good of my soul.' He desired 'to be buried with my ancestors in the church of Welsh Bicknor', and was indeed interred there, on 4 May 1796. Frances survived her husband by eleven years and was also buried at Welsh Bicknor, on 12 November 1807.

· 5 ·

The Nineteenth Century

WILLIAM MICHAEL VAUGHAN – 'THE BUILDER'

WILLIAM MICHAEL Thomas John Vaughan must be regarded as 'The Builder'. No doubt he found Courtfield pretty dilapidated and decided to take Heath's advice and use the 'many flagstone terraces to build a new mansion house'. Still a schoolboy when his father died in 1796, he was educated in Gloucester by the Reverend M. R. Greenway. The restoration of his ancestral home was a splendid challenge to his youthful energy and imagination. The early nineteenth century was a period of much building, so it was an ideal time for this young man to embark on such a delightful and worthwhile project. His Jones cousins at Clytha and Charles Bodenham of Rotherham, his guardian, would have guided him, and his mother was still alive and living at their house in Monmouth with his elder sister, Frances. A charming miniature of Frances painted in 1796 by A. Plimer, exists and shows her as a fashionable young lady.

Charles Bodenham, a banker and family friend appointed by his father, must have administered his estates well and I think it is probable that William's mother was left well off. At all events, there seems to have been sufficient money for his building projects. As well as the new house he had to plan and make a better approach to it up Coppit Hill and a new drive through the deer park (this is lightly pencilled in, one imagines by hand, on the map we have of 1792).

The original approach to Courtfield was by the back road, through pillared gates into a flagged courtyard, as described by Heath,* who

---

* No sign of this remains, though I noticed foundation walls deep in the ground towards the back of the house and on the old tennis court when the Mill Hill Fathers were building a modern block in 1960.

35

referred to the deficiency of this in his criticism of the manor in 1799:

> The ancestors of the late Mr Vaughan were used to make Courtfield their constant residence, keeping up a handsome establishment and living in a manner suitable to their extensive fortune, but by their successors giving a preference to Monmouth (seldom staying at Courtfield longer than an occasional visit) everything around seems to lament the neglect which time and inattention have imposed on it. The only objection (which indeed is a very material one), is the want of a good carriage road to the house – but obstacles of this kind are easily removed when persons of property take an interest in the remedy.

Before he visited Courtfield, Heath had filled his mind with ideas of its magnificence and romance from its having been the nursery of Prince – afterwards King – Henry V, but he was disappointed to find a rather dilapidated manor, with the house divided, part occupied by Mr Vaughan – when on visits from Monmouth, with an elderly domestic in charge – and the rest of the house and outbuildings inhabited by the respectable farmer called Jackson who rented the estate and lived there with his family. Heath mentions a flight of steps and a beautiful terrace overlooking the Wye. And over the iron gate was the Vaughan coat of arms (see jacket) surmounted by their crest.

The manor's dilapidation and decay can be explained by the fact that Richard and William Vaughan, who as we know were outlawed after Culloden and fled to Spain, were unable to return and tend it due to their exclusion from the general pardon of 1747.

William built his pleasant late-Georgian house with a southern aspect overlooking the Wye on the site of the original formal gardens. Not too large, it has a quiet dignity. The central portion projects slightly and has a triangular pediment over a semicircular porch supported on Doric columns and with a ram's mask frieze. The ground-floor windows are set in circular-headed shallow recesses and five of these also embellish the west semicircular wall leading to the stable block. On the eastern side this new block joins the older, fifteenth-century, part, which though refaced and brought into line is lower and has smaller windows. This contains the Henry V bedroom over the library, formally the chapel which in penal days was always inside. The present Gothic church was built about 1850. A beautiful stained-glass window was put in by the late Lord Llangattock in memory of his Aunt Eliza and her husband John Francis Vaughan. There are also memorial stained-glass windows to other members of the family and a set of raised plaster stations of the cross by a Munich

36

artist. As the Vaughan-Weld arms are impaled in the big east window over the altar, it looks as if William Michael may have had to do the building of this too. Certainly he had a very grand funeral there on 22 October 1861.

William married on 22 August 1803 in the Catholic church at Lulworth, when he was twenty-two, Teresa Maria, a year younger than himself. She was the daughter of Thomas Weld of Lulworth (1750–1810) and came from a large family. One of her brothers, Thomas, entered the Church after his wife's death, became a bishop and finally a cardinal. Thomas's elder brother, Edward, was twice married, first to Juliana Petre in 1763, who died in 1772, and in 1775 he married Mary Ann Smythe, later Mrs Fitzherbert and the morganatic wife of George IV. Their father was a large, rich landowner, connected with many influential Catholic families. He rebuilt Lulworth Castle, turning it into a comfortable eighteenth-century house, and also built the beautiful Palladian church, designed by John Tasker, which stands in the park. Tradition has it that George III, who stayed with them, gave Thomas his special permission, stipulating that the outside should look as much like a mausoleum as possible: 'Build a family mausoleum and you can furnish the inside as a Catholic Chapel if you wish', he said. Erected in about 1790, this was the first free-standing Catholic church to be built in England since the Reformation.

William and Teresa embarked on building the new Courtfield shortly after their marriage. They probably lived in Whitchurch, as a letter from William written in December 1805 and still among our family papers came from there and the Old Court does have a Vaughan coat of arms; it would have been close enough to supervise the work, which as William seems to have been partly his own architect would have needed his constant attention. The architect who drew up the plans was William Miles, of Ebley, Stroud, Gloucester and William employed him in all his building projects.

In a letter to Charles Bodenham of 5 December 1805 William says, 'I must not conclude without telling you that Mr Gerard was over here for a day or two and that we laid our heads together and made some alterations to Mr Miles' plan of the intended difficulty ascending Coppit Wood Hill, but must leave this status quo till my return, which I candidly look forward to with impatience.' They were about to set out to spend Christmas at Lulworth – his wife's home in Dorset.

As well as improving the road up Coppit Hill, William Michael built two sets of fine cut-stone gates, the park lodge and probably the charming little Swiss chalet by the top lodge* where he changed the road.

The road up Coppit Hill, winding and steep, must indeed have been difficult before the days of tarmac, but it provides breathtaking views backwards across the flat lands with the river winding down from Ross and the spire of St Mary's Church easily seen four miles away. The lovely arches of Kerne Bridge, and Goodrich Castle, rise in the foreground; the 'Waste Not, Want Not' spring flows refreshingly by the roadside; here and there outcrops of lichen-covered rock, ferns, bracken, willow catkins and a riot of Old Man's Beard festooning small trees; primroses, bluebells and wild cherries flourish in their season, bringing lines from Housman to mind: 'Loveliest of trees, the cherry now/ Is hung with bloom along the bough,/ And stands about the Woodland ride/ Wearing white for Eastertide.'

Further up the river, and looking in the opposite direction over Thomas Wood and away towards Ruardean – of which the Vaughans are also Lords of the Manor since 1692 – the tall spire of Ruardean Church stands out on the skyline. At the top of the hill some lovely old beech trees mark the entrance to the Courtfield estate. In springtime, with their fresh green leaves dappled in sunlight, you feel you are entering fairyland, as indeed you may be. These trees must be about 200 years old so were probably planted by William Michael.

The young couple had their portraits painted by J. Opie in 1805, and they are fine, dignified paintings to hang in a large house. Teresa is in a high-waisted white muslin dress, without jewellery or ornaments, her brown hair is parted at the centre and she has a rather serious, but sweet, expression. William Michael looks handsome and benevolent and older than his twenty-four years, with grey powdered hair, a high white stock, yellow waistcoat and blue cutaway coat with gilt buttons. He is seated on a chair with a leather volume in his hand.

The family still has a marble bust of William which very likely

---

* I gave my eldest son a watercolour of this some years ago; alas now no more, and only an uninteresting but functional cattle grid marks where it once stood. The road used to turn left here and there are still some fine old oak trees, marking the way across the Kiln Piece and Kiln Patch Cottage shown in the 1792 map. Jack Gomery, and his father before him, lived in this cottage for many years.

was done in Rome at the time of his second marriage in 1835. He is considerably older, balding and with side whiskers, but still a very handsome man. It stands in the hall at Glen Wye.* William also collected pictures and there are about a dozen he bought in 1817 in Florence still in the family.

William Michael, as befitted his position in the county, was a Deputy-Lieutenant and JP and was High Sheriff of Monmouthshire in 1833 now that the law allowed Catholics to hold office again.

As well as all this, and his building activity, he and Teresa had eight children – five sons and three daughters, of which five chose religious vocations. Two daughters became nuns and three sons priests. One child died in infancy: in an entry in William's prayer book he writes, 'Poor dear William was born Feb 10th 1807 and died of the croup on Palm Sunday March 26th 1809'. There is an entry in the Welsh Bicknor parish church register recording the burial.

A Royal Elopement

By a curious coincidence it was Teresa Vaughan's brother, Cardinal Weld, who performed the first of the four marriage ceremonies in Rome of my eloping great-great-aunt Penelope Caroline Smyth with Charles Prince of Capua, second son of King Francis I of the Two Sicilies, the richest and most powerful kingdom in Italy. Francis having died in 1830, Ferdinand II was now on the throne and absolutely forbade his younger brother's marriage with a commoner. Penelope was Irish, the daughter of Grice Smyth of Ballynatray, one of the finest houses on the river Blackwater where her family had been established since the sixteenth century and, though of distinguished lineage, was not royal, so not good enough for 'King Bomba', as he was known. So, the young couple decided on elopement, which, with a fine sense of drama, they carried out during a gala performance at the San Carlo Opera House in honour of the King's birthday on the night of 12 January 1836. First they went to Rome where they were married by Cardinal Weld; the next ceremony was in Madrid (Charles's sister was the Queen of Spain), the third, in the

---

* I frequently thank William for building this charming Regency dower house, so entirely suitable for present-day living. We, happily, were able to re-establish the family here in 1955 where we remain. The big house was sold to the Mill Hill Missionary Society along with the park and gardens (about sixty acres) in 1950, but the rest of the estate was retained. William also collected pictures and there are about a dozen he bought in 1817 in Florence still in the family.

best tradition of runaway lovers, at Gretna Green (I have a copy of this Gretna certificate dated 7 May 1836) and their fourth took place in London at the Anglican Church of St George's, Hanover Square, on 23 May 1836.

By this amazing multiplicity of ceremonies Charles and Penelope probably hoped to gain allies in their fight to have their marriage recognised, but seem only to have succeeded in further infuriating King Ferdinand, and when England's Prime Minister, Lord Palmerston, took up the cudgels on their behalf, it proved the last straw, as Palmerston had already enraged the King over the Sicilian sulphur monopoly. Various people tried to bring about a reconciliation between the brothers, and at one stage Penelope wrote to the Queen Mother – who always had a soft spot for the wayward Charles – offering to accept the status of a private citizen if only the King would allow them to return to Naples. However, this offer seems to have been rejected, which was a bitter blow to Penelope's pride and from then on the couple were determined that nothing less than full royal recognition would satisfy them. This led to a life of exile and poverty, moving about Europe to avoid their creditors, and they had to exist mostly on the charity of Penelope's relations. They had a son, Francesco Ferdinand Carlo, and a daughter, Vittoria Augusta Penelope, who both died unmarried.

King Ferdinand died in 1859 and was succeeded by his son, Francis II, who ordered the restoration of Charles's money and estates, but unfortunately the Kingdom of the Two Sicilies was soon overthrown by Garibaldi who confiscated all Bourbon property so poor Charles lost again. All this was probably too much for him for he fell ill and died at Turin in 1862.

King Victor Emanuel granted Penelope and her children an allowance and the use of the beautiful Villa Marlia at Lucca, and on 10 March 1863 the high court in Naples recognised Penelope's claim to the title of Princess of Capua and the rights of her children to inherit all titles and honours due to them as their father's legitimate heirs. Penelope died on 13 December 1882, aged sixty-eight, worn out by a lifetime of struggle against misfortune. She and Charles and their children are buried in the Chapel of San Francesco Saverio at Marlia.

Teresa died on 30 June 1832, aged forty-nine, and was buried at Welsh Bicknor on 4 July. William remarried in Rome on 22 April 1835, his second wife being the Lady Mary Anne, widow of Sir Thomas Gage of Hengrave, Suffolk, the propagator of the greengage, and a daughter of Valentine Browne, first Earl of Kenmare. As so often happens the young Vaughans found it hard to accept their stepmother, who came from a different and more worldly background from that of their own, much loved mother.*

In some notes of his eldest son, John Francis, which I must confess make him sound very priggish, he complains of finding his father imperious and overbearing and his mother is described as:

> that mild angelic being who is now in heaven and was ever the peacemaker. She excused me to my father and my father to me and taught me duty and submission. Well I do remember now that one morning at breakfast my father spoke to her in a manner that made her cry. I knew it was worse than useless to interfere but my blood boiled. I burst into tears of indignation and stalked out of the room. This produced some effect, as I intended. After breakfast that sweet being endeavoured to soothe me; she said there was no unkindness on my father's part and took the blame upon herself.
>
> This did not quite satisfy me. I was young but proud and obstinate in opinion. However, I loved and admired her still more for this noble self sacrifice and devotion. Indeed my affection to her was boundless, and with what pleasure do I now record this love to a saintly angelic being, united to me by the nearest and holiest of ties, and who is now as present to my fond imagination and holds as warm a place in my grateful heart, as when the tender mother's smile was still playing on her sweet and placid countenance. My tears are few and therefore knowing better, but I have yet one left for my own dear Mother, tho' the supercilious Lady Mary Anne succeeds to her place in the hearts of others.

This storm in a breakfast cup suggests William Michael may have been rather a stern disciplinarian, though John Francis by his own account was going through a rebellious stage, but it clearly shows the adoration the boy felt for his mother, later on transferred to his wife Eliza, and apparently handed down to their sons, as both Cardinal Vaughan and Father Bernard in later life could scarcely bear to speak of their mother except to say she was 'the very ideal of everything lovely and holy: we thought, and were brought up to think, that she

---

* Note found among the Vaughan family papers: 'On the 4th July 1832 was buried in the Church of Welsh Bicknor, Teresa Mary wife of William Vaughan Esq, of Courtfield, Monmouthshire. She was a daughter of Thomas Weld Esq of Lulworth Castle, Sister of Cardinal Weld and nearly related to the Lords Clifford and Stourton. A lady of a disposition naturally affectionate, sincerely religious, and of exemplary conduct in all the relations of life. Before the decline of her health she was remarkable for beauty of person and fascination of manners.'

was in every sense perfection. There was never anyone like her.' Both the Vaughans and the Welds were deeply religious families. The atmosphere of their upbringing and the emotional religiosity of the Victorian age contributed to this and possibly to this mystical veneration for their mother, all of which may have contributed to so many of the children going into the Church.

William and his second wife had no children, and indeed had only five years together as Lady Mary Anne died in 1840, leaving William to soldier on alone for another twenty-one years. In his will, of 8 May 1857, he is described as 'of Courtfield, Herefordshire and 2 Gloucester Street, Portman Square, Middlesex', so he must have had a London house and perhaps spent more time there, leaving his married son to carry on at Courtfield.

In her diary entry for 13 August 1841, on her return from the Continent, his daughter-in-law Eliza mentions dining at Gloucester Place, and in William's account book of 1846 there is an entry for half a year's rent of (£135) of 93 Gloucester Place. Certainly when he died in October 1861 his body was brought from London with great pomp and ceremony – there was much black crêpe, plumed horses and candles, three extra-large coffins, the inside of fine pink glazed ruffled cambric, then one of stout lead costing £7 17s 6d and an outer coffin of fine black oak 1½ inches thick, French-polished, with large solid brass handles and two solid gilt crosses and a large solid brass plate with inscription and crest richly engraved thereon at a cost of some £20. The total bill, from Mr J. Taylor, 3 Lower Seymour Street, was £88 9s 6d. Mr Taylor brought the hearse with corpse from Paddington to Ross where he and his assistant spent the night in an hotel and then proceeded with four horses from Ross to Courtfield where William was interred in the vault under the church on 22 October 1861. Mr Taylor made all the funeral arrangements and was away for three days. He seems to have received £20 on account and the remainder of his bill, £68 9s 6d, was settled on 20 March 1862.

For a short time before Teresa's death William lived at Waterloo Villas, Gloucester, and Teresa died in Gloucester. John Francis, their eldest son, was the only boy to marry and his mother was alive for his wedding in 1830 (but not, sadly, for her daughter Teresa's marriage to Thomas Weld Blundell of Ince, Lancashire, which took place in 1839). In a letter to John Francis written in July 1832, shortly after her death, William wrote:

> Accept, dear John, my gratitude and thanks for your truly religious, consolatory and affectionate letter. Indeed, I have so identified myself with your beloved Mother by my constant attendance upon her

during the last month or two, that her dear languid voice and kind and edifying words, and serene, tho' emaciated countenance are ever present to me. This, my dearest John, is agonizing to the heart, but still it brings with it something grateful and consolatory to the soul; and I hope, nay I confidently trust, that she is at this moment happy in Heaven, praying for us all.

It is very kind of you to wish us to go to Courtfield, but God knows when I shall have the courage even to visit the dear spot where we passed our early and happy years. Every chair, etc. within, and every shrub and tree without would remind me of my poor Teresa. But enough. God's holy will be done. I fear your own grief would hardly admit of your administrating much comfort to your amiable wife. My kind love to her and may you both live long and happy.

Ever your affect. Father, W Vaughan.

After this he appears to have moved to London and there are various addresses in Gloucester Street and Gloucester Place. There is a later letter from London, dated 9 May 1859:

Thanks, my dear John, for your affect. and amiable letter, and as I hope and trust that after the expiration of Mr Alloways' lease, you with some at least of your children will be happily settled at poor old Courtfield. It is much more reasonable that your taste and inclination should be consulted rather than mine. I shall certainly never live there, tho' I may wish to be buried there but not at any unnecessary expense, and you will find my will in the little iron chest in my bedroom.

I will send you the Design for the R.S. by this day's post. I think it better to do so. If you reject it and adopt a Communion Rail, it should doubtless be a reasonably handsome one, and in a style suitable to the Church, but I leave it all to you; do just as you like.

I propose leaving Town on Tuesday 'Deo Volente', spend a morning with dear Fanny, halt for 2 or 3 days at Teignmouth and then on to Plymouth. [His son William was then Bishop of Plymouth.]

In case you write to me within the next fortnight, and your letters are always welcome, direct to me under cover to William, No. 2 Victoria Place, Stonehouse, Plymouth. Ever my dear John,

Your affect. Father,
W Vaughan.

This letter was sent to 'John, Lieut Col. Vaughan, Newport, Co Mayo, Ireland', where John must have been on a visit to his Irish property.

Of William's other three sons (a fifth had died very young), William, born in 1814, became Bishop of Plymouth in 1856 and died in 1902; the first of five Vaughan bishops, he served as secretary to Cardinal Weld and was made a freeman of the city of Rome in 1862; Richard, a Jesuit priest, was born at Courtfield 1826; Edmund, provincial of the Redemptorists, born at Courtfield on 26 November 1827, was still living in 1904. Two of their daughters, Frances Mary born on 22 April 1805 and Mary born on 15 April 1810, both became nuns of the Visitation Order.

The next generation was to produce the most remarkable family in the entire history of the Church, has earned a mention in Ripley's 'Believe it or not' series and is also featured on an Anglo-American chewing-gum packet:

> The fabulous Mother – Louise Elizabeth Vaughan of Courtfield, England, was the mother of a cardinal, two bishops, three priests, and five nuns. For twenty years she spent an hour in prayer every day that all her sons should become priests. She was the mother of eight sons and five daughters. Herbert Vaughan became a cardinal, Roger became Archbishop of Sydney, Australia, John became Bishop of Sebastopolis. Three more sons became priests and all daughters became nuns. This record is unequalled in the entire history of the Church.

I think Louise Elizabeth – Eliza – would be surprised, and maybe horrified, to see herself so immortalised!

The Rolls Family Connection

John Vaughan's Eliza was the third daughter of John and Martha Rolls and was born at the Grange, Bermondsey, Surrey on 8 October 1810. The Rolls family came originally from the parish of Penrose in Monmouthshire and are described as 'Yeoman' in 1732. They moved to London in the early eighteenth century, where they made a fortune and became gentry living at the Grange, a splendid country house in Surrey. By marriages with the Coysh and Allen families (Dr Elisha Coysh was a distinguished London physician), the Rollses inherited a lot of valuable property in London and in Monmouthshire and seem to have moved back to The Hendre, one of the finest and largest Monmouthshire estates, about 1830 and so became neighbours of the Vaughans as the estates are only about twelve miles apart. By this time The Hendre had grown from a small shooting-box to a magnificent mansion approached through a thousand-acre deer park and the Rolls were in the habit of entertaining royalty. George V as Duke of York used to shoot and go motoring there. John Allen Rolls, Eliza's nephew, was created the first Baron Llangattock of The Hendre in 1892 and his son, the Hon. C. S. Rolls, became the great pioneer motorist of Rolls-Royce fame.

High in the square in Monmouth is a statue of King Henry V and before it a splendid bronze of Charles Rolls holding an aeroplane. He was the first man to fly the English Channel both ways. On 2 June 1910, he started from Dover at 6.30pm, was over Sangette, France at 7.15pm and after circling around headed back for England and reached Dover at 8pm. It was a wonderful achievement that even the tragedy of his death in a flying accident a month later could not mar. The bronze, by W. Goscombe John, RA, was erected in 1911 and the following inscription is on one side of the plinth:

> Erected by public subscription to the memory of The Hon. Charles Stewart Rolls, third son of Lord and Lady Llangattock, as a tribute of admiration for his great achievements in Motoring, Ballooning and Aviation.
>
> He was a pioneer in both scientific and practical motoring and aviation, and the first to fly across the Channel from England to France and back without landing. He lost his life by the wrecking of his aeroplane at Bournemouth July 12, 1910. His death caused worldwide regret and deep national sorrow.

Monmouth can rightly be proud of her famous sons standing together in Agincourt Square.

Eliza Vaughan's eldest sister, Martha Sarah, married Major Edward Neville Macready of the 30th Regiment in 1840. He was a brother of W. J. Macready the famous actor. An unusually accomplished man and a most gallant soldier, he is described by his brother in the *Reminiscences of W. J. Macready*:

> He was of the very stuff to make a soldier, brave, resolute, clear sighted – and ambitious to a degree of weakness – In any competition he would be first; he was the boldest rider, the best horseman, the truest shot in his regiment, his reading was extensive, his judgement penetrating and clear; abstinent and self-denying in his personal gratifications, he was free and bounteous to all others and so guarded and circumspect that he never lost a friend. He was in a few words a truly good man and only wanted opportunity to have been a great one.

Major Macready fought at Waterloo and as all officers in his regiment were killed or disabled in the early part of the battle, he commanded it through most of the day though just seventeen years old. Then only an ensign, his gallantry earned him promotion without purchase to a lieutenancy.

Courtfield and the Vaughans

JOHN AND ELIZA VAUGHAN AND THEIR FAMILY

John Francis Vaughan married Eliza Rolls at the Protestant church of St Mary's, Bryanston Square, on 12 July 1830 (her parents also had a house in Bryanston Square). Four months after her marriage she became a Catholic and was received into the Church on 1 November, the feast of All Saints.

It was clear that John worshipped his Eliza, and their marriage was wonderfully happy. In his notebook he writes:

> My first acquaintance with Eliza was not accompanied with an impression of her personal beauty or admiration such as lovely features or pleasing smiles impart – it was rather a sentiment of hallowed veneration, that species of mystic attraction, partaking of tenderness and worship which the presence of an angelic nature might be supposed to inspire.
>
> It was as if my spirit foresaw, what was unknown to my grosser part, that thro' joy and sorrow, in youth and age she was to be my guardian angel upon earth; the inspirer of ever pious thought, the prompter of every virtuous action: that my breast was to be her resting place, my heart the sanctuary of her inmost thoughts and aspirations, and that in the pride of her beauty, in the triumph of her loveliness, in the dazzling summit of her attractions, that then her simple faith, her exquisite purity, her fervid devotedness to virtue should endear her more to me than all her other charms. Such art thou too lovely woman, the happy partner of my life. Often hast thou thought I admired thy person less than other suitors, those who spoke not of love. It is that I saw in thee what surpassed all beauty of the body so transcendantly, that it absorbed all love.
>
> I could not know thy heart in all its devotedness, thy soul in all its purity without ceasing almost to prize the fragile case however beauteous, which held such treasure.

Eliza, who came from an earnest Evangelical family, blossomed in the warmth of the Courtfield Catholic life and embraced her husband's faith with such wholehearted devotion that she is credited with spending an hour a day in the church praying that all her children might spend their lives in the service of God. She nearly got her way, with six sons priests who all made their mark in the Church, and four daughters very holy nuns. The fifth daughter, Margaret, or as John refers to her, 'little Dot', seems to have had some sort of disease – it may have been a kind of schizophrenia – and spent her life in a convent nursing home.

No doubt Eliza, religious by nature, was greatly helped by the strength and real goodness of her splendid husband and also her

46

in-laws, particularly Theresa (Weld) who was of a most saintly disposition. Courtfield, too, perhaps by its remoteness from the world, seems to have imbibed and retained something intrinsically wholesome and good so that often one feels one is treading on holy ground, and I believe many people who visit here today are conscious of this feeling.

Herbert, Eliza and John's first child, was born on 15 April 1832, at Gloucester, and baptized there two days later. At that time her parents-in-law, William and Theresa Vaughan, were living at Waterloo Villa (now the Spa Hotel), Gloucester, and no doubt it was considered advisable for Eliza to have her first confinement in the city rather than the wilds of Welsh Bicknor. Subsequent children were all born at Courtfield, with the exception of Gwladys who was born at Bruges when they were travelling – which they often seem to have been doing. Eliza's diary for 1841 gives descriptions of taking their coach and horses, children and tutors on a European tour and one gets an insight into the hotels they stayed at, the people they met, and various difficulties such as horses going lame and John having to go out and buy replacements, or Eliza feeling ill and her devoted John spending the night on the floor by her bedside.

The pair of delightful portraits, still in the family, of two of their sons, Herbert and Roger, aged eight and five, were painted by Wallins, a good Flemish artist, during a stay in Bruges about 1838.

The children were brought up on the ancestral acres of the beautiful Welsh Bicknor peninsula, mixing with the rural community and village schoolchildren who came to learn their catechism in the Courtfield chapel, as well as with their numerous relations – the Rollses at The Hendre, and the Joneses and Herberts at Clytha and Eliza made religion so attractive and the lives of the saints so interesting that the children loved them as their intimate friends, and heaven meant even more to them than beloved Courtfield, where they were so wildly, supremely happy.

Eliza frequently took her children with her when visiting the sick and encouraged them to give their toys to less well-off children. Her love of the poor and sick extended far beyond the conventional bowl of soup and she would sweep their rooms and wash and change the bedridden. When people expostulated with her of the danger of exposing her children to such ills, she would smile and say, 'God will take care of them where my love fails'.

Herbert recalled that at mealtimes, which the older children took with their parents, the general conversation tended to be of cricket, riding, shooting, etc., but his mother often discussed the character necessary to make a good priest, what should be shunned and what imitated. Her family would sometimes tease her, saying she expected too much of poor human nature. She would reply, 'I do not expect a St Francis de Sales, but if only priests would care a little more for the poor people and go among them'. In after years these high standards were outstandingly manifested in her children, who adored her and called her 'the angel of the house'.

But do not think that subdued Victorian piety was the Vaughan style. No, they were a boisterous noisy troupe of growing children – 'Vaughan spirits' – well known in the neighbourhood! They were happiest roving the lovely countryside with dogs and ponies, chasing deer, birdnesting, playing hare and hounds, and theatricals, which their mother encouraged. On the feast of the Holy Innocents they loved to dress up in a sort of general pandemonium ending around the schoolroom statue in clouds of incense and a blaze of candles as they made peace. Eliza liked to play her harp and sing songs and hymns about their heavenly home, or carry them off to the chapel for special visits to the Blessed Sacrament, where on feastdays they were allowed to place their little offerings of flowers.

John Francis Vaughan, Irish Landowner

Obviously John loved Courtfield and had improved the property by numerous purchases of farms in Monmouthshire. Then he turned his mind farther afield. In 1848 he went prospecting in Ireland and wrote every day to Eliza with excellent descriptions of Waterford, Cork and Kerry. It was shortly after the terrible famine in 1845 and he felt sorry for the Irish peasants and appalled for the poverty and desolation everywhere. His dream of acquiring and improving a property culminated in his purchase of a lot of poorish land at Mullaranny in County Mayo, and a delightful little Victorian castle, Rosturk, on Clew Bay, as well as rough shooting over many thousands of acres. But, as is so often the case, he found the Irish impossible to help and he was by no means the first high-minded agriculturist to be defeated by the deceptive beauty of the Emerald Isle.*

On 23 July 1863 John Francis wrote from Lulworth:

It is singular what reactions there are in feeling, in mere temporal and external matters, as well as in the spiritual attractions and the

---

* My great-uncle Sir Horace Plunkett was another. He worked all his life for Ireland and cooperative farming, only to be burnt out in 1923, and had to end his days in England.

sentiments of the heart. The weariness of labour, the fatigue of business, the worry of affairs, often make me long for repose and desire to get rid of external occupations which disgust and harass. I then am impatient to let my farm, to sell any property which gives me trouble, or even to close my house and establishment. A few days' repose, however, a little inaction, a temporary cessation of my usual work finds me impatient with idleness, or even mere amusement and makes me long once more to be up and doing.

I have been less than a week at Lulworth and the time is irksome – more – I note only desire to get back to my occupations at Courtfield, but with restless impatience I want to be on the mountain's side at Sheskin draining lakes, diverting rivers and launching into a series of agricultural or pastoral enterprises which I am well aware will carry in their train much trouble, disappointment, annoyance and fatigue. To all this I open my eyes and experience has taught a lesson which I do not fail to recognise and remember. Still the attraction is present: the fascination is there and I am less desirous, far, of the profit of an advantageous sale of Sheskin (which I have often wished in disgust and impatience I might never see again) than I am thirsting for the congenial pursuit and excitement of a new field of agricultural enter- prise. I try to bring vividly to my imagination, the smoke, the dis- comfort, the dreaming solitude, the irritating monotony which vexes and oppresses the spirit, and the impotent conclusion which seems to follow every undertaking. I remember the oft-arrived-at decision that my Irish scheme has been a failure, that my enterprise has been a mistake, that morally as physically Mayo is an ungrateful soil, that the sooner and more completely I turn my back upon it the better, and that to get well out of the consequence of my folly and invest my capital where it will give some safe return without trouble or supervision was the object which I ought clearly to keep in view – Well! In spite of all this, my mind is now more attracted than ever by the prospect of the broad and wild domain with its savage charm, vague and vast. The possible improvement on an extended scale and at all events, the facile and constant growth of intrinsic value by the agency of its diverted streams – again the old sportsman's feeling of love of possessing a tract of land where wild game is found – all these thoughts and feelings and memories tie me to my barren property of mountain and bay till I begin to feel as if the sale of it would be an unbearable loss.

Still, my judgement tells me if providence sends me a purchaser I must sell. If otherwise, I shall be well content to accept the amusement and annoyance, the profit and loss which it may entail.

Eliza and John Vaughan's ideally happy union was completed by their family of fourteen. Two were to marry, having unsuccessfully tried their vocations for the priesthood, and the remaining six sons and four daughters all were destined for the Church. As John and Eliza's first four sons became priests, and one died an infant, the Courtfield estate was to devolve on their sixth son, Frances Baynham. When Eliza died on 24 January 1853, giving birth to her fourteenth baby (John, who in the course of time was to become a bishop) she was probably worn out with childbearing. Her John was distracted with grief, and soon after went off to the Crimean War. He was colonel of the local militia regiment – the Royal Monmouthshire Militia, which he had joined as a subaltern, and took out to the Crimea where he spent the appalling winter of 1854–5 in the trenches. We still have photographs showing him sitting outside his tent.

John's consideration and affection for his men is clearly shown in the 'Crimea Diary' we still have, along with many interesting comments, often unfavourable, relating to the conduct of the campaign and to the personalities of officers – both French and English – he was meeting. He touches on Miss Nightingale and her nurses, but is far more favourably impressed by the French nursing sisters. The lack of organisation, the terrible dysentery and other disease suffered by our troops, and the cruelty to and starvation of the poor horses horrified him. He considered the French troops better organised and provided for. Among many people he met he mentions Lord Killeen.* 'Lunched with Lord Killen, whom we found looking grave and dingy. He was mixing mustard. His tent looked bare and comfortless. An amiable and unaffected young nobleman, but deuced bad campaigner.'

John survived the war, returned to Courtfield and on 15 February 1860 continued the Vaughan tradition by marrying his cousin

---

* Killeen was a Plunkett (Arthur James, also tenth Earl of Fingall) so a cousin of mine of my mother's side. His mother was a Herbert from Llanarth and her father, Francis Alexis Rio, a French Academician. She was beautiful but died young of consumption. After her death Lord Fingall lived in Paris and his three children had a strange upbringing. Because their mother had died of consumption he was always anxious about the children's health, so they were never sent to school but were educated by a strict governess and later by a kind old priest, Father McNamara whom they loved, and who came from near Killeen, their home in County Meath. Their father did not pay a great deal of attention to them and as Lady Fingall stated in her delightful book, *Seventy Years Young*, writing about her husband: 'The Paris he saw with Father MacNamara was a monk's Paris indeed – he knew all the churches and had even visited the Morgue – very different from the Paris known by other young men of his class. From this upbringing he brought the slight French accent with which he always spoke.' *(Contd opposite.)*

Mary Weld in the Catholic chapel at Lulworth when he was fifty-one and Mary thirty-nine. They had two children, who both died in infancy.

FAMILY CORRESPONDENCE

Reading John's letters (and others from the entire family) one comes to understand their total dedication to the service and love of God. Herbert, cardinal-to-be, writing to his father when Teresa (Sister Mary Magdalen, who entered the Sisters of Charity in 1839) was dying at her convent in London in 1861, repeatedly stresses the joy and happiness they all seem to be feeling at the thought of her being with Our Lord:

> 'I have a feeling of simple joy and refreshment which seems to be in strange harmony with a sister's corpse and the grave, yet so it is. She has herself left the feeling on me. And though I am haunted with the image of her dying expression and her last kiss of gratitude for the spiritual help of aspirations, which I was suggesting to her up to the last, yet the thought of her going off with the freshness of the grace of her second baptism and martyrdom upon her soul, and the being away from the trials and temptations, stays if not weeping, at least all mourning. The first of the thirteen has broken the ice; we may expect to go now one by one. I for one shall be delighted to go whenever it will give God the greatest glory.'

Shortly after she died, he wrote again:

> Kenelm, as he walked with me after her death up to Montague Square, said he used to think that he should go mad if Teresa died, but that he felt that he had good news to give, so consoling and even joyful an

I can remember so well being intrigued by Lord Fingall's unusual voice when as a child I used to accompany my mother on her long-distance driving trips and we sometimes stayed at Killeen Castle. I remember too how greatly he admired 'Tommy', my mother's wonderful Welsh driving pony who could accomplish the 150 miles from Ballynatray to Killeen in three days and be as frisky as a two-year-old at the end.

Sometimes Lord Fingall used to take me with him when he was feeding his cats – of which there appeared to be hundreds – kept in a disused turret of the castle. Cousin Daisy, his delightful wife, had more charm in her little finger than most people in their whole being. When I was older she took me to lovely balls and parties in Dublin and introduced me to all sorts of interesting people, including Yeats and Oliver St John Gogarty. She was always fun to be with and so very kind and good to me.

influence had dear Teresa's spirit left behind her.

She died most beautifully, her last word was Jesus. My own sweet Mother, I am sure was with her.

Writing an account of her death to his grandfather, William Vaughan, he said:

> She was full of joy and happiness and had no pain beyond the distress of congestion of the lungs and shortness of breathing. She feared there might be ether in her medicine in order to stupefy her faculties and on that account she would take no more of it, being most desirous to have the use of her senses as long as possible in order to use them for her greater merit and she was perfectly sensible to the last moment. It was all she had desired – to die young in the perfect possession of her senses, as a professed nun. I am going to bury her today at Kensal Green among the nuns and religious. In half an hour I am going to sing a Mass for her in our church here.

John Vaughan wrote to Reggie in 1869 regarding his son's vocation for the priesthood:

> Dublin
> May 31st 1869
>
> My dearest Reggie,
>
> Whether this will find you at Courtfield is doubtful. I hope it may, that I may have the opportunity of a last chat with you before you take your final leave of this outer secular life and give yourself with the energy and generosity of youth, where generosity and energy never go unrewarded. (On second thoughts, I shall not address this letter to Courtfield, but to Abbotsleigh, and then it will seem as if I were talking also to my beloved May.)
>
> I hope you will be allowed to spend many hours with her, and to talk to her alone, for you will want to pour out your hearts, compare impressions and speak of the future and the past. You were almost a child when May was at Courtfield. The transition from boyhood to manhood and from trifling amusements to earnest purpose is very rapid. I should have liked, my dear Reggie, to have kept you sometime at home; for I do not give you up without a pang. Your manly tastes, and natural character seemed to mark you out for any active life in the world. But, God's Holy Will be done: all are fitted for His service whom He calls, and He calls who He will.
>
> Well, bless you my dear boy. May you bear your trials and crosses with a brave heart, and subdue with a strong will the difficulties in your path.
>
> A loving trust in God, sanctifying and directing your head and will, will lead you right.

Best love to darling May,

> Your affectionate Father
> John Vaughan

A year later, the father is coming to terms with his son's return to the secular life:

> Monmouth
> May 22nd 1870

My dearest Reggie,

Tho' I should be consoled at seeing you called to a high and holy vocation, sacrificing everything that is attractive in this life; yet I have too much of poor human nature left in me not to feel that it will be a great pleasure to have you back again.

You must shake yourself free from all scruples, misgivings or regrets – if they should come across your mind – and struggle resolutely with the trials and difficulties you will be sure to meet with as a citizen of the world.

You must rest a bit and take a vacation at Courtfield; and then I will see what it is possible to do for you by way of a career and business. There is always some way through the world: and if it be that which God by His providence has placed before us, it is sure to be the right one. If it does not lead to heaven it is our own fault. Provided you get there, I care very little for the road.

I shall see you in a few days, so only add,

> Your Affectionate Father,
> John Vaughan.

Reggie went to Australia, where he stayed with his brother, Roger Archbishop of Sydney, and also seems to have worked as a squatter and sheep hand. He married a girl called Julia Shanahan on 5 April 1875 and must have brought her home, as his father's letter of February 1876 indicates. It also implies that she is anxious to return to Australia, but John would prefer them to remain in England:

> 17 Cromwell Place
> February 23 1876

My dearest Reginald,

I must no longer call you Reggy, now you have the dignity of a 'Pater familias'!

I wish you joy on your son, and as one Roger Vaughan is enough in Australia, I hope you will keep the small one in Old England.

Thanks for your cheque. Your future agricultural transactions while you are at Courtfield will be with Farmer Frank! I dare say you help him a lot, to keep his hand in. I look forward to seeing you at Glen

Trothy, and Wolseley at his office before the summer comes.

Father Rowe told me that he 'pitched into an American lady, one day, till she cried, for presuming to think she ought to rule her husband'.

'God', he said, 'has constituted man the head of the family. To reverse that order is to subvert His law, and simply un-christian. It is rebellion in the woman, and degradation in the man. He cannot abdicate his responsibility to God.'

You have an amiable and gentle wife, and it is pleasant to be indulgent to those we love, but the law remains the same.

I am sure you will feel you have other duties to your children, of a higher order, than making money for them; and therefore I feel pretty confident that, after well weighing the question before God (the only true test and standard), you will decide against bringing up your children in the bush. This, of course, is only my view. You must act on your own judgment and conscience, and whatever you do I shall be content. Only looking back at the experience of half a century I see how much oftener men take a wrong turn in life from amiable weakness, than from perversity or erring judgment.

I did not intend ever to allude to this subject again but it has escaped me, and I cannot unsay it. I am in hopes of getting my 3 brothers to dine with me on Tuesday. William and Edmund are going to Rome together, and Dick is in town –

Mary slightly better – I am still shaky.

Love to Julia and small Rodge –

Yours affectionately,
John Vaughan

His little homily on man being the head of the family must have been intended to stiffen Reggie against humouring his wife's desire to go back to Australia. Anyway, they remained in England, lived at Glen Trothy, reared a large family and suffered disastrous financial loss in 1884, which May and all the Abbotsleigh nuns were to be so busy praying about (see page 125).

In a very private letter to his daughter Mary, Mother Clare Magdalene, Prioress of St Augustine, Newton Abbot, John writes:

17 Cromwell Place
S Kensington
Jan 20th 1873

My darling little May,

I write, not because I have anything special to say, but because I think it may give you pleasure to have a few lines from me. Do not let my letter be shown about.

I like to speak to you as the thoughts well up from my heart, and the thought of my letters being seen by others puts a restraint upon me, for I know those kind charitable nuns would think I was as good as my sentiments, the result of which would be that I would be (undeservedly) a regular imposter. With my children it is otherwise. It is a sort of 'grace d'état' that I should be able, in a degree, to direct and cheer them to heaven. Your saintly mother had but one thirst on earth – to make her children saints – to make them love God with every fibre of their being. Can I desire otherwise? I have entire faith in prayer and in the loving guidance of God's providence when trust is placed in Him. I have always believed that it was my Mother's holy prayers which provided her son with a saintly wife and drew down a blessing on us.

That love which is in God is perfected in heaven, and I strongly feel that I now have especially two who watch over me and mine, in spite of all my worthlessness. I have always felt so strongly that to attain heaven – that is to do the will of God – is, in so paramount a degree, the object of existence, that I have felt a sort of satisfaction in the midst of my anguish, at the death of a child. It is as if we were all tossing on the sea, ever liable to be drowned and I saw one safely landed on the shore. So you see, my darling May, much as I love you, I am resigned when God wills it, to give you up to Him.

Johnny appears bent on the priesthood and full of fervour. All but little Dot seem to be now provided for and my only care is now – somewhat tardily – to prepare myself, with terror, for my awful and great account. Even when young I had rather a contempt for this trumpery world, and my astonishment now is that any old fellow like myself can care for it at all. Happy are those who, like yourself, in youth and health have abandoned all for God. The hundredfold promised will assuredly be paid.

You have heard how poor Lady Wolesley has been dying of cancer the last year. Her agonies were fearful and on last Saturday, she sank, suffering tortures to the last – paying, it is to be hoped, 'the last farthing' here on earth. What a long talk I have had with you! If you can, without pain, let me have a few words to say how you are. God bless you my darling child. He is very good to you, for he draws you near to Himself.

Yours most affectly,
John F. Vaughan

Late in 1879, John was writing of lighter matters, from France where he – with Mary – was making a protracted stay at Biarritz, for the good of his health:

Hotel de Paris
Biarritz
Bapes
Pyrenees

November 28th 1879

My dearest Reggy,

I have no bailiff, no woodman, or gardener, or housekeeper to bother me, or take up my time; so I have more leisure to read, to meditate – and to write to my sons and daughters.

I think I sent you a postcard from Arcachon, just to give our address. We spent a week there, not unpleasantly; though the Church was more than half a mile distant to walk, which does not quite suit me before breakfast.

We were in an enormous palace – like hotel, not a quarter filled this season of the year. There were some pleasant people there, however. Not the least amusing of them was the Japanese Ambassador and his suite. He spoke both French and English; an unaffected intelligent young man.

We arrived here the evening before last, but yesterday was so wet that we were unable to hunt up our numerous relations.

We have this morning blue sky and soft air, so we shall walk out presently, and make our round of visits. Agnes Weld called here last afternoon and told us that C. Weld Blundell's wedding was expected to take place that day. So many difficulties have arisen from the fact of its being a mixed marriage, and two of the Cooper family were reported to be so ill, that they seemed to be altogether in a state of perplexity about the intending transaction.

However, I have no doubt but that 'the young people' console themselves with the popular saying that 'the course of true love never did run smooth'.

If they really are spliced, I expect that we shall see them in the course of a month or so, at this place.

We have capital quarters here; very comfortable rooms – the church just before us – and the sea, with its rugged outline of rocks, within 30 yards. The woman who acts as chambermaid on our floor, was delighted to find that I was the father of Abbé Vaughan (Kenelm). She said that while he was with Mr Palmer she had nursed him through a three months illness.* She spoke of him with the greatest admiration and reverence, and declaimed that he was quite a saint. He said to her one day, 'Katherine, have you got a watch?' She replied 'No', but said she she hoped some day to be able to buy one. 'Well', said

---

* Kenelm was for a number of years chronically, even critically, ill with consumption (see pages 91–6).

56

Ken, 'within a month your guardian angel will send you one.' Ken got well; and she thought no more of what he had said. But within a month he sent her a handsome gold watch, which she showed us in triumph. He was a 'veritable saint' she protested!

December 1st

Since I began my letter, which you will see by the date was some days ago, a Fr Mathew has called on me. He is from Maitland, Australia and says that he knows you well, and John. He has also lent me some numbers of the *Freeman's Journal*, with various clever and amusing speeches of Roger's on the education question. Fr Mathew is here for his health. He was in Ireland during the summer but found it too cold and damp this time of the year. He is a somewhat rough unshaven specimen of humanity. The Weld Blundells have a fine large house, so also have the Hornyolds, who have a private chapel with Mass daily. There are a good many other English Catholics here, so there is no lack of society.

I suppose that you are busy as ever with your farm, your autumn wheat looking well and your sheep already fattening on your turnips. I am writing today to the Gloucestershire Bank to know the state of my account. I am rather disappointed that Dale has not written to report the payment of arrears.

I am told that Frank is doing a great deal at Courtfield in various ways. Whether he has returned here, or is still in Paris I have not an idea. My health, on the whole, has slightly improved, but I never expect to walk over your farm again. Mary is in excellent health and spirits. She enjoys having the choice of half-a-dozen Masses within 20 years; and a host of relatives to amuse her leisure hours. She writes in love to Julia and yourself and hopes the baby is better.

Yours very affectionately,
John F. Vaughan

By the following March, John was ready to return home, if somewhat apprehensive as to his future there:

March 19th 1880   Hotel de Paris
                                                                  Biarritz

My dearest Reggie,

Here we are at almost the last week in Lent and as far as climate goes, in the midst of summer. It is time to begin thinking what our next move must be. We have no plans. The only reason why we should desire to set up an establishment in London this year would be for the pleasure of having yourselves, alternately with Frank and his family, with us.

57

There are difficulties, however, in the way. Frank* will be with his Regiment the next three months and Carrie** absent most of the time, so that a visit to Courtfield is out of the question. Between ourselves I should be quite resigned never to see the old place again. I have made the sacrifice. I have felt the parting (however voluntary) for it closed the principal era of my existence – the rural life, with little interval, of half a century – and I have no desire to renew the pain. I have more satisfaction in leaving Frank in the full employment of what I hope may be, for many years, his happy home.

To me the visit would be somewhat like returning from my grave. A thousand memories would crowd upon my heart. The plantations are my children: the trees are my old friends. There is not a spot which has not been familiar to me from my boyhood – not a field, nor a bit of woodland which is not associated with happy days that never can return.

It is better to accept the present, and prepare for the future, than to cling to what is inevitably past. I have far more reasons to be grateful, than to repine. My latter days will, I hope, be better, perhaps more cheerfully spent, cut off from the pleasures and interests of an establishment and an estate, than if I 'stuck by my acres to the last.'

Well, all this my dear Reggie, is not very lively. In truth our family horizon is not very bright at present. Dear, bright, little Gwladys† is gone. Poor Margy is hopelessly separated from us,‡ and Kenelm fills me with anxiety.

It is good news to hear that you and family are flourishing and I have no doubt but that after so long an adverse time for farmers, there will be a return of prosperity. I expect that this year you will reap advantage from the land you have laid down with so much labour, and that you are even now getting a good price for the beef and mutton you send to market. Are your cattle doing well – and the sheep you put so early upon turnips? Those who kept their stock most liberally, I have no doubt, will pull through best. Mary says that she is going to add a leaf for my envelope so it is time for me to 'shut up' literally. Are you giving Johnny Rolls your support? The Conservatives are now our best friends.

Yr affct.
J. F. Vaughan

---

* Francis Baynham, the sixth son, Colonel of the Royal Monmouthshire Militia.
** Frank's wife, Caroline.
† His eldest daughter, who had just died.
‡ Mentally ill, perhaps schizophrenic, she spent much of her life in a home.

This letter shows how dearly John loved his Courtfield and the farming life. His heart always remained there.

John and Eliza's eldest daughter, Gwladys, a Visitation nun, died on 3 February 1880. In a letter about her death to his son Reginald, John wrote:

> It is a pang to lose a sister, but is a deeper pain to lose a beloved daughter, so devoted to me as dear little Gwladys was. Her life was one of sacrifice and suffering. She gave up the home she loved to become a nun, among foreigners with whom she had no sympathy. With her it was truly 'All for Jesus'. For more than twenty years she bore, with brave and gentle patience, the intense trials of a wearing religious life and the acute sufferings (they were many) of constantly failing health. And now, dear child, the worries and pains are past! I have one tie less to earth; one motive more to think of heaven.'

John did not, in the event, long survive his daughter Gwladys. In September 1880 he and Mary went to Biarritz for the winter and both died, within ten days of each other, that December.

John's sons – Herbert, Bernard, John, Reginald (Reggie) and Francis (Frank) – all seem to have gathered at Biarritz as their father and stepmother lay dying. Herbert, writing to his great friend Lady Herbert of Lea, said:

> I do not think he can last many days for he has become sensibly weaker and the action of his heart feebler and more painful. God has poured his graces into his soul in a torrent during his last illness. His humility, simplicity, gentleness, faith and love form the most consoling spectacle I have ever witnessed. The Lord seems to be sensibly purging away the dross and purifying the gold in the crucible of suffering before taking him. The poor human heart is crushed. Still it rejoices to witness such an end for one to whom I and all his children owe unspeakably more than anyone knows and whom I have always loved most tenderly. Mary is paralysed. It is a race between the two, each wishes to survive the other, if only for a few hours, so as to spare the other the shock of being left alone.

So this perfect, splendid English gentleman was seen off by five sons, three of them priests. The following letter John wrote to their sister May Vaughan, Mother Clare Magdalen, Prioress of St

Augustine's, Newton Abbot, two days after their father's death, is worth quoting:

Hotel de Paris
Biarritz
December 18, 1880

Darling May,

At the time of my father's death I had been just twelve days at Biarritz and during all that time he was suffering incessantly. Imagine a man condemned to pass *months* in a chair without once leaving it, even to go to bed! How terrible to think of! Yet add to this, weakness and exhaustion! An inability even to breathe without pain, suffering from the heart and the torture of immense swollen legs which he seemed to feel more than anything else.

If he could have slept a little and forgotten his pain it would have been some alleviation, but he could not sleep for his heart would not let him, however much he longed for it. When in this state he had to bear up also against the heavy cross which was laid upon him in the form of Mary's illness and helplessness and death, in the very next room; yet he bore all for the love of God, and without a murmur or a complaint. He was perpetually praising and magnifying God, and not so much His justice or power, but His unfathomable compassion and unutterable love. The greater the suffering the greater seemed to be this love of God, the more he felt the divine hand of God afflicting him, the more tenderly he pressed it to his lips. He would take the little crucifix and press it again and again to his mouth and his whole countenance would light up and his love seemed to overflow his heart, until at last he would break forth into some beautiful burst of fervent prayer. The words he used were truly most exquisite, but the tone and accentuation, the manner and stress he put on them was what was most wonderful and spoke, as a revelation from God, of the greatness and depth of his emotion and feeling. I had many long chats, tête-à-tête when he opened out his soul as he had never done before to me. He spoke of his early life; of our saintly mother; of his home and family life during her lifetime; of his happiness, strength, prosperity and how God had blessed him during his whole course upon earth; of the way God had blessed him in his children and all his family relations, etc.

He would relate a hundred little incidents and events of his past life to show how much he had received from God and how much he owed Him. Curiously enough, though he was often fearing the attacks of the evil one, and severe temptations, he was entirely free from them; he told me he felt no fear, no anxiety about his conscience at all. He was at peace with his conscience and troubled by no misgivings. His confidence in the compassion of God seemed boundless. 'Do not think me an innocent man', he said 'because I am a poor fragile miserable sinner. I have sinned greatly, but had I sinned less I do not think I *could* have loved God so much.' He often referred to the wondrous change that must come over a man at the moment of death. 'How completely', he said, 'one must become severed and cut off from the whole earth, and all amid which one lived and moved!' 'To be face to face with the Maker of the Universe! How wonderful! I do not mean', he added, 'of this earth only, but of sun and moon and stars and the vast limitless wide-stretching heavens, etc.'

He said one very strange thing once, and I almost fancy he must have been wandering a little in his mind, though he spoke quite sensibly enough that moment. We were remarking that the self-same swollen body he had would one day rise again beautiful and immortal. 'The bodies of the dead', he said, 'rise in a state of youth.' I said, 'It is generally believed about the age of Our Lord's risen body, which is considered about the plenitude of manhood, viz. about thirty or three and thirty'. 'Oh yes', he said, 'I thought so, I always thought so. . .' We then waited to see why he thought so and felt so secure on the point. As however he seemed reluctant to speak, Bernard asked him his reason, to which he replied slowly, 'Well, it was a curious thing you know, but I was at my prayers one time, and I saw an old grey-headed fellow die, and go to purgatory, but bless me! When he came out again he was quite a smart young fellow.'

He said all this so seriously that we did not know what to think; I know I simply burst out laughing.

The last four and twenty hours of his life he lost consciousness almost completely and wandered a good deal in his mind. He said our Blessed Lady was coming to fetch him on the octave day of her feast, if he were well enough to go.

Then he thought the sisters, whom he called 'those two girls' were keeping him from going to Heaven. I said, 'Oh! You do not wish to go yet if it is not God's will, do you?' 'Ah, no', he said, 'but is it God's will? I suspect it is the will of these two girls! Why! If they go on nursing these two worthless legs, they may keep me here for months.'

He breathed his last just when he said he would between six and seven on the evening of Thursday. We were all around him, Frank, Bernard and myself, the two sisters and the footman.

He received Holy Viaticum that morning. The last Mass at which he was present on earth was mine, offered up for himself. Bernard, who said Mass just before me gave him the Blessed Sacrament.

We are going to have a solemn requiem Mass in the parish church this morning at ten o'clock. Both bodies are to be conveyed to Courtfield together where they will await the resurrection in the family vault.

I hope these few hurried lines will be of some interest to you.

Your fond brother,
John

Their coffins were brought by steamer from Bordeaux to Bristol and they were interred in the vault at Courtfield on 11 January 1881.

A letter of condolence, from their friend William Partridge to Frank Vaughan at 49 Gloucester Place, Hyde Park, 22 December 1880, gives some idea of the high regard in which John was held by all who knew him:

Dear Vaughan,

My wife and I most truly condole with you and Mrs Frank Vaughan and the rest of your family in the very sad bereavements which have fallen upon your house. I fear that Friday next will be a trying day for you all. You have our sympathy.

If the departed ones could have had a wish it would have been to have been united in their deaths as they were in their lives, leaving behind them as they have done a bright example of conjugal love and union, and of exemplary action in the discharge of every social duty. Since my boyhood I have been accustomed to look up to your Father as the personification of everything good and noble. The ripe scholar, the finished gentleman; and you must pardon my giving expression to these feelings. Ever since the days of our Grandfathers, our Families have been friends and neighbours. With kind remembrance to you all, Believe me,

Sincerely Yours,
William Partridge

HERBERT VAUGHAN

Herbert Alfred Henry Joseph Thomas, Eliza and John's eldest child, was born on 15 April 1832 at Beaufort Buildings, Gloucester and baptised there two days later by Father Francis Daniel, then chaplain at Courtfield. His godparents were Mrs Vaughan, his grandmother, and Mr Joseph Weld his uncle (Eliza kept a note in her missal of all the names, birth dates and godparents of her children).

Herbert was very much the leader of the children, the apple of his father's eye (he delighted in the bold, eager, adventurous spirit of his eldest son), happiest when roving the Courtfield estate hunting rabbits with his dogs, or breaking-in wild Welsh ponies from the hills. He became an excellent horseman and loved partridge shooting with his father – indeed shooting was perhaps his favourite sport. Years later he wrote to a nephew, 'giving it up cost me more than anything else, when I took to the Church'.

He received his earliest Latin lessons from Father Abbott, the priest in Monmouth, and at the age of nine was sent to Stonyhurst, the great Jesuit college in Lancashire where his father and grandfather had been before him and which had been given to the Jesuits by Thomas Weld, a relation on his grandmother's side. The four years he spent there seem undistinguished and in 1847, owing to some disagreement, he was removed to the Benedictines at Downside for a year and subsequently to another Jesuit school, Brugelette, in Belgium (after transferred to the Rue Vaugirard in Paris) where he spent three pleasant years and learnt more than he ever did at his English schools. The boys worked much harder and took a greater and more intelligent interest in their studies. He always felt that the tone and spirit of the college were very high, and raised him after the ordeal of an English school: 'They always made you feel they were treating you as a gentleman.' He was nicknamed 'Milord Roastbeef' and did not much like the French boys, 'for I was an English boy and sometimes had to assert myself with my English fists'.

It was there at Brugelette, when he was sixteen years old, that he made up his mind to become a priest. He conceived a burning desire to consecrate himself to the Welsh mission and deeply regretted being unable to speak Welsh. Herbert made this decision in 1848, but in a letter of his mother's written in 1846 to her friend Madame Rio she says, 'Ever since I read the account of St Bernard and his four brothers leaving the world and retiring into a monastery I have prayed that all my sons may follow their example. I am confident Herbert will become a Priest.' It therefore caused her no surprise when he told her his decision to renounce everything and become a priest. She said simply, 'I knew it, dear'.

It is impossible to imagine how difficult a decision this must have been for an idealistic, romantic, sensitive and in some ways lonely boy. He loved Courtfield, the country life, riding and shooting, and he also knew his father, to whom he was devoted, had great expectations of him making a career in the army and succeeding him at Courtfield. Indeed his father was bitterly disappointed when he heard the news, exclaiming, 'well if Herbert goes, all the others may go too'. And this was what very nearly happened – Herbert, Roger, Kenelm, Joseph, Bernard and John becoming priests and Gwladys, Teresa, Mary and Clare nuns.

His Mother Eliza had of course been delighted by this so obvious answer to her prayers. A favourite saying of hers was that as she had received everything from God she would like to give everything back to God and what more precious than her children? She never tired of telling her children stories about the wonders the love of God and devout prayers could work. A note in her missal records the date she did indeed give Herbert to God: 'Our beloved child Herbert left us on Monday 13th Oct. 1851, and crossed to Boulogne on his way to the Eternal City on 23rd Oct.'

In Rome, Herbert shared lodgings in the Piazza de la Minerva with the poet Aubrey de Vere, who described him thus:

> I like my companion better every day. He is a Mr Vaughan, the eldest son of one of the great old Catholic families of England. He renounces prospects as brilliant as almost any man in England can command to be a priest in some out-of-the-way village in Wales, and seems as happy as the day is long in his studies and devotions. He is very handsome and refined and as innocent as a child.
>
> He sits up half the night reading Thomas Aquinas and tells me the next morning that he has been dreaming that people have been burning him alive and that it has given him no pain.

In the same year de Vere visited Courtfield to introduce himself to Colonel Vaughan's family, and remarked later, 'I have never seen such simply noble, generous, devout and humble people. The beautiful mother of twelve children cannot feel satisfied unless her sons all become priests and her daughters nuns. Though this would cause the extinction of one more of those old English families which for centuries have held their own in stormier days.'

Eliza's death in 1853, when Herbert was twenty-one, had a most devastating effect on the whole family, who felt they could not live without her. Herbert abandoned his priestly studies and travelled back to 'dear Courtfield' to be with his stricken father. Back in Rome again after a few weeks, his diaries have a melancholy, unhappy trend, filled with doubts about his fitness to serve God. Restless and unable to study, his health became so bad friends feared for his life. But he *knew* it was God's will to use him to accomplish great works and prayed he might live to become a priest: 'I pray that I may live for so happy an hour – not so happy an hour but so divine, so heavenly an hour – for that it be attended with sweet comforts and joys I do not so much care . . . I cannot know whether he wishes me to have two or three or five talents, but surely I may pray fervently to have five talents'. And he asked God to give him the grace to double them. As always, he was piercingly aware of his faults and thought that ill health might be God's way of taming his impetuous and critical disposition:

> Were my constitution stronger and equal to the energy of my character, I should be going very wrong in very many ways. And now even as things are what a host of bad habits have I not to rout out! How hasty I am in speaking – how sweeping in condemnations, how positive in assertion, how persevering in my own opinion, how little yielding to others, how wayward and obstinate! . . . My line is to arrive. I cannot walk but I must run – I am imprudent because I have not time and patience to consult people's feelings and ways of thought. I am hasty and rash because I do not care for my own comfort. . . . If I live for over fifty years, and by that time have learnt never to criticise, to become quieter and gentler in manner, I shall have done something. If I don't succeed even then, I shall have had a good battle with myself, I shall be able to confirm the prophet's words, 'the life of man upon earth is a perpetual warfare'. At all events, fight I will (by God's grace and goodwill) and never cease until I have completely gained a triumph. The very impetuosity I would suppress shall supply its own steam for its direction into a more useful channel. I must remember, as my dear Father used to tell me last summer, that I am to be careful not to break the various powers of nature, but to master them and use them for what is good. Great energy is too valuable a quality to be killed.

In 1852 Herbert moved into the famous Accademia Ecclesiastica frequented by the sons of aristocratic families. Here he met Manning, one of the most brilliant converts from the Oxford Movement, and began what was to be a lifelong friendship. Manning, educated at Harrow and Balliol, where he was President of the Oxford Union, was twenty-four years senior to Herbert and was to have a profound effect on his life and career. Recognising Herbert's deep spirituality, high ideals and zeal for the salvation of souls, he felt he had found the man to help him improve the standard of secular priests, and recommended him to Cardinal Wiseman for the important post of Vice-President at St Edmund's College, Ware.

Herbert was ordained at Lucca on 28 October 1854, when twenty-two years old, and said his first Mass in Florence at the Church of the Blessed Virgin Mary of the Annunziata two days later. Charles Plowden served. Curiously, after so many years of longing to be a priest, his diary says nothing of his feelings at this supreme moment. Perhaps to his sensitive nature it was too holy and intimate for mere words.

At this age he did not have the necessary experience for his first appointment, to St Edmund's. Trying to remedy this, he went on a sort of 'Grand Tour' of principal colleges in France, Germany and

Italy (he was a fluent linguist), endeavouring to gain knowledge about the training of priests and the management of seminaries.

Though unworldly, and at no time in his life interested in ecclesiastical politics, Herbert had plenty of common sense and the ability to get things done. His constant wish was to serve God better. When he became a cardinal he chose as his motto 'Amare et Servire' – to love and to serve.

At the time Herbert was preparing to join St Edmund's, the college was going through a difficult time with ecclesiastical in-fighting and Cardinal Wiseman was having difficulty in getting help with work he considered needed to be done among the teeming masses of London's poor. Religious orders he approached were unwilling, and pleaded such work was contrary to their rule, so he brought in the Oblates of St Charles to assist. St Edmund's however took a dislike to them as foreigners who they feared might try to take over. Manning, Vaughan and some other priests joined the Oblates and when this became known Herbert's position at the College became next to impossible. Also at this time the Oxford Movement, full of enthusiastic converts with newfangled devotional extravagances and Roman practices, was proving obnoxious to hereditary Catholics, who had stuck to their simple faith throughout two hundred years of persecution, only to be now branded as uneducated old fuddy-duddies. That Herbert came from the oldest of old Catholic stock, but had received an up-to-date training abroad, that he was a gentleman with a burning desire to do great things for God, qualified him in the Cardinal's eyes for this important post, but in reality placed him in an impossible position. And Dr Weathers, the President, was decidedly against his appointment. However, Herbert did his best, and perhaps the trials and frustrations he encountered during his seven years here were of value to him in later life, as was the lifelong friendship he formed with Wilfred Ward and his wife (Ward was a lay teacher at St Edmund's).

Tall, handsome* and a beautiful horseman, Herbert's students idolised him, and loved to see him come galloping across the park on the fine charger his father had given him. His kindness and enthusiasm endeared him to the boys and he was able to do a good deal to

---

* Wilfred Ward used to speak of 'Herbert Vaughan's extraordinary personal beauty', and a journalist writing about him on his seventieth birthday said, 'he is still the most handsome man in England'. Probably he had a high degree of sexuality and found it necessary to keep himself on a tight rein until able to sublimate this into acceptable channels.

improve discipline and the tone of the seminary. From this untenable situation he sought work outside the college, founded much-needed missions in neighbouring country towns and with money from his family and friends built a church and school in Hertford where he said Mass on Sundays. It was probably during this time that he changed direction, giving up his idea of missionary work in Wales, for the wider scope of the foreign missions.

After prayerful deliberation and soul-searching, conversations with Wiseman and Manning who encouraged him – and a visit to Spain where he learnt Spanish and also met a saintly Spanish Jesuit, Father Medrano, who advised him to carry on – he went to Courtfield to pray at his mother's tomb and seemed to hear her advising him to begin very quietly and humbly. He now felt ready to start on the first great work of his life – St Joseph's College for Foreign Missions, from which would flow a never-ending stream of missionaries for the conversion of the heathen. But for this he needed money and he decided America would be the best place to get it. So, armed with letters of approval from the bishops, Cardinal Wiseman and the Pope, he set sail from Southampton on 17 September 1863 on the SS *Atrato* and after a rough voyage and storms which smashed the paddle-wheel, limped into Colon (Panama) twenty-one days later.

Here he witnessed the horrific sight of one of the sailors being eaten by a shark – he had tried to get ashore down a rope, but the wind moved the ship, the rope went slack and all that remained was a trunk bobbing on the waves.

Herbert had to wait a week in Colon, a small town of 2,000 inhabitants, for a ship to take him on to San Francisco and was scandalised by much of what he saw. Smallpox was raging, but the civil powers, at war with the Church, had forbidden priests to administer the Sacraments – so people were dying without spiritual help. Churches were closed and weeds grew through the pavements.

He was deeply shocked by the state of the Church and the priests encountered in Colon: 'I have been several times told of priests taking their cocks into the sacristy, hurrying disrespectfully through their Mass and going straight off from the altar to the cockpit. They are great gamblers', he wrote. Herbert did what he could, attending the dying, hearing confessions and baptizing. Finally he got himself arrested for saying Mass in the house of a dying woman. As this was a criminal offence he was forbidden to leave the country, but was allowed out of gaol on a payment of $50. With the help of the British Consul he jumped bail, got across the isthmus and was smuggled aboard the *St Louis* which took him up the Pacific coast to San Francisco.

Arriving in San Francisco on 1 February 1864, Herbert received a serious setback, for Archbishop Allemany received him coolly and told him he might as well return home for on no account would he permit this 'spiritual poaching' in his diocese: they were poor and needed all available money for themselves. Undaunted, he redoubled his prayers and also got the local nuns of the Presentation Order to implore St Joseph's help, though they told him the Archbishop never changed his mind. They agreed to pray during the whole of March, and on the last day and almost at the eleventh hour, he received a letter from the Archbishop granting permission for one sermon in each church and one collection only. His first sermon raised £200, the second £250, and the other churches in proportion, and from San Francisco he sent home between £2,000 and £3,000 and promises of much more, 'All the effect of prayer – St Joseph did the work'.

Herbert travelled about California, becoming popular with the people as he journeyed, and his mission so caught their imagination that they gave generously and he seems to have collected as much as £7,000 during the five months spent there. For himself, he grew to love the country and the people and for the rest of his life was partial to everything American – their energy and spirit of adventure struck a chord in his own nature. He thought the Sacramento River rolling into the Bay of San Francisco more beautiful than anything he had seen in the old world.

In July he left for Peru aboard the *Uncle Sam*. On board he found everyone in a state of consternation because the redoubtable Captain Semmes of the *Alabama* had just captured a San Francisco vessel, the *Golden Age*, and it was feared *Uncle Sam* might suffer the same fate. In his diary Herbert noted that should this happen he would try to interest Captain Semmes in the foreign missions! However, the voyage proved uneventful.

Arriving at Lima on 20 July, he found conditions similar to Panama with religion at a low ebb. 'The monks here are in the lowest state of degradation and suppression of them would be an act of divine favour', he wrote. One wonders what he found in the monastery. But he set to work in this strange city, begging from street to street, from door to door. 'There is much humiliation and many little crosses in begging', he reported, but humiliation was sweetened by success. In vain did the government try to stop him, becoming alarmed at the activities of this young priest who seemed likely to take so much money out of their country. They passed a proclamation forbidding him to collect from the inhabitants of Peru. But, 'as laws here are of no consequence, so was this inhibitory decree. The President's wife, in the presence of her husband, gave me $250 when I went to the palace to try my luck with the President's purse, and he actually apologised for the disgraceful decree he had passed against me, saying I could collect privately', he was happy to relate.

From Lima, Herbert's pioneer spirit took him long journeys into the interior. Once he started at 2.30am and rode thirty-three miles before breakfast. At Arequipa he notes, 'it had the best Bishop in Peru but alas! he was buried just before I got there'. Still he managed to collect $2,000 there all the same.

The account of his ride across the Pampa Grande or Great Desert of Peru is interesting:

> The road, or rather pathway, is strewn with the bones of horses and mules, and after the vast plain of sand is passed the track between and over the Coast Range of the Andes is covered with the remains of animals that have fallen by the way exhausted by fatigue or thirst. As soon as the animal can no longer go on, he is relieved of his burden (everything that is carried into the interior has to be borne by mules – there are no roads for carts or carriages), he is necessarily left behind by his owner, and then before the drove of Mules is out of sight, great vultures, gathering from all parts, come down upon him. One alights on his head – the poor animal seems to have lost all sense of self-preservation – and plucks out his eye. The poor beast is soon despatched and the next day the carcass is dried up and abandoned by man and beast. Not always, however, by man, for whether it be to remind him of death, or as an ornament in the wilderness, these dried horses, mules, and asses are made to stand up, some headless, some on one or two legs, in every shape and form that a dried broken-up carcass can be turned into.

After Peru, where he had collected $15,000, this indomitable priest rode hundreds of miles on horseback down into Chile where he found Santiago 'the most Catholic town for its size in Christendom'. The civil authorities, unlike Lima and Colon, allowed him to travel where he liked and collect what he could, sometimes meeting with extraordinary generosity:

> I went up and down the country, preaching in the churches and begging alms of the faithful from door to door. One day as I was walking along the street a man came up to me and said in Spanish – 'Are you the person who is begging for the establishment of a Missionary College in London?' 'Yes, I am', I replied. 'Then', said he, 'take these $100.' 'Who are you', said I, 'that I may put your name in my book.' 'I am nobody', he replied and away he went and I saw him

no more. Another day I was begging from house to house and a poor washer woman gave me the coppers that were standing by her soap suds. The next house I went into was that of a rich man. I asked him for alms and he put his name down for £1,000.

Altogether Herbert collected $25,000 in cash, and the promise of 35,000 more to follow. The money came from all sorts and conditions of men: Señor Rafael Larrein, President of the Senate of Santiago, gave $500, José Ramón Ossa $250, the Bishops of Concepcion and Coquimlo $250 each, the Archbishop of Santiago $200. Some are entered as 'pobres' (poor people) $1. Though very successful at it, Herbert all his life hated begging. For him, 'Begging is not a thing which comes easily to an English gentleman, even in a good cause'.

In March 1865 he left the cities of the Pacific and sailed with Captain Turner RN on board HMS *Charybdis* bound for Rio. The weather became so rough the captain was afraid to try the voyage through the Straits of Magellan, so the *Charybdis* rounded the Horn 'with royals and studding sails'. On this thirty-three-day voyage they encountered more bad weather off the Falklands and Herbert records that he was 'lashed to the table'.*

Arriving in Rio, Herbert heard the news of Cardinal Wiseman's death, which left him 'broken down with sorrow'. Wiseman had been his great friend and supporter, 'giving me help and sympathy in my hateful mission of getting money in these countries'.

He was a spectator at a slave market in Rio where he saw a black girl of about twenty sold to the highest bidder – $510; he walked away feeling sick. But, however harrowing it was, his visit paid enormous dividends. In Brazil he was equally successful, the money poured in and soon he felt he had collected enough to return home and start his College.

After almost two years of his wandering life and freedom to work in his own way, Herbert could not but help feeling apprehensive of the trials and frustrations awaiting him at home. He wrote to Mrs Ward telling her he would be returning soon, bringing with him ten burses to maintain students for the foreign missions: 'I have collected about £10,000 and have some other promises which must not be counted until they are realised. My wish would be to make a start at once hiring a house in or near London for that purpose. If we have not Oblate Fathers for the work, then horse the coach from

---

* My husband Joe and I also had this experience during a stormy Atlantic crossing in the *Princess Irene* in 1962.

some other stable, jobbing our horses until we can keep our own.'

News of Manning's appointment as Archbishop of Westminster filled him with joy. He wrote at once, congratulating him and offering his obedience to serve in any capacity. He had a begging trip planned for Pernambuco where he expected to make a big collection, but abandoned this when a sudden summons from the new Archbishop called him home. He reached England at the end of July 1865 and was received with great kindness by Manning who advised him to go ahead with the work on which his heart was set.

Mrs Ward told him of a possible home for his college, Holcombe House, Mill Hill, and directly Herbert saw this Georgian house (which may have reminded him of Courtfield) it seemed to him the ideal situation. That it was not for sale did not deter him – he stormed St Joseph with prayers and the story of how he left a small parcel containing a figure of the Saint in the hallway is well known, and very soon the house was his! So a start was made, and Herbert opened his seminary on 1 March 1866 – very quietly and humbly, with little or no furniture, one professor and one student. They were so poor they slept on hay and for a time lived on cold tinned food to save the expense of a cook. Herbert wanted all available money for setting up burses for the training of his students, and he felt missionaries should accustom themselves to leading spartan lives!

Herbert Vaughan's was the first Catholic foreign missionary college in England; American generosity had made a beginning possible, and now it was up to the Catholics of England to support it. Archbishop Manning helped with a great public meeting at St James's Hall, Piccadilly, in April 1866 when the hall was thronged, ten bishops on the platform and dozens of distinguished laymen. Manning made one of his finest speeches explaining the important work the Missionary Society was engaged in. He also introduced Lady Herbert of Lea,* who virtually adopted Herbert Vaughan and his Missionary Society and was to do so much for the success of the college among her rich and influential friends.

The spiritual affinity which developed between Herbert Vaughan and Lady Herbert they likened to that between Saint Jerome and Saint Paula, and in Herbert's many letters to her during forty years of friendship their tender love and caring for each other shines as their lodestar leading them towards God. A remarkable woman,

---

* Elizabeth Herbert (1821–1911) was the daughter of Lt.-General Charles Ashe à Court Repington, CB, and niece of the first Baron Heytsbury. By her marriage in 1846 to Sir Sidney Herbert (1810–61) she had four children.

her zeal and activity matched his own, and not for nothing was she known as 'Lady Lightening'. The widow of Sir Sidney Herbert* of Crimea fame – as Secretary for War, he was responsible for Florence Nightingale's going out and setting up her hospital there – when she became a Catholic in 1865 there was a desperate struggle at Wilton House, the family seat, to prevent her taking her children with her. They were made wards of chancery and the Lords de Vesci and Clanwilliam, the trustees, saw to it that they were brought up in the Church of England. This was agony to poor Elizabeth Herbert, who eventually found comfort and solace in helping Herbert Vaughan with his schemes for the newly started Mill Hill Missionary Society. He wrote to her on 13 January 1867 from Mill Hill:

> How strange that the Queen sitting in the midst of her splendours and fashionable appliances at Wilton should so singularly think and feel with the poor Head of this poor beginning of a Foreign Missionary College, which looks out on a field of 800 millions of heathen and says 'Here is my work and my harvest!' A singular contrast in outward life and as singular a harmony and conformity in that interior life, which alone is life. Blessed be God! In more ways than either of us have said, I perceive that our thoughts and ways are one . . . and so you and I are drawn close together in mutual sympathy and love, and our home here below shall be Mount Calvary, and our occupation to gather Our Blessed Lord and our studies and interest how to make each other more like to Him, and then how to serve Him in His living images; His poor, and those perishing souls for whom he wept and died.

In October 1867 Lady Herbert took her seventeen-year-old son George, thirteenth Earl of Pembroke, on a voyage to Jamaica for his health and Herbert sent her a present of a portable altar, and a letter explaining, 'The little chalice in it was used for centuries at Courtfield and was hidden in a wall in the age of persecution, bring it me back'. He also gave her advice on books to take, clothing, American folding armchairs – 'All "knowing people" crossing the Atlantic take them' – and introductions to people who may be of use to her. He also provided an antidote to sea-sickness, as well as a lot of spiritual advice, ending up with the comment that sea voyages open the mind and heart to the love of God for all souls, especially the most abandoned, and the salutation:

> And now, good bye, may God Bless You always, train you and keep you. Change of scene, the necessity for activity and occupation,

---

* Son of the eleventh Earl of Pembroke, by his second marriage, and half-brother to the twelfth Earl. He was created first Baron Herbert of Lea in 1861.

humanly speaking, will help to keep you up. I pray that you may have many consolations in your dear son and that you may soon come back to those you have left behind, and that you may love and serve Him more and more every day, whose arms are always stretched open to receive you in His embraces. Pray too, for me and for the development of this work here begun in poverty and difficulty.

I almost fear to send you these lines, lest you should think me 'preaching', but, dearest child, I can only write you out of the abundance of my heart what is in it. And you must take me as I am if we are to be on such terms as may help one another to Heaven like brother and sister. Write me a good scolding – do.

Lady Herbert returned home in December, and on the 18th Herbert wrote to tell her of his relief at getting her safely back:

Dec. 18th 1867, Mill Hill.

Thank God, my darling sister, that you are safe again in England. I can't tell you the joy your arrival is to me, the relief! I have been, ever since you left, under the most horrible presentiment that fever or the sea would end your life, and it has been all I could do to shake off an impression, so unfounded and unreal. God only knows what I went through the night of 20th November.

The chief houses in the City thought that evening that the ship was lost. I was awake the whole night, and prayed for you as I'd never done before, and I broke down next morning, three times in my Mass. The server could not make out what was happening; but that evening the good news came . . . I feel as though I don't care a bit to see you, I am so thankful to think you are safe back to continue.

Womanlike, she was upset by his letter, as Herbert's reply to her answering letter shows:

Dec. 20th 1867. The Mill

Indeed dearest sister mine, I would be at York Place between 12 and 1 tomorrow, even though I had all the *Dublins** on my hands in order to see you. You little knew the meaning of those words of mine, which disappointed you. Never since 1853 [the date his mother died] had I suffered so much in heart and mind as during the last two months. The *knowing* was and is so great a happiness that in its first presence, the *sense of seeing* felt it could wait.

Though Herbert writes to her as 'dearest sister', or 'darling child', Lady Herbert had become for him the perfect substitute for the adored

---

* The *Dublin Review*, with which Herbert Vaughan was helping his friend and its editor, Wilfred Ward, at this time.

mother he lost in 1853. In another letter he writes:

> I hope we may have some little time together before you go Rome-
> wards. Why not a quiet day at the Mill. I think we can do one another
> some good. Today I said to the Archbishop (Manning) that we under-
> stand one another well and I said something of what I thought of you,
> and why I loved you, etc. He said 'I am very glad' and saw great good
> in our intimate relations. I told him a little of the good you had done
> me: but of course I was silent about what is and must be so secret to
> each other, if we are to be a mutual spiritual help. Tear this up and
> don't show it to the Weld-Blundells!!!!
>
> Your devoted son!
>
> See what I have written by accident for brother, and yet there is more
> in the slip than one would think, perhaps?

His letter to her of 9 January the following year perfectly illustrates
the depth of their mutual love and understanding:

> Jan 9th 1868. The Mill.
>
> My dearest Sister, I have read your letter through and have had
> a good cry, like a fool! You have quite caught the history of those
> letters, one after the other. I love you with so true a love, with better
> than a human love, that I *would* write them, though they cost me not
> a little. You see I did not quite know when you said once before that
> you would be 'humble and obedient', how far it was a *facon de parler*
> or a fact.
>
> I did not quite know how far I could venture on remarks which
> might, I thought perhaps, lead to your misunderstanding me. And I
> was not sure whether, from the fact of our having been so differently
> placed in this world: you, surrounded by *such* an atmosphere and
> brought up in the Church, whether the tone and spirit of our thoughts
> would be in discord or harmony when brought together. And now
> you have *completely* satisfied me, that I am not deceived in what I, in
> my heart believed. I shall now feel towards you as I do towards the
> Archbishop in the matter of his writings. When they are important he
> has always shown them to me and made me censor, and I have cut
> out *frightfully* some times. Once he re-wrote a long Pastoral because I
> was able to show him something against the line he was taking. This
> is only for your ear, for nobody else's, but I say it to show you that love
> and reverence do not mean (and I knew you would be the last to think
> they did), that we are simply to praise, and to be afraid of speaking
> when we catch another and perhaps a larger and more practical face of
> a many-sided truth. As chance to discern a greater prudence, or what
> may be more for the good of our alter ego, or what may be nobler or
> more pleasing to God.

And we can often judge these things for one another. (Though we may be less gifted and less wise or good) when we cannot discern them ourselves, because they are too close under our eyes, having run out of our pen, and as it were inadequate representations of our real self. Do you the same for me and never be afraid of saying all to me, as I was almost afraid of speaking to you. But now I know better. And your letter does not contain a sentiment with which I do not heartily agree and admire.

I think this letter shows something of the depths of spirituality and mutual help this wonderful friendship gave these two remarkable people. Surely the good Lord was kind when He created these two saintly souls to sustain and comfort each other in the difficulties of life.

Often described as a 'proud prelate' on account of his good looks and authoritative manner, Herbert Vaughan was in reality a sensitive and humble man with a lifelong desire to bring souls to the knowledge and love of God. In this he was greatly helped by the blessed spiritual love and friendship he shared for so many years with Lady Herbert. They were kindred souls and worked side by side – she was called the 'Mother of the Mill' and poured out help financial and practical in an unstinted stream. Sir Shane Leslie edited the Cardinal's letters to her, which were published by Burns Oates in 1942. Unfortunately, her letters to him appear to have been destroyed. She is buried beside him at Mill Hill under the simple epitaph 'The Mother of the Mill'.

While quoting from this correspondence, I hope I will be forgiven for taking a great leap forward in Herbert's story and including here his last letter to Lady Herbert. On it she wrote 'Precious letter':

March 22, 1903

I received the Last Sacraments on the 19th and thought St Joseph would come for me: but he saw I was not ready then. Perhaps I may be on the 25th – perhaps later.* A good son delights to enjoy the presence of a good Father, to share his company, his interests and even his nature and his happiness.

We are always saying 'Our Father who art in Heaven', and then secretly adding, but whatever you do leave me where I am! Do we believe? We weep and wail over the death of those we love, because we do not sensibly believe that they have gone home to their real Father and to all their best friends.

*Cardinal Vaughan in fact lived on until 19 June. Lady Herbert survived him by some eight years, dying in October 1911, aged ninety.

Of course, I know that Our Father wished us to do all we can by natural and ordinary means, to prolong our life of work and probation, and I have nothing to reproach myself with in this matter. I have got a good male nurse and every care needful. But a man of over seventy has a right to look with a certain yearning towards the end. And we who are 'slaves' have our own little rights and hopes, which our Mother and St Joseph will keep an eye on . . . you may be sure if I get home before you, I will do more for you there than I ever could on earth.

During his travels in America Herbert had learnt to appreciate the power of the press – he thought one newspaper article worth ten sermons. When the ailing Catholic periodical *The Tablet* looked like folding up in 1868 he bought it and, without any journalistic experience, decided to edit and run it himself, which he did for three years. His friends supported and helped him and from a shaky start he transformed the paper into a widely respected weekly. At one time he also helped Wilfred Ward with his quarterly, *Dublin Review* (see his letter of 20 December 1867 to Lady Herbert, page 73). She also took an interest and often helped with advice and articles, being herself quite an experienced writer. Afterwards Mr Snead-Cox – later the author of a two-volume *Life of* Herbert Vaughan (1910) – was given the editorship.

In 1871 the first consignment of St Joseph's Foreign Missionaries were sent by the Holy See to the negro population in America. Four missionaries sailed for Maryland with Herbert Vaughan and were received there by the Archbishop of Baltimore. Herbert's society was starting to bear fruit. He found the negro slaves in total ignorance of Christianity: on being shown a crucifix and told it represented the death of Jesus Christ an old man said, 'How wicked of those Yankees to treat a poor Southern General like that!'

Herbert travelled about the Southern States and was saddened by the callous way negroes were treated, even by the priests who regarded them as so many dogs. Slaves had only recently been set free which he felt was a step in the right direction. Given time it would all come right, and he had a distant hope of American negroes evangelising Africa itself. He must have been encouraged when, in December 1891, the first American coloured priest, Father Charles A. Uncles, was ordained by Cardinal Gibbons; he had been trained by the Mill Hill Father of Baltimore. Herbert's hope was being realised. A little later a party of Mill Hill missionaries set out for Uganda.

On his return to England in 1872 Herbert, at the young age of forty, was elected Bishop of Salford to replace Bishop Turner who had died suddenly. He would have preferred to remain with his newly founded Society at Mill Hill but, obedient to the Pope, he appointed Canon Benoit as Rector, while himself remaining Superior General of St Joseph's Missionary Society. He took himself off on a ten-day retreat with the Redemptionists at Clapham in preparation for his consecration and then travelled to Manchester and presented himself at the Cathedral House, Salford, on foot and carrying a carpet bag. On being asked by one of the resident clergy who he was and what he wanted he replied, 'Oh, I'm Herbert Vaughan and I've come to be consecrated'. This tremendous ceremony was performed the next day, 26 October 1872, by Archbishop Manning in St John's Cathedral in the presence of a great gathering of Lancashire Catholics.

Thus began the third important chapter in Herbert's life.

His first public appearance as a bishop was at a temperance demonstration in Manchester's Free Trade Hall with Archbishop Manning and Father Nugent, who was known as 'the Apostle of Temperance'. Herbert, though he hated drunkenness, made it clear that he could have no part with those who spoke as though total abstinence was a commandment of God. He told them he was not himself a teetotaller, and even believed that alcohol taken in moderation could have a beneficial effect. While admiring the heroism of many who took the pledge, they must not regard it as a necessity and look down on those who had not taken it. Understandably, his speech caused consternation among the teetotal leaders on the platform, but his honest and fearless approach was received with delight by his audience in the crowded hall.

Drunkenness was common in Manchester at this time and one of his first acts as Bishop of Salford was to organise a 'Crusade of Rescue' and he hoped to establish a branch in every parish in his dioceses in his war against the 'Demon Drink'. He was particularly concerned at the plight of the children, whose first and frequent errands were fetching drink from public houses – 'they grew up with drink in their blood', he said.

Next Herbert instituted a seminary, a sort of finishing school for the training of young priests who had often received their education abroad – in Rome, Paris, Valladolid, or Lisbon, say – and lacked practical experience or work in an English parish.

He expected high standards of his clergy, and insisted on his priests visiting people in their homes, saying 'a house-going Priest makes a Church-going people'. He approved of Church services in the vernacular as he thought people could pray better in a language they understood. Writing to Lady Herbert, he commented, 'it is only you converts who know Latin so much better than English: you see we old Cats are not so well educated! Very few of the lower classes in Salford and Manchester talk Latin and still fewer understand it!'

The new bishop did not neglect the secular education of his flock. His travels on the Continent had made him aware of the advantages of a college where young men could learn a trade to fit them for the growing industry and technology of rapidly expanding Manchester. Accordingly, St Bede's Commercial College was founded. He was also much concerned with children in public elementary schools and teaching them Christianity, for, as he said, they are the strength and hope of the future – they form the young democracy that is going to rule our country to make or mar the future of Christianity in this land. We know not what may lie before the Catholic Church in the present century. But we do know the future depends upon the child. The greatest service we can render to God is by training the young to become Apostles of Catholic truth.'

The Jesuits, who already had a fine church in the city, now wished to build a school and claimed their right to do so under a sixteenth-century law. Their bishop objected as he did not want a rival establishment close to the one he intended building. The Jesuits thought such a young and inexperienced bishop could easily be persuaded to give way, but they had misjudged their man. Once Herbert was convinced he was doing God's will, no thought of surrender or compromise entered his mind. He was a Galahad in defence of his Holy Grail.

Mr Snead-Cox has told in his *Life of Herbert Vaughan* the story of this dispute with the Jesuits during the six long years it took the Bishop to establish his authority. No doubt he found this protracted, hard-fought battle and his necessary frequent absences in Rome exceptionally exhausting and his straightforward, direct nature must often have been saddened by the devious methods of his opponents in regard to their alleged privilege. The Bishop won his case, and in his farewell audience with the Pope His Holiness reminded him that a victor should go more than half way towards peace and reconciliation. Herbert's first act on reaching his dioceses was to go into retreat at Stonyhurst, and to ask the Jesuits to conduct the Salford clergy retreat – but Archbishop Manning was not so forgiving.

This struggle was but the prologue to a much wider dispute with the Jesuits in 1877, conducted by the now Cardinal Manning and the bishops against the religious orders who claimed exemption from diocesan jurisdiction. Manning went to Rome, determined to get the position clarified, but the delaying tactics employed by the Jesuits eventually wore him down, and in 1880 he asked Herbert to take his place. Herbert, with his cousin Clifford, Bishop of Clifton, arranged that one of them should always remain in Rome to counteract the Jesuits' delaying tactics. During this period he unearthed some important papers which caused dismay in the enemy camp. In November that year he received a letter from Cardinal McCloskey stressing the importance of the case for the United States. He had copies of this letter distributed to the Commission of Cardinals. And either he or Clifford saw each of the ten cardinals at least once. By January the Commission sent its findings in favour of the English Bishops to the Pope. In May 1881 the Bill, 'Romanos Pontifices', established a complete victory for the English bishops.

Herbert waited outside the printer's office for the first copies of the bill. He was given three and wrote in his diary: 'I took them down to St Peter's without opening them, offering them to St Peter from myself, the Bishop of Clifton and the Episcopate, promising to conform to its decision in the letter and spirit to the best of my ability . . . on Sunday the Bishop of Clifton and I went to St Peter's to give thanks.'

Once again Herbert's tenacity of purpose had won the day, greatly enhancing his standing with his fellow bishops in England and America. In Rome the curia had a saying, 'Manning the diplomat, Clifford the lawyer, Vaughan the devil!'

After the fray, and a month's rest on doctor's orders at Bad Kissingen, Herbert was impatient to get back to Salford and continue with St Bede's Commercial College. He loved Lancashire and Lancashire folk and thought them 'the grandest people in England for popular energy and piety'.

When the aquarium next door to St Bede's came up for sale the Bishop bought it for £6,800 and for a short time tried to run it, importing an alligator, snakes and cockatoos as added attraction, but alas the Mancunians still remained uninterested so he had the architect incorporate it into the college as a museum and assembly hall.

As well as his work in Salford, Herbert was in continuous touch with his growing Mill Hill missionaries where Father Benoit was carrying on his work and Lady Herbert also being of the greatest help. At one stage when his brothers John and Bernard were also in Manchester they were referred to as 'Thought, Word and Deed', and certainly Herbert was a glutton for work. The joke used to be that, when he had a spare five minutes, he would ring the bell and ask his secretary what new thing he could start.

In 1878 he approved of Alice Ingham joining the order as Mother Mary Frances of the Franciscan Missionaries of St Joseph, and soon Mill Hill had 'sisters' to cook and clean and look after them.

Herbert Vaughan, a man with a vision, a total love of God and dedicated to saving souls, was indeed the proverbial grain of mustard seed. During his twenty years in Salford he took an active interest in all matters affecting the life of the city, became friends with the Protestant bishop, and did everything possible to alleviate the lot of the poor who grew to love him and regard him as their friend.

He also set about reorganising the failed Catholic Truth Society. Writing to Lady Herbert on 24 October 1884, he asked, 'Would you mind a committee of the Catholic Truth Society meeting at your house on November 5th at 3pm and taking part in it yourself? We are reviving it and this time I think it will succeed.' And of course he was right. The many publications on a wide variety of subjects on sale in most churches for a few pence testify to its popularity and have brought enlightenment and help to millions of souls throughout the world.

In January 1892 Cardinal Manning, Herbert's oldest friend, lay dying at Westminster and Herbert was with him for the last five days. Inevitably, two men of such strong character had sometimes had differences of opinion, but the bond of friendship remained unbroken to the end. Writing to Dr Casartelli, who succeeded him at Salford, he said, 'it has been a great consolation to me to help my old friend of forty-one years to die'; and later, on his first public appearance as Archbishop of Westminster, he proclaimed his lasting indebtedness to his 'dearest father and friend': 'I owe him obligations, intellectual, moral and personal of a more deep and enduring kind than I can find words to portray'. When it became apparent that Herbert would be elected to succeed Manning he took it on himself to write a private letter to the Pope stating his unsuitability and begging His Holiness to find someone more worthy for such an important position.

It was not to be. The cardinals met on 20 March 1892 and nine days later Herbert Vaughan was elected Archbishop of Westminster.

Unlike Wiseman and Manning, Herbert Vaughan was not an intellectual and had little understanding or interest in contemporary Catholic thought. Not particularly diplomatic and often tactless, he appears to have lacked a certain sensitivity for the feelings of others – one of his letters to Lady Herbert reveals this (see page 73) – and his impatient nature and hastiness with ecclesiastical ceremonies earned him the nickname of the 'Scarlet runner'. He also had difficulty in recognising people he knew only slightly – a serious disability for a man in his position which could create an unfortunate impression if, for instance, he failed to recognise someone who had donated a lot of money to one of his projects. This often caused misunderstanding and offence, and much of his supposed haughtiness of manner was due to this. Nor was he by any means universally popular with his priests, who seemed rather afraid of him. Singularly direct and simple, he spoke his mind unhesitatingly and had no gift for adroitness when dealing with difficult situations. So unworldly and holy a man whose chief concern was prayer before the Blessed Sacrament, or talking of the love of God, must have been difficult for ordinary mortals to get close to. He seems to have had little interest in food or creature comforts or any aesthetic feeling for his surroundings, nor can I find evidence of the latter in any of the nineteenth-century Vaughans.

At sixty, Herbert considered himself too old for the metropolis, but after hearing a sermon about St Patrick starting work on the conversion of the Irish in his sixtieth year, he took heart and felt assured it was God's will for him. He was enthroned in a simple ceremony at the Pro-cathedral (Our Lady of Victoria, Kensington) on Sunday 8 May 1892 as third Archbishop of Westminster. This was followed by a far more magnificent ceremony at Brompton Oratory on 16 August when the Apostolic Delegate, Archbishop Stoner, invested him with the pallium brought from the Eternal City, in the presence of all the English hierarchy, heads of religious orders, 400 priests, the diplomatic corps, and most of the English Catholic aristocracy. Francis Vaughan, his nephew (and later Bishop of Menevia) carried his train. The Oratory was packed, even standing room hard to find. Nothing like this pageant of the Catholic church had been seen in England for over 300 years.

Herbert, in himself the humblest of men, was destined to rise even higher, and swiftly too. The next year he was made a prince of the Church: on 19 January 1893 he knelt before Pope Leo XIII to receive the Red Hat.

Mill Hill had celebrated its silver jubilee on St Joseph's Day 1891 and someone remarked to Herbert, 'You must see today the travail of your soul and be satisfied My Lord'. 'I never think of what has been done', came the reply, 'but of the vast amount there is still to do.' His next undertaking was to build a cathedral. Both Wiseman and Manning had agreed on the necessity of a metropolitan cathedral to complete the restoration of the hierarchy, but it was left to Herbert Vaughan to build it.*

In the face of much criticism he set about this gigantic task with his usual zeal. He chose John Francis Bentley – who was also a poet – as architect and sent him to Italy to study their basilicas as he wanted the cathedral built in the Byzantine style. He wrote hundreds of letters to potential donors, in this way collecting £75,000 which enabled him to start work. The foundation stone was laid on 29 June 1895 by Cardinal Vaughan, assisted by Cardinal Logue, Archbishop of Armagh. Eight years later it was sufficiently advanced to be opened for the first time for the funeral service of its founder. Herbert, as usual, had put the matter of building this great work in the hands of St Joseph and money poured in. His brother Kenelm undertook a begging trip in Spain and South America and collected £18,000, which built the Blessed Sacrament chapel.

The enormous amount of work entailed in organising, staffing and running the choir, clergy, etc., for this great new cathedral must have been very taxing on the ageing cardinal, whose health was failing. At seventy-one he had no great desire to go on living, as his last letter to Lady Herbert shows (see page 76). But in 1902 he went to stay with old friends Lord and Lady Talbot at Derwent Hall where, surrounded by loving kindness, his health improved. Lady Talbot recalls that on arrival he was so weak he could only sit in the chapel for a short time – saying Mass was out of the question – but he seemed always to be praying and engrossed with God all day long. As he got stronger to his great joy he was able to say Mass twice a week though his doctors insisted on his retiring to bed afterwards. He was constantly in the chapel praying before the Blessed Sacrament.

Improved in health, Herbert left Derwent Hall in December. In his letter thanking the Talbots for their 'kindness and care lavished on their poor old patient during all these months' he voiced his fear that business will prevent his return 'to the dear nest at Derwent' for some time. Hard on himself as always, Herbert used to say 'God has given me a great work to do and I have not done it well'. His depression was no doubt caused by physical weakness after a life of unremitting toil, prayer and work. He found enforced inactivity frustrating and at times was very sad, but accepted it as the will of God: 'We are so active in the service of God, so busy and inclined to trust to self, and forget to spiritualise our work – and then God sends us a sickness like this'.

---

* For details of this great building, see *Westminster Cathedral, A Popular Guide*, published by the Catholic Truth Society.

Feeling he was dying, Herbert decided to go to Mill Hill, so he left Archbishop's House on the feast of the Annunciation, 25 March 1903. His strength was failing fast, his energy and drive gone. Daily he could feel himself growing weaker. He could no longer walk any distance but had his male nurse push him in a bath chair around the grounds. Life was almost over – he was marking time until his beloved St Joseph came for him. On 19 June he expressed a wish to make a public profession of faith. Though very weak he had himself wheeled to the College church with his scarlet cappa magna on his shoulders and his red tasselled hat on his head. On the way he insisted on stopping to tell Miss Hamner – an aged lady who lived in a garden cottage and was the moon to Lady Herbert's sun. The procession then wound on to the church where in the presence of the Vicar General and canons of the diocese Herbert solemnly made his profession of faith and asked forgiveness of all whom he may have offended or scandalised through hastiness or want of judgement.

He died peacefully the next night, the feast of the Sacred Heart, 19 June 1903, at ten minutes to midnight. But not before an extraordinary assault of the Devil in which he felt himself doubting the faith he had dwelt in all his life. Could there be no God? No hereafter? This attack troubled him profoundly but that wonderful man Father Daniel Considine,* an Irishman from Derk, Pallasgreen, County Limerick, came to talk with him and quietened his mind, enabling his valiant spirit to go forth and meet his God in peace.

The Cardinal's body was taken to lie in state at Westminster and his Requiem Mass was the cathedral's official opening. By his wish he was buried at Mill Hill under the shadow of the calvary. At seventy-one, worn out by his strenuous, striving life and the vast amount he had accomplished, he was only too ready 'to go into the next room'.

> St Mary's Church
> (Paulist Fathers),
> 628 California Street,
> San Francisco.

My dearest 'Sister Editha', June 21st 1903

So God has given beloved Herbert wings to fly away to our Eternal Home above!

---

* Father Considine, quite independently, has also been a source of help and enlightenment to me. His precious little book, *Words of Encouragement*, is often dipped into in the watches of the night.

How glorious for him – but for us all what a terrible loss, especially for you, dearest Lady Herbert! No words can say how deeply I feel for you and how I realise the truth of the saying – 'mourn for the mourners not for the mourned!' For I know how very dear he was to you – dearer than a more human friend – for you were so united to him in our Lord and in all works for His glory and for the salvation of souls. But this union can still go on and even become stronger now than ever.

A few weeks ago I sent him a poem that has given me quite a devotion to brother death – I am sending you a copy [reproduced below] for I think it is so beautiful.

John told me a few weeks ago that Herbert was quite happy, because he felt he could not be in better hands than in God's hands.

It is an immense consolation to know that and to know that he died so happily and calmly and so well prepared.

Dearest Lady Herbert, I fear that the news of his death will affect your poor weak heart. But I pray God to give you strength to stand bravely resigned to His adorable will, who arranged all things in our eternal interest. Let us pray much for him, though I feel his purgatory will be short.

Thank you ever so much for your delightful letter sent on to me here where work detains me still. Do send me a line.

> Your devoted
> Kenelm of the Blessed Sacrament

Brother Death

I think of death as of a friend and brother
Who, some bright day, will come and call for me,
And lead me to the presence of Another
With whom I long have pined at home to be.
I know not in what form or 'mid what guises
He will approach me, only this I know,
If he at midnight or at noon surprises
I shall clasp hands with him and gladly go.

Have I then nothing that to earth can bind me?
Has all my oil of gladness been consumed?
Shall not I cast one lingering look behind me,
Regretting flowers that but for me have bloomed?

But oh! To go to be with Christ forever!
To see His face, His wondrous voice to hear!
Never again from Him I love to sever,
Never to miss His accents on my ear!

84

So then, my brother, Death, for thee I'm ready,
I wait, yet woo thee not, abide God's time;
My heart is fixed, my footsteps calm and steady;
So lead me on to destiny sublime.

Lead me to Christ, lead from all power of sinning,
Lead me to those who in His image shine,
This will of life be only the beginning
And birth, not death through thee, shall then be mine.

ROGER VAUGHAN

Roger William Bede Vaughan (called after his ancestor at Agincourt), John and Eliza's second son, was born at Courtfield on 9 January 1834. His godmother was Mrs Bodenham and his godfather Mr Vaughan. As he was not strong he was educated privately at home; then, like his brother Herbert before him, he attended The Rev Thomas Abbot's School in Monmouth for three or four years, but he preferred shooting, fishing and riding to his studies. He was sent to the Benedictines at Downside when he was older and there became a Benedictine novice and a professed monk. Later he went to Rome and on 9 April 1855 was ordained priest at St John Lateran. He returned to England in 1859 and did mission work at Bath and two years later, in 1861, was appointed Professor of Philosophy to the Benedictine monastery of St Michael, Belmont, Hereford, and a year later was elected Prior. He held this post up to the time of his nomination as Archbishop of Nazianus and coadjutor to Archbishop Polding of Sydney. It was while the ageing Archbishop Polding was on a visit to Belmont that he met Roger and was so impressed with his capabilities that he petitioned the Pope to be allowed to have him in Sydney. Roger was duly consecrated Coadjutor Archbishop on 19 March 1873 at the church of St Vincent de Paul, Liverpool, and arrived in Sydney on 16 December 1873, where he was met at the quayside by Archbishop Polding and the two prelates drove together through enormous crowds in an open landau to the pro-cathedral.

Roger's first task on arrival in Sydney was to collect money to complete St Mary's Cathedral. The aged Archbishop Polding had – and these quotations are from letters to his father and step-mother: 'let things run terribly to seed and disorder', in what might have been the richest archdiocese in the British Empire had it not been 'most diabolically mismanaged'. He also believed that Polding had, for many years, failed to defend 'Catholic rights' and to assert the 'Catholic position'. Yet Roger also stressed the great potentialities of the position he had taken on: the colonial population were 'a rough lot caring nothing for manners, but much for money, but the local Catholics were very generous even if a regular lot of rhinoceroses who needed basic points constantly repeated, and cannot feel unless absolutely hammered. Cardinal Manning's polished frigidity would, I will not say not be understood but would simply not be noticed.'

Roger quickly established a reputation as a controversialist. The Anglican Bishop Barker was one of the first challenged. In a letter to his father he wrote: 'The Protestant Metropolitan, from the moment I landed in this place began to peck and clap his wings and crow – I let him go on two years 'til he came out thoroughly and then I came down upon him. You will see his speech in reply; really simply vulgar claptrap.'

Roger found the run-down Catholic church staffed exclusively by Irish who resented the fact that he was that virtually unknown thing, an English Catholic gentleman:

> This is true misery – that our clergy are almost exclusively Irish, ignorant and with extremely little zeal for making converts and saving Saxon souls! Had I a dozen or half a dozen English Oratorians here, or Redemptorists – we might make endless conversions. Besides I find the English laity have no confidence in the Irish priests: they fear to ask them to their homes for fear they might say some stupid or offensive things. And thus the work I want to do is paralysed. I hope in time to get a new school of educated men, fit to cope with the errors of the day and to meet educated Protestants on their own ground.

Writing to his stepmother Mary the July following his arrival in Sydney, Roger treats her to an exuberant description of a diocesan tour:

> Last month I made a tour in the southerly portion of the Archdioceses of about 200 miles. My progress was an uninterrupted ovation. Every town turned out to meet me with bands of music and carriages and horsemen. I was never without an escort of between 50–60 horsemen, sometimes nearly 500. Protestants and Jews caught the infection and joined the rest. They say never before has such a thing occurred in the Colony.
>
> All my movements were in the Sydney Telegraphic news next morning – just as if I were a King of this Cannibal Island! The Governor, they tell me, never gets anything like the reception I have received. When I was in Queensland the City of Brisbane gave me a

public banquet – the Marquis of Normanby in the Chair, and all the Government swells and Legal dignitaries taking part in the affair.

What is most surprising is that all this is done, I may say, in spite of my preaching and teaching the unvarnished Catholic truth and putting forward the full Catholic claims without any reserve. The fact is I believe people like courage and honesty and if they do not believe in what you *say* they believe in you. (Of course, I mean me!)

But life was not all cheering crowds. On the contrary. Roger outlined for his father, succinctly but not without humour, a somewhat lonely existence:

They say the inhabitants of this country are divided into two classes: those who came out at the expense of their country; and those who *ought to have* come out at its expense. Rather a severe saying but not without some grain of truth. Still for my work, Church work, there is a wide field, and much to do, and a large and impressionable population to work upon. The Governor (Sir Hercules Robinson) and his family are pleasant people, and there are one or two others whom I know. But my time is fully occupied with work and I am familiar with nobody; which I find works best. I think I can say that I have not such a thing out here as what is generally called a friend; so I am in no-one's hands but my own; and I keep my own confidence. I was very much amused by your description of Herbert and myself in your diary of 18—. Who would have thought that we should have developed into Lordships and Graces!

He must indeed have often been very lonely, but no doubt his energetic nature and the enormous amount of work he undertook kept him going and this increased when Archbishop Polding finally died in 1877 and he succeeded him and at last had a free hand. Of Archbishop Polding, Roger wrote:

He died full of years, and having been one of the Fathers of the Colony, he had what they call a 'splendid' funeral; the whole city turning out to show respect to his memory. He had lived a spotless life for 42 years here; and, as he did not take an active part in any religious aggressive movements, conciliated to himself, the good will of all denominations. Now I hope to take up the running, which will be much easier for me to do now than when he was alive: for then, practically, I had him, and those who hung on him, to look after as well as the general interests of the Diocese and I feel now much like a donkey on Coppet Hill with the log off his leg – not so easily caught! Practically, I have been, during these three years, studying my ground, taking stock of my men, and waiting 'til it came to my turn to take the box: and I think all has happened very providentially. Three years have not been too long to give me a fair insight into affairs and to prepare me for real work – and now I hope to begin. I have the priests and people quite with me; and I believe I could, if necessary, talk any amount of opposition into a cocked hat!

I was anxious to let the little world in which we live learn that Bishops are spokesmen of the Great Divine Institute of the Church, and not mere little penny trumpets singing self and nothing deeper, higher or better.

I believe if one talks enough and with careful preparation an impression must at last be made. And I know that I have very many silent followers in the opposite camp who will eventually be moved to do more than listen and approve. One great thing I have gained is: that by carefully preparing everything I say, and never saying anything unless I have something to say, I have won the ear of the public and get fully reported in the leading Protestant and Imperial newspapers. You may imagine that the irreligious and heretical world would greatly prefer an octogenarian to myself – and thus they hold me in a certain fear, not knowing what hammer I shall bring out next.

As well as his chief work of continuing the building of St Mary's Cathedral with the architect Wardell, and fundraising for this purpose, Archbishop Vaughan organised a tremendous month-long 'Ye Olde Tyme Fayre' in 1882 (possibly modelled on the St Patrick's Fair in New York of 1879), which netted almost £6,000 for the building fund. He was also intimately concerned with Church education and sixty-eight new schools were established during his ten years as Archbishop. Education had long been a preoccupation, for in 1874 he had written: 'I am now Rector of St John's College within the university and thus hold the reins and whip of the Educational department of the Church here. I bought my predecessor out – a most objectionable, whisky-drinking purple-nosed little Irish priest. The Jesuits had offered him £5,000 down for his position – I offered him £400 a year for life.'

In 1880 he started his own weekly newspaper, the *Express*.

Having cleared up the 'administrative mess' in Sydney he made a great push to get enough money to finish the cathedral which he estimated would be in the region of £150,000 and for this purpose he toured his diocese with great success. His talks and sermons caught the imagination of the public and even Jews and non-Catholics contributed generously, and he seems to have been royally received and fêted wherever he went. Sufficient funds raised, building went ahead and in 1881 he presented the bells to St Mary's Cathedral.

Among his many activities while Archbishop, Roger took an

1. Richard Vaughan of Courtfield (1600–97).

2. John Vaughan of Courtfield
   (1675–1745).

3. Elizabeth Vaughan
   (wife of John Vaughan).

4. John Vaughan of Courtfield (1707–80).

5. William Vaughan of Courtfield (1738–96).

6. Frances Vaughan, wife of William.

7. William Michael Vaughan of Courtfield (1781–1861).

8. Bust of William Michael Vaughan of Courtfield (1781–1861).

9. Theresa Vaughan, wife of William Michael Vaughan.

10. John Francis Vaughan of Courtfield (1808–80).

11. Eliza Louisa Vaughan, wife of John Francis Vaughan (1810–53).

12. Herbert Vaughan of Courtfield (1832–1903).

13. Herbert Vaughan in the Park at Courtfield.

14. Roger Vaughan of Courtfield (1834–83).

15. Kenelm Vaughan (1840–1909).

16. Francis Baynham Vaughan of Courtfield (1844–1919)
17. Caroline Ruth Vaughan, wife of Francis Baynham Vaughan
    (married 1871, died 1922).

18. Frank and Carrie in Rome.

19. Bernard Vaughan, SJ (1847–1922).

20. Mary Lavender Vaughan (1910–1989).

21. Joseph Herbert Vaughan of Courtfield
(1910–1972).

22. Patrick Vaughan of Courtfield (1942–).

23. Left to right: Mary, Joseph, Richard, Thomas, Patrick and Oliver.

interest in Mother Mary Mackillop's educational work with the Sisters of St Joseph of the Sacred Heart and her establishment of orphanages and homes for the poor. She had encountered a lot of opposition and difficulty with the Australian hierarchy and was even excommunicated for a period in 1871. However, when she discussed her case with Archbishop Vaughan he was sympathetic and assured her of his willing support.

Roger appears to have become an appreciated and beloved personage during his ten years in Australia and when in July 1883 he left for his first holiday in England there was a tremendous turnout to see him off, and a fleet of vessels stood out to sea in beautiful Sydney Harbour to wave farewell. His devoted parishioners also presented him with a large sum of money for his personal use.

On his return to England the liner docked in Liverpool and he went to stay at Ince Blundell nearby where his Aunt Theresa lived. He had sent her a strangely prophetic little note written from the Adelphi Hotel, Liverpool:

Dearest Aunt T,   Saturday August 18th

I have just arrived by the *Arizona* from New York, and I am glad to find from Uncle Richard that you are at Ince – I propose being with you by luncheon time tomorrow, Friday, and need use no italics or CAPITAL letters to tell you how I long to see you, and have some real rest. We had a rough passage, and as my berth was not so big as the coffin I shall be measured for some day, I did not sleep so calmly as I shall then! With this grim joke, fit for an undertaker, and with love that has been pent up for ten long years,

I am your devoted Nephew Roger

After an evening with family and friends, the next morning he was found dead in bed. Perhaps the emotional experience of his return to his beloved family proved too much for his great but tired heart.

Archbishop Vaughan was temporarily interred in the vault in Ince on 23 August 1883. Then controversy arose over his burial. The diocese of Sydney wanted his body sent out for burial, and Dr Sheridan, Vicar General of Sydney, cabled the family with an expression of the general wish that the remains should be sent to Sydney for burial. But an Irish bishop, Dr Moran, meanwhile was appointed his successor and wrote (apparently quite untruly) that the people of Sydney did not want Archbishop Vaughan's body and that he himself refused to pay a penny for the burial – this in spite of the fact that as successor to the see Roger had made him his sole heir and he had received all the balance of the money the

Archbishop was given for his journey to England. Replying to letters from Herbert Vaughan asking for his decision about Roger's burial, Cardinal Moran wrote from Ireland:

> 17 Mountjoy Square, Dublin
> September 10, 1885

My dear Lord,

In reply to your Lordship's letters I have but little to add to what I have already written. The public papers announced the fact, which everyone knew to be correct, that Dr Vaughan's remains were interred with due solemnity in the family vault. If there has been any mistake in the matter the blame must rest upon somebody's shoulders. It certainly does not rest on mine. It appears to me that there can be no more appropriate place for the late Archbishop's repose than the family vault at the mansion where he died. If the family desire to transfer his remains elsewhere, I have no objection to their doing so, but it certainly will not be done at my expense.

Believe me to remain yours faithfully, Patrick F. Card. Moran

Archbishop of Sydney

What can one make of such a discourteous, ungentlemanly letter?

Eventually, in 1887, Roger was buried at Belmont – the Benedictine Abbey he had been Prior of – but in 1946, fifty-nine years after his death, Cardinal Gilroy, on behalf of the people of Sydney, petitioned the English Benedictine congregation to have the body of their beloved Archbishop brought back to Sydney where he now lies buried in the crypt of St Mary's Cathedral. Here is just one letter from among the numerous expressions of sympathy received when he died, sent to his youngest brother, Reginald, at Courtfield:

> Mundanah Towers
> Little Congee
> Sydney
> August 20, 1883

My dear Vaughan,

It will be some satisfaction to you in your great sorrow to know how all Australia deeply and unspeakably mourns today for their irreparable loss on the death of the loved and honoured Archbishop. For myself who enjoyed his confidence and his friendship to a degree not attained by any other Protestant in this country, I can only say that I can hardly write this without weeping for my noble friend.

His numerous letters to me I treasure beyond all others; and while I live I shall look upon them as the connecting link with one of the purest and highest and most generous minds we have ever had in this country. With deep regard,

Believe me,
J. Henniker Heaton

KENELM VAUGHAN

Kenelm David Francis Vaughan, John and Eliza's fourth son, born at Courtfield 12 August 1840, can be described as the mystic of the family. When he was sixteen he took the Cistercian habit at Mount St Bernard Abbey but had to give up after four years owing to ill health: he was consumptive. In 1862 his doctor sent him to sunny Italy, in those days considered the best treatment for his disease and he spent three years there, but without benefit to his health. When he returned to England in May 1865 he went to St Augustine's Priory, Newton Abbot (where his sister later was a nun) and that summer it seemed he was near his end. As his great desire was to die a priest, his uncle William, the Bishop of Plymouth, hurried things up by raising him to the subdiaconate on 27 August, to the diaconate on 3 September, and to the sacred priesthood on 21 September that same year. His doctors and all the community fully expected him to die and in a letter to his father in 1865 Kenelm said:

Dr Gillow examined me thoroughly yesterday. His opinion is that my right lung has withered up, and that my left one is diseased and wasting from overwork. He says that humanly speaking my life cannot hang long upon one wasting lung, though I might get over the winter, with extreme care and precaution – and live for a year. His positive conviction is that nothing can help to stay the advance of disease and keep me in life but alcohol. It is better for me than meat, milk or anything. He has therefore doubled the quantity of brandy per day. What a brandy bottle I shall be! I hope I shall not die of delirium tremens. He tells me to go out as little as possible. The prospect of an early death does not deject me – indeed it would rejoice me if I was better prepared. For I feel that the hour He fixed for my death will be the very best for me! Dr Gillow advises me to winter here. He says that in my case climate would avail little. I am delighted to hear it, for I could not wish to be dying in a better place than this, where I have such easy access to the Altar, where I find even Him whom the Angels find and adore in Heaven.

Towards the end of October 1865, at the suggestion of Mother Margaret Stone, he joined in a novena in honour of St Winifred of Holywell and on 3 November, the last day of the novena, he experienced a miraculous cure. He describes this in detail in a letter to Father Mason dated May 1866:

> You ask me for an extent and detailed account of the cure obtained for me through St Winifred's intercession. Well, to begin, I must tell you the nature of the disease of which I was cured was consumption. This disease seized hold of me six years ago, and in 1862 so pulled me down that Dr Monk sent me to Italy as the only means of keeping me alive. There in Rome I passed three winters without much betterment. In the May of 1865 I returned home to Courtfield with the disease increased upon me. There I began so to fall to pieces that my father sent me to London to see if the doctors there could cobble me up. But Dr Monk whom I consulted found my lungs in a state that he dared not examine them, lest by so doing he might cause vomiting of blood. In a fortnight's time, however, by dint of doctoring, he fitted my lungs to go through an examination, which having made, he pronounced that serious mischief was going on in both lungs and my life was in a most precarious state. He ordered me to Torquay. Near there in the Convent of St Augustine, I stayed, grew worse and wishing to die a Priest, received Subdeacon's and Deacon's Orders. A month later I trained down to Plymouth to be made a Priest. But then I relapsed and so ill was I on the eve of the day fixed for my ordination that the Bishop thought that on his return from Liskeard that evening, he would have to arrange for the next day, not my ordination, but my funeral service. However strength was given me for the occasion and on the following day I was ordained a Priest.
>
> I then went back to St Augustine's half a corpse, to die and be buried. There Dr Gillow attended me. He said however he could do nothing for me – that all human remedies were useless and that my case was hopeless – indeed he used to speak of me as 'the dying man of Abbotsleigh'. He ordered me a little brandy as a stimulus – that was all the medicine I took. Indeed my inside was so rotting that motion of the arms or loud speaking caused blood expectoration. Yet I managed to crawl down each morning to offer up Holy Mass. But immediately it was over I was forced, owing to the violence of perspiration, to change all my clothes, and from extreme weakness to throw myself on the sofa, thinking sometimes that I should never rise again.
>
> Now that I was given up by the doctor, Mother Margaret turned to St Winifred, the Saint of her protection (?), and besought her to obtain for me my cure of a sister of the Perpetual Adoration Convent, who by the way now enjoys never failing health, for she died soon after and went to Heaven.
>
> The Novena to St Winifred began October 26 1865. Each day I joined in public prayer to her and drank of the water from Holywell. On the last day of the Novena, November 3rd, her festival day, I felt more

than usually miserably ill and with difficulty I crept down at a snail's pace to the Church. There I found the Bishop of Plymouth who had come overnight to say Mass for me on St Winifred's day. He began his Mass at seven o'clock – I followed soon after him into the Church where I began Mass at the side altar of the Blessed Virgin.

Before the consecration down came a shower of water (from where I don't know) which so bedewed the corporal chalice and host, that I called Canon Agur to know if I would continue Mass and consecrate the ruined host. But as he told me to take no notice of it, I continued the Mass. After the reception of the Blessed Sacrament I felt an inward change for the better, yet was not directly conscious of a cure. After Mass, having unvested, I poured the remains of the Holywell water I had by me into the chalice which the Bishop having blessed, I drank. I then entered the Church and made my thanksgiving – kneeling without fatigue – a feat I had not accomplished for months. A short time afterwards, the Bishop said to me as he entered the sacristy, 'Well, how do you feel?' It was then that, conscious of a cure, I exclaimed 'Perfectly well'. Indeed then I experienced sensibly that my works inside were put right and that a new life was given me. I now no longer crawled up to my sick room like a dying man, but walked with the Bishop with firm step, as a man in health to the breakfast room chatting aloud as I went, and surprised all at my performance there. My instantaneous cure soon spilled over the house, and all were astonished with a great astonishment, and joined with me in returning very great thanks to Our Lord for showing, through the intercession of His Blessed Servant, Saint Winifred, such mercy to me. It was indeed a mercy for I was unfit to die. After the elapse of a week the doctor visited me, examined my lungs, found not a vestige of disease remaining in them, and is persuaded that my cure is an undeniable fact.

In a month's time I was sent to do duty for a Priest at St Mary Church, where I am now stationed, but in a few weeks I returned to St Augustine's Priory where I caught a violent cough and cold which confined me to my bed for five days. But wonderful to say, the Divine Hand of our Lord had so completely healed my lungs that they were prooof against all such attacks which fact only served to strengthen the faith of my friends in the veracity and permanency of my cure.

Since my cure I have, assenting to my promise to St Winifred, made a pilgrimage of thanksgiving to her shrine at Holywell.

And now in conclusion I beg of you to pray that I may make good use of the life that is given me, and to ask St Winifred to preserve my health for a short time, that I may be able to do a little work for Our Lord and His truth in this unfortunate Protestant land.

Yours very truly in Jesus Christ,
Kenelm Vaughan.

Kenelm wrote to his father on 3 November, the Feast of St Winifred, giving the briefest account of his miraculous cure:

My dearest Father,

I went down sick and ill to the Church to say Mass this morning (the last day of the Novena) and I came out of the Church feeling wonderfully well and vigorous as though Our Lord had heard the prayers of the nuns, and had through the intercession of St Winifred cured me of lung disease.

The house all consider I am cured and are lost in wonderment and I in gratitude to God for I was not fit to die. Will you thank Our Lord for thus restoring me to health and ask Mary and May to do so too.

Your devoted son,
Kenelm Vaughan

I have kept back this letter from post 'til I had seen the doctor. He came today, November 10th; on examination he tells me that my lung-disease has stopped, that my chest is quieter and that he considers the medicines have been wonderfully blest.

Subsequently Kenelm travelled the world, collecting a lot of money in particular for the Blessed Sacrament Chapel in the enormous Westminster Cathedral his brother Herbert was building. His zeal and enthusiasm opened the purses of rich and poor and constantly the Cardinal is exhorting him to take more rest and care of his health: 'you must put a bit into your mouth and hold yourself in with a strong rein, otherwise your mind and body will not stand the strain of this constant effort to collect money for your noble work'. And again, 'I hope you will try to take a little more care of yourself. I have just been reading in the life of B. John Colombini that his wife one day reproaching him for bringing all sorts of beggars into her house and even filthy lepers, he replied, "But did you not yourself pray that I might learn to practise virtue and charity?". "Yes", she retorted, "I prayed for rain but not for the deluge". Apply this to yourself.' Kenelm's fundraising became a tireless, never-ending task. In a letter of 1899 the Cardinal writes,

Before you depart from the hospitable and generous city of Buenos Aires and for Argentina, I hope you will express in my name the gratitude which I feel to those who have received you with so much genuine kindness and have responded with so much alacrity and good will to your appeal . . . their generosity will bear fruit by stirring up Faith and Charity here in Europe and especially in London, where it will be known, because it will be commemorated in the Chapel of the Blessed Sacrament. The records of the noble contribution of their names and of their gifts will perpetuate the memory of their generous response to your appeal, here in London long after you and I have passed away. All posterity will speak with praise and admiration of the way in which distant Argentina by the faith and generosity of her sons and daughters in this, our day, helped to raise the largest Church built in England since the sixteenth century, and chose as the special object of their gifts the Chapel of the Blessed Sacrament.

I hope that before you return you will have collected enough to complete this Chapel, so that it may be truly said that the entire cost of this Chapel has been defrayed by the children of that grand old Catholic race with which we are connected by ties of blood and of affectionate admiration. I bless you and I bless all who have been associated with you in your work of zeal and charity, and I thank all clergy and laity alike for what they have done for my Cathedral.

Kenelm extended his begging tour to Spain and attended the eucharistic conference at the ancient city of Lugo in 1890. He spoke and wrote Spanish fluently. Indeed both he and his brother the cardinal were very conscious of their Spanish connection:

Besides these reasons for veneration of the Church in Spain, there are feelings of a personal and domestic kind which turn my heart towards that great Catholic land. It was to Spain that our family fled in exile during the days of persecution in England, and I recall with pleasure that our ancestors served in the Spanish Army, married into a Spanish family, and that we are therefore connected with the Peninsula by blood as well as by faith and charity.

In 1896 the Cardinal wrote to encourage Kenelm:

Dearest Ken . . . I trust you are getting on well; so far I think you have been singularly blessed – crosses and coins fairly mixed together. When I was a tramp round America I used to keep two pockets, one for alms and one for crosses: so that I every day got one or other of these pockets filled – sometimes both!

And I have often thought since then that the crosses and mortifications of those years went far further to bring about the success of Mill Hill than the money which enabled me to buy the site and erect the College. The Chapel of the BV in Westminster Cathedral will also be built up by you in the same blessed way. Take good care of yourself. I am often anxious about your health, but I have a great confidence that you will live to finish your great work.

Kenelm's untiring work trudging around South America collecting money for the building of the cathedral and his excessive zeal for expiation understandably sometimes caused anxiety among his friends. His letters home to his father and to his greatly loved sister,

Clare Magdalen, a nun and later Prioress at St Augustine's, Newton Abbot, are on such an entirely spiritual plane, that it is hard for us to understand them. But, writing to his father on the eve of a trip to Mexico City, his subject was much more down to earth – bricks and mortar in fact: 'I have been very occupied all these months in raising funds to realise a work, the idea of which was in me, I believe, when I was born, ''The Work of Expiation'''.

He wanted to build a chapel, if possible from the stones of ruined churches, where perpetual adoration and propitiation might be offered for all the insults and sacrileges committed in England since the days of Henry VIII. Also he tried to found Orders devoted to penance but with such strict rules that no-one except himself could keep them.

During his years of travel in Chile, Peru, Ecuador, Mexico, and elsewhere throughout South America, Kenelm went through hardships and dangers which few stronger men could have endured. I once met a lady who told me she had lived in South America as a girl and remembered her family befriending Kenelm when he was ill, and though not Catholics they regarded him as the nicest and holiest man they had ever met. His brother the cardinal also thought of him as a saint. Once, while staying on a ranch in South America, where the family always gathered together for their night prayers before a picture which Kenelm took to be the image of a saint, he was greatly surprised when he looked more closely to find it was a portrait of his mother, Eliza Vaughan. How they had come by it, no one knew, but they had venerated it for years.

After almost forty years of travelling, Kenelm's last work was for Cardinal Bourne at Hatfield in Hertfordshire and he called his presbytery 'Anatoth' in honour of the prophet Jeremiah for whom he had a great devotion.

In the church at Courtfield Kenelm erected, in 1907, a delightful stained-glass window depicting an aged Jeremiah and a crowned and youthful King Kenelm of Mercia (812–20), knight errant of Christ. He died there on 19 May 1909, the vigil of the feast of the Ascension, and was buried in St Alban's cemetery on the 22nd.

The Travels of Kenelm Vaughan through Spain and South America

The Brotherhood of the Divine Expiation had offered to provide the Chapel of the Holy Sacrament (also referred to as the Spanish Chapel and the Hispano-American Chapel) in Westminster Cathedral and to man it in perpetuity. Cardinal Archbishop Vaughan thought of the idea that Spain should be invited to provide funds for this purpose for several reasons: Cardinal Wiseman, his predecessor, was born in Seville; the Church built by the former Spanish Ambassador, the Marques del Campo, in Spanish Place had recently been demolished and the Chapel could be its replacement; and Cardinal Vaughan himself had Spanish blood in his veins. So he sent his brother Kenelm to Spain to solicit contributions.

Kenelm reached Spain in November 1895 and was well received by the mortally sick Cardinal Archbishop of Toledo, by the Archbishop of Madrid-Alcala, by the Papal Nuncio and by the Queen Regent herself, Maria Cristina. Madrid proving too cold for Kenelm's health, he went south to Seville where he was again well received. There he recruited five founder-members (minimum £50 donations) and a further seven in Jerez. He then proceeded to Cadiz and thence to Tangier, Gibraltar, Tarifa and Algeciras.

In July 1896 Kenelm went north. He was granted an audience by the Queen Regent who presented him with a gold chalice to be used for the first Mass to be offered in the chapel. King Alfonso XIII became a founder-member. Kenelm was also well received in the Basque country and in Navarre.

The projected visit of Cardinal Archbishop Vaughan himself to Lugo had to be cancelled but Kenelm and his deputation were well received there nevertheless. The Bishop of Lugo donated $1,000. They then proceeded to Santander where they were again well received. However, the difficult domestic situation and the fact that Cardinal Archbishop Vaughan had made a statement apparently supporting the USA in the war between Spain and the USA in 1898 made it impossible to continue Kenelm's mission throughout Spain and he had to leave Spain, having collected £5,000. The target figure had been £18,000, to add to a similar figure which had already been raised in Britain.

Cardinal Archbishop Vaughan instructed his brother to continue his mission in South America. So, having obtained the blessing of Pope Leo XIII, Kenelm set out for South America and arrived in Buenos Aires in November of 1898. As a tribute to the memory of Cardinal Vaughan's great-grandfather, the President of Argentina, General Julio Roca, became a founder member. Initially the mission was faced with a hostile press but they gradually came round to supporting it. The President of the Republic of Paraguay also became a founder member and made a solemn public profession of his Catholic faith.

After a difficult journey Kenelm arrived in Santiago de Chile, where he was well received by the Archbishop and the President of the Republic became a founder member. Kenelm received some criticism in the press at this point and was sent a dud cheque, but he also received a lot of support, recruiting thirty-one founder members and thirty-one benefactors in Chile (the latter category contribute a minimum of £10).

In Uruguay the law prohibiting the entry of foreign priests into the country was waived for Kenelm. The President of Uruguay became a founder member, but the mission met with only moderate success.

In Peru too they had a mixed reception. The President had become a founder member the previous year and was presented by Kenelm with a diploma, but some newspapers attacked the mission. However, the results generally were up to expectations.

Kenelm next travelled to Bolivia by boat and train. He suffered on the journey a bad bout of mountain sickness and his doctor said he was mortally ill, but Kenelm proved him wrong by recovering quite quickly. Some Bolivian newspapers were critical of the mission, saying that charity ought to begin at home, but the overall reception was quite good. He had problems in obtaining official permission to solicit donations in Sucre but was successful eventually. Equally, he was at first refused permission to solicit donations in La Paz, but successful on appeal. General Pando, the President of the Republic, became a founder member.

Kenelm returned to Peru and there ended his tour in 1903 because of the troubles in Ecuador, Colombia and Venezuela.

The total sum collected in Spain and South America amounted to £14,600. Kenelm ended his mission saying that despite his age and poor health he would be prepared at any time to undertake a further mission in the attempt to raise the £3,400 still needed for completion of the chapel and the further £20,000 estimated to be needed to provide for its manning in perpetuity.

JOSEPH VAUGHAN

Joseph William Jerome Vaughan, born at Courtfield on 24 September 1841, was John and Eliza's fifth son. His godfather was William Jones, his godmother Mary Weld. He was educated by the Benedictines at Downside and entered the Benedictine novitiate at Belmont in 1859 when he was eighteen. In due course he was sent to Rome where he made his solemn profession as a monk of Downside on the tomb of St Paul, studied in Naples for a time and later at Monte Cassino under Abbot Carlo de Vera, Prince of Anagona and a most lovable and saintly man for whom Joseph formed a tremendous regard.

He too seems to have suffered from consumption and experienced a miraculous cure after visiting Monsieur de Pont, 'the Holy Man of Tours'. On his return to England he was ordained priest at Belmont by Bishop Brown of Newport and Menevia on 15 June 1867. For the next eight years he remained at Belmont, teaching and writing. During this time the Marquess of Bute made a retreat there before his marriage and Dom Jerome sometimes discussed with him his hopes of founding a Benedictine abbey near London. However, this project changed when Lord Bute promised a primary donation of £5,000 provided the monastery were founded in Scotland and when the Lovats proposed the old military barracks at Fort Augustus and an adjoining 200-acre farm with an annual rental of £400, Dom Jerome accepted and on his first visit to inspect the site (on 10 February 1876, the feast of St Scholastica, sister of St Benedict) jumped from his carriage enthusiastically crying out, 'Hic Habitabo!'.

So began his life's work which was to occasion him much toil, joy and sorrow. Henceforth his mission was to revive the Benedictine order in Scotland and build the great abbey of Fort Augustus. He went to Rome in the winter of 1877 to obtain the Pope's blessing on his project, which Pius IX was pleased to give and also informed him he would make him the first Abbot.

On 14 September 1876, 'the Exaltation of the Holy Cross', the foundation stone of the abbey was laid by Lord Lovat, that of the college by the Marquess of Ripon, and of the guest house by the Hon Joe Maxwell-Scott and Mr Monteith of Carstairs. Jerome's first task was to collect money for the building fund which by 1878 had reached £23,000, exclusive of a large donation by Mr Hunter Blair, given at a later date. On 15 October 1878, the feast of St Teresa, the celebration of the solemn opening began and was kept up for three days, and the monastic chant, after a silence of 300 years, was heard once more in the Highlands. Pugin was the architect, the building operations had occupied about four years and cost between £80,000 and £100,000.

On 12 May 1878 Jerome Vaughan was nominated Prior of Fort Augustus. He was dissatisfied with what he and some of the younger monks considered to be the lax rule of the English Benedictines, and begged the Pope to send delegates from the strict German Benedictine community to instruct the monks. Accordingly, an abbot and a prior were sent to Fort Augustus. The very next day, to Jerome's surprise, a chapter invested the German abbot with full authority in the monastery and from then on the Germans, having sensed a good thing, schemed for the removal of Jerome from Fort Augustus. Complaints were made against Jerome's zeal for the rule, and opposition was stirred up against him among the young monks. Things were not helped by the English Benedictine community, who accused Jerome of trying to have Fort Augustus placed directly under papal authority. He was also accused by the Scottish hierarchy of attempting to poach Gaelic-speaking priests from their seminaries. All this infighting and petty persecution proved too much for him, and in 1887 he repaired to Rome, a broken man, and never more returned to Fort Agustus. He spent a year at Monte Cassino, from where in a letter to Lille, his sister-in-law, dated 29 August 1887, he said:

> I came here resolved to clear myself before the Holy See and expose the conduct of those who have slandered me and usurped my place. Nor am I wanting in documents that would establish the truth. But all that is changed. I have now taken another view. All has been *permitted* (I do not say 'willed') by an overruling providence.

Jerome saw in a side chapel a picture of Christ being scourged at the pillar. Judas, the traitor, and many others whom Our Lord had served and loved, are looking on approvingly. Of this, he commented, 'My favourite devotion is to go and kneel before this picture and pray for those who have most injured and afflicted me. This brings me great peace of soul, and seems to heal all wounds.'

Jerome dreamed of founding a congregation of priests called the Congregation of St Gregory, to whom he had a great devotion, dedicated to prayer for the conversion of England, but this, alas, did not come true. He made his headquarters at the Benedictine mission of Chorlton-cum-Hardy and he died there on 9 September 1896. By his own wish he was buried in his beloved Monastery of St Gregory at Downside.

It was entirely due to Jerome Vaughan's energy and his stirring up of the hearts of men to generosity that the Benedictine order was established in Scotland.

FRANCIS BAYNHAM VAUGHAN

The sixth son, Francis Baynham, inherited Courtfield. For an account of his life see pages 119–32.

BERNARD VAUGHAN

Bernard Vaughan has his niche in nineteenth-century history as a famous preacher, wit and raconteur. Born at Courtfield on 20 September 1847 and christened Bernard John on the 22nd, his godparents being John Steinmetz and Elizabeth de la Pasture, he was the seventh son of Eliza and John's large family.

In 1859 he was sent to Stonyhurst, like the rest of the family (Thomas Weld, Bernard's great-grandfather, had given Stonyhurst to the Jesuits in 1794). Bernard was a born mimic and up to endless pranks during his schooldays and it was of him that Pope Leo XIII later exclaimed, 'He was born on the top of Mount Vesuvius and we sent him to England to cool down'.

Bernard remained at Stonyhurst for seven years and by then had decided to become a Jesuit. By nature exuberant and extrovert – the complete opposite to his brother Kenelm – but with the same deep religious fervour of all the Vaughans, he found it hard to give up his family and friends and the pleasures of the world. At a dance the Duke of Beaufort gave at Troy House he astonished his partner by telling her he was going to be a priest. 'You!', she exclaimed, 'who love the world and dancing so much.' 'It is because I love it so much I am leaving it', was his reply.

Writing to his stepmother Mary in 1866 from Manresa House,* he said:

> This life is most happy, most blessed and rendered more so by the continual little trials we are called upon to make for the love of the Sacred Heart, though repugnant at times to flesh and blood, yet most sweet and savoury to the spirit. The novices are all most perfect and exemplary, while as you know full well, the reverse is depicted in grand relief in me – always wild, never with that recollection which I should have. Pray then fond Mary for me that I may be more assiduous in this noble work.

Bernard loved sport, particularly shooting; writing from Kylemore in Ireland, he enthused:

---

* Manresa House was built for the second Earl of Bessborough by the great architect Sir William Chambers. When the Jesuits bought it after the death of the third Earl they changed the name from Parkstead to Manresa, but made as few alterations as possible to the structure, the beauty of which has in no way suffered.

I never was in such a lovely place before this – it is to my mind quite perfect, the house situated on the side of a great mountain which is covered with timber, and the lake is stretched in front of the house so that one can get a salmon at any time . . . I am out the whole live-long day, sometimes in the Bay killing great numbers of wild fowl. I killed five golden plover with a single cartridge one day. I shall not be able to have any shooting in England so I think it wise to have a little here where all manner of game are to be found.

In a later letter he writes, 'How about my gun? I must sell it, because I must have a watch at Manresa, now I can't get this watch without the wherewith'.

His letters home were cheerful and newsy, full of gossip and information about the people he is meeting or staying with. On 9 December 1866 he wrote home from Manresa:

You will be glad to hear I arrived here in due time to keep the feast of the Immaculate Conception; and though somewhat depressed in spirits, yet am quite thoroughly happy. Certainly it is very hard to give up one's relatives and friends and bid adieu to the world and its pleasures, and yet considering for whom it is done, how very little it is! Now that I am about to become a Religious I am *determined* to fight tooth and nail, hand and foot, to crush every evil and surmount every difficulty for the love of the Sacred Heart of our great and noble Master, Christ Jesus. And what example have I before me in my eight brothers and sisters who have devoted their lives to religion to urge and cheer me on. But beloved Father pray that I may have great generosity, a large big heart and that all its love may tend to one aim, a greater love of Our Lord and His Holy Will. As yet I am but a postulant but in a day or so I commence my retreat and a few days after I hope to take the habit. How I long to take the habit and keep it for ever!

Bernard liked to keep his father in touch with the other members of his family. In 1866, after visiting his sister Gwladys at her convent of the Visitation order in Boulogne, he reported home:

Sunday I sailed for Boulogne where I remained with the Cliffords for a few days, seeing Gwladys for several hours each day. She is just the same as ever, as bright as a little sun, and so full of joy to think of my being a Jesuit. It was delightful to see the Darling little thing again. From Boulogne I proceeded to Paris where I saw everything and many friends. I was only there for 24 hours and the whole time was occupied in sightseeing – rushing from one Church to another. I dined at Vicomtesse Santander or some suchswell party. I also met and

spent some time with the celebrated Fr Mani Ratisbonne who was converted by a vision of Our Lady. He is a remarkably clever kind man.
Yesterday I spent with the Bishop of Amiens who nearly cried when
he saw me, so strong is his affection for Clare.* Nothing can exceed
his kindness to me; I breakfasted with him at 12 noon and that over
he took me to see Fr Frelix, the great Jesuit preacher of the day who is
at the Jesuit house of Amiens. After remaining an hour or so with Fr
Frelix, whom I like and admire immensely, we went to St Eschoul and
saw the French Jesuit Provincial – a most sanctified mortified man. Of
course we went to the Poor Clares who are so wonderfully poor and
yet so rich. The Poor Clares kept the grating open the whole time so
that I saw the whole community and the place where Clare prayed so
fervently.

The Mother Abbess told me that Clare used to stand on a chair in
order to be nearer Heaven. The Bishop was given a small lock of her
hair which he kissed with the greatest devotion. His Lordship would
be delighted to see you at his magnificent Palace anytime you should
chance to pass there. He asked me to remain with him a week, and
said that should any of our family chance to pass Amiens without
making his Palace their home that he would feel much hurt. The
Bishop gave me his photo, and begged me to procure him one of
Clare. Today or tomorrow I go to Roehampton;** I am dying to be
there.

Bernard was not ordained until after long years of preparation,
at Stonyhurst, Manresa, Beaumont – where he taught boys for four
years – and St Bennos, where he studied theology for another four.
Finally he was ordained on 20 September 1880 and his life as a
preacher began, first in London where he preached the Lent of 1881
on 'The Divine Life of Our Lord'; he was next sent to Manchester
where his brother Herbert was Bishop, and soon started to make a
name for himself with his sermons at the Church of the Holy Name,
and his zeal and activity found endless scope in this comparatively
new parish. He collected large amounts of money with bazaars, etc.
and built the beautiful chapel of Our Lady della Strada from designs
by W. Bentley, the architect of the cathedral.

In 1895 Bernard preached a course of sermons at the packed Free
Trade Hall in Manchester, defending the Catholic position against
Bishop Moorhouse's attack on papal supremacy. This proved so
popular that on the last night the vast crowd dragged his horseless

---

* His sister Clare, who had joined the Poor Clares at Amiens, and died
there at the age of nineteen, in 1862.
** That is, Manresa House.

carriage home to the triumphant strains of the band.

In 1901 he was appointed to the staff of the Jesuit church at Farm Street, Mayfair and his fame as a preacher really took off. Usually there was standing room only at his 12 o'clock sermons which the beau monde as well as the costers and his friends from the East End flocked to hear. His most famous sermons, 'The Sins of Society', were delivered in 1906 and set Mayfair blushing and the rest of the world talking. A Spy cartoon depicted him as a modern Savonarola: 'The accomplished enemy and yet best friend of the smart set comes – as all the world knows – of one of the oldest Catholic families in this country, namely the Vaughans of Courtfield'.

Madame Tussaud's made a striking effigy depicting the great priest in action just as he was seen in the Farm Street pulpit denouncing the sins of society; he stood between Princess Mary and the Duke of Wellington, making quite a contrast to them. His commanding presence and the elegance of his oratory caught the imagination of the press and his sermons and discourses were widely reported. Bernard knew the value of publicity – he was often called the 'Limelight Priest' – but he felt convinced that by speaking out boldly on the evils of the day and endeavouring to make the Catholic church better known to his countrymen, was the way for him to serve almighty God. He was blessed with a spontaneous, happy sense of humour which endeared him to the public. King Edward often came to hear him preach and the congregation at Farm Street included Sir Stuart Coates, the Duchess of Norfolk, the Duke and Duchess of Newcastle, Lady Trowbridge, Don Carlos Dominguez, Mr Edward Eyre, the banker, Lady Alice Dundass, the Hon Joe Maxwell-Scott and many other notables. His critics accused him of caring only for the higher strata of society and 'confessing countesses', but he was equally at home in a Mayfair drawing-room or an East End tenement. It was not generally known that he spent two nights a week based in a bare room in Commercial Road, going out into the byways of Whitechapel – often into courts and alleys that even the police avoided. Here he preached to the sick and needy and the children, and organised relief for the hungry and suffering. The furniture of his room consisted of a camp-bed, a deal table, two chairs, and a frying-pan! Visitors to Commercial Road might find him cooking liver and bacon, a portion of his own meal, for some destitute old woman. Yet this was the man who could write, thanking a Duchess for a gift, 'You are not an Angel; you are a whole choir of Angels!'

During the War, in January 1916, Bernard created a sensation with a speech at the Mansion House, the gist of which was 'keep on killing Germans'. This caused a furore, but Father Vaughan turned on his critics in slashing style: 'The Rev F. B. Meyer and the Rev J. H. Newsham Taylor blame me for advising our troops to kill the enemy instead of being killed by him', he said. 'In my simplicity I was under the impression that our troops had gone to the front, not to take up and handcuff the aggressor, but to do for him. Unless our troops are out at the front to kill Germans, let them come home and be killed with us. They won't have to wait long.' At another conference he convened on 'the call of the War to Prayer', held in London in April 1916, he quipped, 'While our khaki men are in the trenches, I have felt that we ought to be in the benches', and added, on a rather more serious note, 'while they, with their quick-firing guns, are mowing down the enemy, we with ours ought to be storming heaven. But I fear we lack the munitions of prayer.' He delighted to visit camps and barracks during the War, and German aggression and cruelty made such an impression on him, that this militant Jesuit issued the slogan: 'Keep on killing Germans'. He adopted an uncompromising hostility to anything that savoured of a premature peace, and publicly expressed his disagreement with the papal peace proposals.

Bernard was a sturdy champion of Britain and the Empire, and his patriotic discourses roused the nation. He helped forward various charities such as St Dunstan's, the Starving Children Relief Fund, etc. His talks to the troops were an immense success and they loved his witty stories.

Once, in Wimbledon, he witnessed the unedifying spectacle of civilians pushing their way onto a tram and elbowing wounded soldiers off the step. He simply swept the intruders away and helped the men to mount. A cheer arose. 'Don't cheer me', he snapped, 'hiss yourselves.'

Bernard's oratorial powers were remarkable and actors frequently came to listen to his delivery. He did not mind the rough chaff of two Protestant pitmen in a train, who began jeering at him as a Jesuit: 'Haven't you horns and a tail?' they challenged. 'Well, no', he replied. 'I am a freak. But you should see the others!' It ended in one of the men offering him half a crown for charity and asking for 'a prayer for me and the kid that's sick'. However, on another occasion, also in a train, rudeness proved too much for him and when a passenger who had been most objectionable finally got out, as he walked off Father Vaughan put his head out of the window and called, 'Hi, come back, you've left something behind.' 'What?', called the man, hurrying back. 'Merely a very bad impression', replied Bernard.

Father Bernard began a world tour in 1910: he visited slums in New York, he was the preacher at the Eucharistic Congress in Montreal, and in Tokyo he lectured in the Imperial University and spoke in the House of Peers. He travelled thousands of miles and spoke three or four hundred times to some half-million people. He found America stimulating and thought it a splendid country for young people if they were prepared to roll up their sleeves and really work. The hospitality of Americans greatly impressed him too and he found that never during his visit did he have to pay for a railway ticket or a room in an hotel. To a lady who offered to secure for him anything he required, a motor car, a steam launch, or anything of the kind, he replied that he had only two wants – to have a jolly good time on his death-bed and a new toothbrush.

On his return to London Bernard was presented with the following address from members of his Guild of the Blessed Sacrament:

Reverend and dear Father,

The Guild of the Blessed Sacrament representing nearly a thousand men in this parish of St Mary and Michael's join most heartily in this welcome home to you, its founder, and wish by this address to place on record some appreciation of your work and character.

Your close association with this part of London extending over a period of fifteen years, so full with activity and zeal in the steps of your Master, has left numerous monuments and gifts which will endear your name to the hearts of our people for many years to come. The Hall in which we are assembled, built and furnished at considerable cost, is a gift we are not forgetful of.

The Cavalry in Commercial Road, its reminder of many promises, the message to those who pass on that highway of labour and hard toil, are typical of your own life – showing forth the great ideal of manhood in sacrifice, forbearance and love, equally to those who struggle by before the dawn and those who would forget in the midday hours of sunshine and pleasure.

Your earnest and kindly labours in the back streets, the courts and alleys here, have sown the seed of many a better and more hopeful life. Here has been the garden where you have found your flowers to be tended and watched with care and shown with pride to all who come to see – the struggles with poverty and the children of the poor.

The little ones here have learned to know and love you with trustful, joyous hearts, because they feel you are truly a father to them and one

106

who will never forget. Your talks to them week by week, the treats and schemes for their happiness have brought, you know not what an amount of joy into their tender lives.

To the sick, the sad and broken here you have carried your message of love, of healing, and the sunshine of your great and generous heart.

In your great Mission of two years ago and in the foundation of our Guild, you have raised a monument to God, which has stood firm and strong in spite of many influences. Strikes, poverty and domestic trials have swept over our ranks, yet not scattered them – rather have we found greater strength in meeting them with co-operation, provision and striving, under the watchful care of our leader.

We might continue at great length mentioning actions of your life for the good and uplifting of our people – of your struggles to bridge over the gulf between East and West, between poverty and riches. How much we appreciate them and honour and respect you is beyond our power to adequately express: we can never thank you sufficiently for all you have done, but whatever your new friends in the great continent of America may think of you – your old friends in Commercial Road give place to none in their pride and love for you as a Father, a Guide and most dear Friend.

We have read with pleasure of the honour and respect shown to you by all classes and creeds on your great American tour. You have delivered your message throughout that mighty country, raising up the minds of men to higher and more noble things – and now you are home again, our hands and hearts go out to you with warmth and sincerity in bidding you 'caed mille failthe'* with a prayer for every blessing and health for yet many years to come.

This address we present to you unframed and unadorned – but the sentiments it conveys are framed with the love of hearts and illuminated with feelings of soul, more precious than rare wood, more rich in colour than the hand of artist could devise.

> T. J. Ring (Chaplain)
> Charles Berg (Master)
> Thomas Whelton (Hon Secretary)

This testament to his work among the poor must have pleased Bernard mightily, and gave the lie to his detractors and those who accused him of toadyism to the rich and powerful. Anyone who knew the whole man and his untiring work and love of the poor and destitute soon came to see he was employing all the gifts God had given him to the greater glory of his beloved Master. Above all he was intensely English, as he showed during and after the War,

* Irish Gaelic for 'a hundred thousand welcomes'.

and he always said what he thought. Thus, in 1910, he was much criticised for expressing the hope that King George V, who had then just succeeded King Edward VII on the throne, would keep up his late Majesty's racing stud. To his critics he replied that he was in favour of all sport, not excluding racing under proper conditions, for he considered that every true Englishman had in his character a trend of sportsmanship. Naturally what is generally called modernism was abhorrent to him.

He was rather pessimistic in his outlook on the future of Christianity in this country, for he considered that unless England speedily roused herself and fed the fires of religion with the fuel of faith and prayer, she might wake up to hear a passing bell tolling her soul's death.

Bernard's last tour of South Africa was not a great success and he returned home in July 1922, a sick man, to spend his remaining months at Manresa House, Roehampton. Here he died peacefully on 31 October, aged seventy-five. His last words were, 'I am not very well, but I am in His hands as I have always been'.

Princes and prelates, dukes and dustmen packed the Farm Street church for his requiem on 3 November 1922, and many were crying openly as they followed the cortège through the London streets to St Mary's cemetery, Kensal Green, where he was buried in a humble grave where six other priests of the Jesuit order already lay.

The Wit and Wisdom of Bernard Vaughan

'Protestantism may be a good religion to live in, but the Catholic religion is the best one to die in.'

'If you have to choose between a good time and a good eternity, do not hesitate about which it is going to be.'

'When you go hence leave this planet brighter and happier because of your passage through it.'

'To educate the rising generation without religion is to arm a mob and not to drill an army.'

To someone who asked if he still rode, he replied, 'No. A Jesuit has only one horse and he keeps his towel on it.'

Once, when he offered a non-conformist minister a cigar, the minister remarked that he was not sent into this world to smoke. 'I quite understand, but as I belong to a Church which prefers to get its smoking done in this world, I hope you won't mind me lighting up', replied Father Bernard.

'If you want to build character do not hope to build on whipped cream under a coronet. It must be formed and moulded like a block of marble, under the chisel and hammer of suffering.'

'One way of partaking of another's sin is by silence. It is the sin of a coward.'

'Never have misunderstandings without making them up at bedtime.'

'In days gone by ladies dressed for dinner – now they undress for it.'

He was particularly severe on 'the aggressive type of woman who had ceased to be a lady and had not yet become a gentleman'.

'I object to the sea-front go-with-the-times girl. The girl with even less in her than on her.'

He was once staying with a brother priest for whom he had been preaching. Next morning after Mass the priest asked him if he would care to accompany him to the schools. The priest anxious that Father Vaughan should see how well instructed the children were, asked them to explain the Sacrament of Holy Matrimony. One boy replied, 'Holy Matrimony is a period of suffering and torment man has to go through in order to prepare for higher life'. 'You silly boy', said the priest, 'that's purgatory not matrimony, you're describing.' 'You never can tell', said Father Vaughan, 'the boy may be right after all.'

On one occasion a bishop said to him, 'They tell me, Father, that your congregation never knows what you are going to say next'. 'My sermons', said Father Vaughan, 'would not be of much use my Lord, if they did.'

'I believe in the God who created Mr Wells. But not in the God Mr Wells created.'

Once, when on a ship that was in great danger of going down, the ladies rushed to him asking, 'Shall we be saved?' 'That depends on you my friends', he replied. 'But I have the best authority for assuring you it is as short to heaven by water as by land.'

During the War the Kaiser complained to Rome that Father Vaughan had called him 'an electro-plated Napoleon', with the only result that the Father apologised abjectly – to Napoleon!

A young man was airing his agnosticism. Turning to Father Vaughan at the end of his tirade against his like, he said, 'And pray, what do you think of me?' Like the crack of a whip came the reply, 'Nature made you an entity, abuse of her gifts, a nonentity'.

Father Bernard's wit did not always win. Once he asked a Rabbi friend, 'When are you going to eat ham?' 'At your wedding', replied the Rabbi, with a simplicity that gave it greater force.

He was once asked by the Master of Trinity College (Cambridge) as they stood beneath Holbein's famous portrait of Henry VIII, 'What would you do Father, as a Jesuit, if his Majesty were to step out of the canvas?' 'I should ask the ladies to leave the room', was his prompt reply.

Preaching one day on behalf of a hospital for incurables, he was asked not to refer to its depressing title. To this he replied that the world was a hospital for incurables – at least, he never knew anyone to go out of it alive.

On one occasion he was saying his office on top of a bus, when a militant Protestant interrupted him by exclaiming in a loud voice, 'When I pray, I enter into my chambers, and pray to my Father in secret!' 'Yes', said Father Vaughan, still apparently engrossed in his prayers, 'and then you get upon the top of a bus and proclaim this fact to everybody.'

He was giving a Church 'At Home' when a guest was mistakenly announced as 'Lady Dash'. 'No, no', she corrected, 'just plain Mrs Dash.' Instantly Father Vaughan stepped up saying, 'MRS Dash it may be, but plain, never!'

Bernard was destined for the Army but, as he used to say, he 'Put his money not on the rouge, but on the noir!' and so changed the red coat for the black cossack.

'Life does not consist in holding a good hand, but in playing a bad one well.'

A bigot, intending to 'floor' him, asked did he believe that the 'end justified the means'. Father Bernard replied it did in some circumstances. Then he told his questioner that on being informed that a 'fallen woman', a Catholic, lay dying in a house of ill fame, he went to the den of iniquity at half-past one in the morning and heard her confession, adding 'I believe she is in heaven now'.

'Love has a thirst which nothing can quench but the fountain of living waters – God.'

A boy called on him one evening. 'Father', said the lad, 'I want to see you special and private – somewhere quiet.' Father Vaughan asked him into his study, prepared for fearful revelations and spiritual difficulties. Then the boy said, 'Father, you ain't got such a thing as a pair of trousers, 'ave yer?' 'Yes, I have, old chap', replied the priest, 'and what's more I've got them on.'

He was once tackled by a young lady in a train, who asked 'Father Bernard Vaughan, would you mind giving me your autograph?' He took the book which she held out and complied good-naturedly. Then he said, 'How did you know who I was?' 'I have just seen that lovely model of you at Madame Tussaud's.'

On one occasion, after the King, then Prince of Wales, with some fifteen other royal personages had been present at one of his Cannes sermons, he was asked, 'Did you not feel nervous before so much royalty?' 'No', replied Father Vaughan, 'for you must know that I have been accustomed to preach before the King of Kings.'

'Personally, from my reading of theology, moral and dogmatic, I should not feel entitled to administer the rites of the Church to anyone, no matter what his nationality, who was deliberately dying of hunger strike.'

REGINALD VAUGHAN

The eighth son, Reginald Aloysius Joseph Mary, was born on 15 June 1849. His godfather was Reginald Jones and godmother Mary Weld Blundell. He gave up his attempt to become a priest in 1870, married in Australia and eventually settled at Glen Trothy in Monmouthshire (see pages 124–5).

JOHN SPENCER VAUGHAN

John Spencer, John and Eliza's fourteenth child, was born at Court-field on 24 January 1853 and his mother died giving birth to him. He was educated at Downside and wished to become a Carthusian monk but his health did not permit, so eventually he became a secular priest. He studied at the English College in Rome, and also at the Bruges Seminary and on his return to England was ordained priest on 4 June 1876 by his eldest brother, Herbert, then Bishop of Salford. He was appointed to the staff of St Bede's College but his health was not good and soon his doctor, the celebrated Sir James Paget, recommended a warmer climate and a long sea voyage. Accordingly, he was sent to New Zealand and Australia where his older brother Roger was Archbishop of Sydney (see pages 87–91) and his cousin, Sir Frances Weld, Governor of Tasmania.

John devoted his time to preaching and missionary work in the backwoods of Australia, throughout New Zealand, the Sandwich Isles, San Francisco and Canada. Like all his brothers, he seems to have been exceedingly fond of travelling and his health as well as his education greatly benefited. On his return to England he resumed work at St Bede's College for a time until Cardinal Manning sent for him, desiring to have this accomplished priest near him in London. They seem to have got on well and he became a tremendous help to Manning at Archbishop's House and also spent time with his saintly brother Kenelm at the House of Expiation in Beaufort Street, Chelsea. In 1896 he was appointed Domestic Prelate to Leo XIII and two years later a Canon of Westminster.

His excellent sermons and the many books he wrote brought him much into the public eye. He appears to have been of a thoughtful,*

* Clearly a universal perception of John for, in the Vaughan fraternal triumvirate 'Thought, Word and Deed', John comes first (followed by Bernard and Herbert respectively).

well-balanced nature, less excitable and volatile than his brothers, and his writing is always clear even on obscure theological subjects. He published some twenty-five books, the best known probably being *Life after Death*, which ran into nine editions and was translated into four languages. Other well-known titles were *Thoughts for all Times*, which was very popular in America, *Faith and Folly* and *Happiness and Beauty*, a delightful little book published by Longman Green in 1913, which deals in a most comprehensive manner with the creation and purpose of mankind. He also edited for Herbert a book the Cardinal was working on at the time of his death called *The Young Priest*, which was intended to serve as a guide to his Mill Hill Missionaries.

Monsignor John Vaughan was created Bishop of Sebastopolis by the Holy See in 1909 and Auxiliary to Dr Casantelli, Bishop of Salford. He also, at Cardinal Vaughan's request, organised a Lecturing Crusade among the non-Catholics of the Westminster diocese, the idea being to give at regular intervals lectures in public halls on Catholic subjects, doctrinal and historical. Admission was to be free and every effort made to encourage the attendance of non-Catholics. This was an innovation that proved very successful and was joined by some of the most learned controversialists of the day such as Father Luke Rivinton, Monsignor Moyes, Croke Robinson and Howlet, and many others. Many districts of London were visited and thousands of non-Catholics availed themselves of these occasions to hear from the priests something of the doctrine and teaching of Holy Church and a great deal of discussion and conversation took place.

From 1912 to 1915 the Bishop was rector of St Bede's College, Manchester, and later during the last ten years of his life he gave retreats to the clergy both in England and Ireland, and helped in the different parishes of the Salford district. Finally, he was put in charge of the parish of Great Harwood near Blackburn. He died there on 4 December 1925.

GWLADYS VAUGHAN

Gwladys Teresa Elizabeth Filomena Mary, John and Eliza's eldest daughter, was born at Bruges on 27 February 1838, during one of the family's European tours. Her godmother was Mrs Jones (of Llanarth) and her godfather, Mr Digby. She made her First Holy Communion on Easter Sunday, 8 April 1849, aged eleven. Gwladys and her nearest sister, Teresa, made their first Confession on 11 March (the feast of St John of God) 1847. From her earliest youth, she seems to have had a special love of God. When a toddler she used to follow her mother to the chapel when she was praying, and one day asked her why she looked so much prettier when she was praying, and why she shut her eyes so that she could see nothing. Her Mother laughingly replied, pointing to the tabernacle, 'Jesus is there', which greatly impressed little Gwladys, who fell to her knees and kept on repeating, 'Jesus is there, Jesus is there'.

When she was six, Gwladys had a serious illness which affected her spine and her general health for the rest of her life. It also brought her very close to her mother as she had to be educated at home. Her mother taught her drawing and painting and an ardent love of Our Lord, explaining to her how it was possible to offer up her sufferings and limitations with joy. Eliza's death, when she was fifteen, must indeed have been a heavy cross for this child to bear; but she found her consolation three years later when she joined the Visitation convent at Boulogne at the age of eighteen; she had got to know them during the three years the family lived at Boulogne after Eliza's death. For the rest of her life she struggled manfully against continual suffering, with resignation, and always learning to love Our Lord more and more. Her father's second marriage seems to have made her very unhappy, and she wrote him the following letter on New Year's Day 1860, in reply to his in which he told her the news that he would shortly – on 15 February – make Mary Weld his second wife:

De notre Monastere
de Magnetra

My very dear Papa,

Your letter has quite knocked me up and I can not tell you all the tears that it has caused me. Still you know my beloved Father, I have never had an opinion contrary to yours, and your sentiment is always mine. You are as ever my only Father and my only Mother is she who gave me birth.

I have nothing to do but pray. O yes, pray and pray that things may turn out well and as you wish, for I quite consider you beloved and very dear Father, as sacrificing yourself in the most heroic way for your children and can never believe that any other thing would have made you take such a step.

All you say about 'Mary Weld' is very consoling. I should like very much to know her age, as I have never seen her.

My dearest Father, how I thank God for having called me to

114

His divine service before such an event came to arrive. I should be miserable were I at home. There is no chance of my seeing you before you are married, I suppose?!

Poor Ken,* I do not think he will ever be strong or vigorous enough to do anything but suffer as he does, with fervour, patience and resignation, till the loving Providence arranges what is best. By Clare's** letter, she seems to wish to make a retreat here; how much pleasure it would give me who am for ever your truly devoted daughter.

Soeur J. Clementine Elizabeth Vaughan DSB

Clearly she adored her father and could not understand his wishing to marry again, but resolved to make herself accept it.

She died on 3 February 1880, after many years of increasingly poor health. Her father paid tribute to her in a touching letter to Reggie (see page 59).

HELEN VAUGHAN

Helen Teresa Mary, John and Eliza's second daughter, was born at Courtfield on 7 August 1839. Her godparents were Mrs Blundell and Mr Edward Weld.

Always called Teresa, she seems to have been a sweet, attractive child, much beloved by her brothers, and would have been fourteen when her mother died. Early she started to work among the poor, and while living in London, on cold winter nights, liked to go out with her sisters, laden with food and other things for the sick and needy. She was called by God to the religious life and early in 1861 entered the Sisters of Charity of St Vincent de Paul, to work among the poor and destitute in London. Within a few months of taking the habit, she was stricken with a mortal disease and died peacefully in her convent as the handmaid of the Lord, on 28 May. She was buried at Kensal Green by her brothers, in a plot set apart for nuns. Letters from Herbert Vaughan to his father and grandfather give a vivid account of her holy death (see page 51).

---

* Her brother Kenelm, two-and-a-half years older than she, at that time suffering from chronic ill-health (see pages 91–6).
** Her sister, who had joined the convent of the Poor Clares at Amiens (see page 103).

CLARE VAUGHAN

Clare Mary Vaughan, John and Eliza's third daughter, was born at Courtfield on 22 February 1843. Her godmother was Mrs Edward Weld, her godfather Edmund Vaughan. She made her first Confession on 30 November 1850.

Having read Lady Lovat's life of Clare Vaughan – Sister Mary Clare of the Infant Jesus, as she became – I am afraid I find her excessive piety so completely nauseating that I feel quite unable to write about her, though others may consider her a saint. This child seems to have had an iron will for getting her own way; she badgered her father, her uncle and all her friends into consenting to her joining the Poor Clares at Amiens so that her passion for abasement, humility, and finally her will to die could be appeased. What this child can have known of life is impossible to say. One is inclined to feel very sorry for her. Her vapours and vomiting when she had to sweep a room or wash the dishes and determination invariably to belittle herself, seems hardly like true humility. A day with Mother Theresa would probably have killed her; and doubtless she would have given that great lady a pain in the neck!

One wonders where this excessive desire for self-inflicted punishment got into these Vaughan children – perhaps if one could untangle the skein there might be an old nurse at the bottom? Clare died, as she wished, at her convent on 20 January 1862, when only nineteen years old.

MARY VAUGHAN

Mary Elizabeth Barbara, John and Eliza's fourth daughter, was born on 23 November 1845 and baptised in the Courtfield chapel three days later by the Rev. J. Dawson. Her godparents were Mr and Mrs Plowden of Plowden Hall, Shropshire.*

Very early in life Mary talked of being a nun, but her brothers used to laugh at her and say she was too fond of every kind of amusement, to which she replied, 'Well, the more I enjoy everything, the more I shall have to give up – the more I shall be able to do and bear and suffer for the love of God'. She was beloved by the whole family, particularly her father (see his very private, moving letter to

---

* Their great-great-grandson became godfather to my son Richard.

her) and was herself especially devoted to Bernard.

Mary made her First Communion on 13 March 1855, but the same day was taken seriously ill with scarlet fever. Her governess, Miss Pole, wrote on the 14th, 'Dear little Mary is dangerously ill; she does not suffer much pain and looks like an angel. This morning she received the Last Sacraments with full consciousness . . . our only hope is in prayer.' She recovered, though remained delicate for a long time. In 1865 she joined the community of the Canonesses of St Augustine, Newton Abbot, and took the name of 'Clare Magdalene' when she received the novice's habit on 12 July 1866.

Sister Clare Magdalene was professed on 16 July 1867 and for a time continued in tolerably good health and enormously enjoyed her religious life, especially the time spent in adoration before the Blessed Sacrament. But sadly, she too seems to have suffered the consumptive complaint inherent in the family and three times had serious haemorrhages of the lungs, from which she always recovered to the astonishment of her doctors and everyone around her. Her convalescence following these attacks was almost wholly given to prayer and spiritual reading; but she eagerly resumed her duties in the community the moment she was allowed to. She seems to have been artistic and fond of singing and needlework but, as with all the Vaughans, her devotion to the Blessed Sacrament was the core and centre of her life, and her idea of rest was to go off to the Divine Presence in the chapel and keep Jesus company. In winter she suffered intensely from the cold, but if any of the sisters sympathised with her about it, she used to say 'Well, we must keep the fire within burning. I am just going into the Church where Our Lord will warm both soul and body. Shall I give your heart to him, too?'

Mother Clare Magdalene became prioress of her community in spite of increasing ill-health and for the few years that were left her proved an efficient administrator and beloved Mother to them all. She died from haemorrhage of the lungs on 28 December 1884. Her Uncle William, Bishop of Plymouth, performed the funeral ceremony at her convent.

MARGARET VAUGHAN

Margaret Mary Magdalene, born at Courtfield on 8 May 1851, was the fifth child and last daughter of John and Eliza's family. Her godparents were Helen de la Pasture and the Rev. H. Vaughan.

She seems to have had some sort of mental disease, probably schizophrenia. In a letter to Mary dated 3 November 1879, John wrote:

> You ask about poor little Dot. It is a very sad case. She is greatly to be pitied and I am sure quite irresponsible. Her present humour is to be devoted to Father Ryan, whom she was so violent against, and to take an antipathy to me.
>
> When she heard I was at the point of death, she expressed no interest. And when I saw her, she turned away. All this I am told is simply characteristic of her disease. It is distressing to us and must be painful to her. Poor Child! With all this she is, in her way, extremely religious and devout and God, who sees the heart, may sanctify her by her sufferings and good will.

In another letter, this time to Reggie, written on 5 March 1874 from 17 Cromwell Place, South Kensington, her father gave some idea of the difficulties of looking after her:

> The most noteworthy occurrence in the family since you left was Margie's return from Abbotsleigh. If she was eager to go there and delighted at the prospect – she was doubly eager and doubly delighted to get away. I was afraid to trust her even in the 'Ladies Carriage' for the journey, for she might have got out and lost herself and stepped into a wrong train – so instead of meeting her at the station, Mary went all the way to fetch her home. I do not see her the slightest degree altered, but in good health and spirits and looking forward to our returning to Courtfield. Poor little Dot!

The family seem to have been fond of her and often sent messages in their letters. Margaret lived mostly with her father and stepmother. After they died Frank and Reggie were her guardians and she had an allowance of £200 a year. The Cardinal, in a letter to Lady Herbert written from Rome on 15 January 1881, said,

> It would be exceedingly kind if you went to see her sometimes when you are free, I should be very glad to have your report. Whether it would be possible, or desirable, for her to return to Courtfield is a very delicate matter, even if it were her wish to do so. The real question is: Is she well taken care of where she is? And would she be better off elsewhere?

The rest of Margaret's long life was spent in a convent nursing home, where she died aged eighty-five on 6 May 1936.

FRANCIS VAUGHAN

Francis Baynham William was John and Eliza's sixth son. Born on 18 March 1844, he had as godparents the Rev. William Vaughan and Mrs Segrave. He was brought up – as they all were – to the hunting, shooting, fishing life of an English country gentleman, though no doubt it must have come as a surprise when his four elder brothers entered the Church and he inherited the beautiful Courtfield estate and on his father's death became lord of the manors of Welsh Bicknor and Ruardean.

He was also Deputy Lieutenant for Herefordshire in 1880 and a JP for Herefordshire and Monmouthshire, and Colonel of the Royal Monmouthshire Militia. He seems to have been the first of the Vaughans to go in for papal duties and was a Chamberlain to His Holinesses Pope Leo XIII and Pope Pius X and Knight Commander of the Order of Pius.

Francis Baynham was also the first Vaughan to marry an American, his wife, Caroline Ruth Pope, being the daughter of one of the most distinguished surgeons in American medical history and head of a school famed throughout the country for its high standards and thorough methods of teaching. Caroline Ruth Pope, eldest of his three daughters, was born in 1848 and brought up in the luxury of her wealthy home in St Louis in a Protestant Episcopalian household – a completely different background from the entrenched and immovably Catholic Vaughans of Courtfield.

The Pope Family Connection

Charles Alexander Pope was born in Huntsville, Alabama, on 15 March 1818, the son of Benjamin Stokesley Pope, a native of Delaware and grandson of Colonel Charles Pope who served with distinction in a Delaware regiment in the American War of Independence. In the museum at Stonyhurst, there is a paper signed by George Washington stating that Lt.-Col. Charles Pope was admitted into the exclusive Cincinnati Club for gentlemen. No one who was not from a good family was received into this club.

This Colonel Charles Pope married Jane, daughter of Benjamin Stokesley, in 1772. She was of Quaker stock connected with Warner, Mipplen, and prominent members of the Society of Friends. She died on 9 July 1793 aged forty-one and was buried in the Presbyterian Church at Smyrna, Delaware and a tomb was erected to her memory in 1842. Benjamin Stokesley Pope, the fourth son, was born on 29

August 1783 and is described as a man of rare literary taste and culture. He married in 1815 a Miss Eliza E. Wyatt, a descendant of Sir Francis Wyatt, Governor of Virginia, and made his home in Huntsville, a beautiful town amid a cultured community.

Charles Alexander, born in 1818, was Benjamin and Eliza's only son and he began his medical studies with Doctors Fern and Erskine of Huntsville and with Doctor Daniel Drake at the Cincinnati Medical College, for whom he entertained the highest regard. He received his medical Degree in 1839, at the age of twenty-one, from the University of Pennsylvania and departed for Europe for further study. In Paris he was acclaimed as the most expert and neatest operator on the cadaver and a brilliant future was predicted for him in the noble and daring art of surgery. He returned to America and settled in St Louis, Missouri where in 1843, at the age of twenty-five, he became Professor of Anatomy and Physiology. His meteoric career continued and in 1849, when still only thirty-one, he was elected Dean of the Medical Department of St Louis University. He married in 1846 Caroline O'Fallon, the only daughter of Colonel John O'Fallon, the most successful and prominent citizen of St Louis and a well-known and wealthy philanthropist. With his help he built the finest medical college and school of surgery in St Louis.

For twenty-five years Charles Pope was the most brilliant surgeon in the western states and immensely popular. Tall, handsome, of a genial disposition and agreeable manner, he was also a man of sterling integrity. The crowning honour of his career came in 1854 when he was elected President of the American Medical Association at the St Louis meeting.

The tremendous pace of his career probably burnt him out and in 1865 he resigned his post as Dean and Professor of Surgery in the St Louis Medical College, owing to ill health. He and his delicate wife and family then removed to Europe – chiefly on her insistence because she thought it would benefit both him and the children. He resigned all his important medical positions in the autumn of that year and was given a splendid farewell dinner by his many friends at the Old Lindell Hotel, St Louis on 8 October. His farewell speech was tinged with sadness and regret at the prospect of leaving his friends and his life's work, though he expressed a hope of 'returning again invigorated and improved to minister still at the sacred altar of medicine'.

The Popes settled in Paris and their son John came as an under-graduate to Oxford in 1868 to study law. They were very rich, had a fine house, and moved in the best circles.

The Aclands were friends from St Louis days when Dr Henry Wentworth Dyke Acland was travelling as personal physician to The Prince of Wales on an official visit to Canada, and an unofficial tour in the United States. Writing from St Louis in September 1860 to Sarah his wife he said:

> After an exhausting day I went to tea with Dr Pope. His house was about twice the size of ours and more splendid with considerable space at the back – three entrances and stables; everything well arranged, in good taste tho' very handsome – and such a nice wife. The son and three daughters and some young ladies – names unknown – were there. The boy is 10 and they propose to bring him in a year or two to Eton and Oxford. Mrs Pope, a clever, well read person, made me feel wonderfully at home and in about half an hour we had set the Professor to sew on a sewing machine in illustration of what I had better learn to do as an evening amusement. Every American lady now has all the household work done by a machine.

Sarah Acland, writing from Paris on 29 May 1870 to her son William Dyke Acland, reported:

> My dearest Willie,
>
> . . . Mrs Pope is most kind, she has a fortune of her own, I suppose a large one, for she persuaded Dr Pope to give up a professional income of 25,000 dollars (£5,000) at St Louis and come to Europe because she thought it would be better for the children: Mr Pope [John] who is at Oxford, and the three daughters, who are here with her. And they are very rich still. This apartment which is furnished costs 1800 francs a month (£864 a year). They have a carriage in which they take me about and indeed do everything possible for us. They live in one of the splendid new boulevards. . .

Dr Pope was in America at the time, but due to return to Paris that same week. Charles had gone on a short visit to St Louis where he was received with open arms and much fêted by his old colleagues. He rejoined his family in Paris as planned, but died suddenly on 5 July. Caroline and her sisters were in England, probably staying with their friends the Coopers at Torquay, and John went over to Paris to look after his mother and bring her to England where Captain Bernard Cooper RN and his wife befriended them. Charles Alexander's sudden death at the age of fifty-two must have been a shattering blow for his family, far removed from their roots in St Louis and not long settled in Paris. He was interred in the O'Fallon plot in the Bellefontaine cemetery there. A granite cross bears the simple inscription 'Charles A. Pope. Requiescat in Pace.'

The Coopers, who were Catholics, probably had a lot to do with first John and then his mother and sisters converting to Rome. They were staying in the Plymouth diocese and no doubt soon got to know the Bishop, William Vaughan, and it was he who introduced his nephew Francis Baynham to Caroline Ruth Pope at Dartmouth and subsequently married them on 16 August 1871 at the Church of Our Lady Help of Christians, Priory Road, Torquay. No doubt, owing to their recent bereavement, they had a quiet wedding. The Popes appear to have lived at Torquay for a time.

The romantic Catholic history of the Vaughans and their beautiful home in the Wye Valley must have exercised a tremendous influence on the newly converted Popes. However, Caroline seems to have been of an analytical turn of mind and did not possess the unquestioning love of God peculiar to her husband's family. In a curious little 'Report', written in January 1881 by a Father P. Fotheringham while the Bishop of Plymouth and other members of the family were assembled at Courtfield waiting for the coffins of John and Mary Vaughan to arrive from Biarritz, we get glimpses of Caroline, whom he seems to have held in the highest regard:

> I have often noticed that Mrs Vaughan uses very few words in expressing her opinion, but the words are always well chosen – there is never a word too much either in speaking or writing – the meaning is invariably clear, and the manner very charming, making anyone quite merry.
> . . . One might have thought that when Mrs Vaughan has – as is so often the case – distinguished company she would be more or less ashamed to acknowledge a humble individual like the writer as a friendly guest or visitor; and it is to me a source of great pleasure and eternal gratitude that Mrs Vaughan never seems ashamed of showing, as far as I may be allowed to say so, friendly disposition towards the writer.

On a walk through the park as far as the milestone they had a religious discussion and Caroline confessed:

> she has always entertained a great terror of death; that it was only a question of time, that she hoped she would have grace to resign herself when death came, that the late Mrs Vaughan had not such fear of death, that we ought rather to wish for death since it is the means of going to God, but that she did not 'feel this love to God'; life was a dream.
> I asked if she was strongly attached to life. 'Yes', said Mrs Vaughan, 'I wish to live as long as God allows me to.' She thought the love

of God was the best preparation for death. Her difficulty appeared to be twofold: 1) 'It is difficult to love the Unseen', 2) 'I don't feel this Love of God'. I briefly pointed out the theological arguments for overcoming these difficulties and Mrs Vaughan said in reply that the subject was not too abstruse.

Caroline had been married and living at Courtfield for ten years when this conversation took place. Charles, her eldest son, named after his maternal grandfather, was a boy of eight and appears to have been keen on sport, shooting and riding. He took Father Fotheringham to see his 'black horse', which he said his grandfather John Vaughan had given him; also a litter of puppies and the poultry yard where the fowls were perching on the branches of trees which the good Father thought very nice and Charles said he had collected fifteen eggs that day. They seem to have had quite a happy conversation about the company gathered for what Charles refers to as the 'fulial'. Charles stated that he enjoyed company and preferred gentlemen to ladies 'because they go hunting'. One gets a picture of happy domesticity, with 'Captain Vaughan [who had been in some trouble over a shot dog with the Ross magistrates] taking his troubles very lightly being as cheerful and merry as ever'.

Caroline Ruth's brother, John O'Fallon Pope, was born in St Louis on 26 December 1850. Charles and Caroline's only son, he had moved with his family to Paris in 1865 and went to Christ Church, Oxford where he read law, and matriculated in 1868.

In 1871 he left Oxford and became a student of the Inner Temple and later went to study philosophy with the Benedictines at Belmont. He received his MA from Oxford in 1876 and went to Rome to be ordained. On 7 September 1878 he joined the Jesuits at Manresa House, Roehampton. He seems to have gone in for teaching, both at St Benno's College, St Asaph, and also at Beaumont. Pope's Hall, Oxford was named after him and later became Campion Hall. John was a master there from 1902 to 1915, when he retired.

He often stayed at Courtfield and seems to have been popular with the family. When his mother died in 1915 he paid a visit to St Louis in connection with her large estate. On his return he spent several years at Beaumont and eventually retired to Manresa House where he conducted retreats until 1931.

John O'Fallon Pope's considerable fortune played a large part in the purchase of Heythrop Hall for use as a Jesuit College. In his retirement he was described as an austere and unbending theologian, very set in his ways. He died at Manresa on 31 October 1934, aged eighty-three, and his funeral was attended by Dr Herbert Vaughan and a daughter of their old friend Captain Cooper.

Francis Vaughan and the Courtfield Estate

Francis Baynham (Frank) was fond of travelling and he and his wife Caroline often seem to have been in Paris, where Mrs Pope lived, or in Rome fulfilling papal Chamberlain duties.* One suspects he preferred the life of Paris and Rome to farming at Courtfield. Letters from his father, who had moved to London in 1872, seem to indicate this and are full of advice on farming matters and keeping the rabbits down and occasionally a reminder of his luck in inheriting the Courtfield estate. It looks as if he may not have been so good and careful a farmer as his father, or astute about money matters. At one stage, he seems to have lost a lot of money – perhaps in Pearson's Fire Alarms – and there was talk of disentailing the estate in order to avoid bankruptcy in 1906. Luckily this seems to have been avoided. Pearson, described by the solicitors as a most unreliable character, seems to have led him into this mess. His brother Reginald Vaughan, of Glen Trothy (see page 112), also seems to have suffered a major financial disaster in 1884 and there are many letters of condolence from various relations. One from his brother Jerome, then Prior of Fort Augustus, says he had a horrible shake and severe blow on receiving the news and he is horribly afraid:

> that Frank may be in the same boat – has he also lost a lot of money? And what has the Colonel [their father, John Vaughan] been doing up in heaven to let all the money he gathered together with so much trouble be lost so quickly! There is some meaning in it all and we must accept the dispensation of God's holy will. You have hit the main thing when you say pray that we may be able to live at the Glen [Glen Trothy] and have the Blessed Sacrament and a Priest. I shall begin a Novena of Masses for this tomorrow morning. It used to be a great pleasure to me to think that you and Francis were well off – at all events comfortably off – but now I fear you will be much pinched and my heart bleeds for you.

Your ever devoted Brother,
Jerome Vaughan O.S.B.

So both Frank and Reggie must have suffered some dreadful financial

* We have an oil painting of St Peter which used to hang in Pope (now Saint) Pius X's bedroom in the Vatican. He gave it to Prior Jerome Vaughan, who left it to Frank.

crash. Frank had a rich wife but it is doubtful Reggie was so lucky.

A lot of letters commiserating on the terrible financial loss came from his sister, Clare Magdalen, a nun at St Augustine's Priory, Newton Abbot, where the entire community seemed to be praying day and night for his 'money matters' to come right, but didn't seem to have much hope of success. The burden of the letters was that God had permitted this terrible misfortune,

> and so it is naturally, but supernaturally I am certain it is even for your good – it is to make you more like our Lord in poverty and make you suffer in that way and so get you a higher place in Heaven – Oh! it is a fearful sum to lose! Is it not wholly your fortune? What will you do? Perhaps go to France somewhere to economise. How is Frank faring? I suppose he too has lost something. Oh dear me! £10,000 is such a fearful large sum. God has permitted it. A soul told me our Lord will bless you with a good harvest.

Reading his father John's letters one gets the impression he is watchful and rather anxious of Frank's management of the estate. In a letter to Frank about money matters, written on 5 June 1872, he said:

> Your management of your Irish property is certainly, as you say, not successful, nor, unless you exhibit more judgement, prudence and decision of character, will it, I fear, become so.
>
> I know, my dear Frank, there is not much use in offering advice to a man of seven or eight and twenty, who is married and takes his own course, but I acknowledge that I feel anxiety and misgivings when I look forward to your future.
>
> You will inherit, at all events, (beside the Irish property), all the estate I received from my father, increased by many small purchases and greatly improved in value. But you will not administer that property successfully, nor take your position and discharge your duties, as a country gentleman, without acquiring the necessary knowledge and experience.
>
> I secured you my life interest in Glen Trothy, that you might have a house in a county where you had a standing and where you might have a useful career. As for Mrs Pope's objection, or your own reluctance, to lay out any money in improving the Glen for fear that one of your brothers might benefit by your expenditure – that difficulty is easily met. I would ensure you, by Deed, a full repayment for all improvements you might make if you were ever deprived of them.
>
> I think, almost with dismay, of you living without a profession, at some watering place or abroad; either leading a totally idle life or with no object (beyond your wife and children) but amusement and

society. Ireland, for reasons that will occur to you, will not be a suitable residence.

I believe Harris* to be an honest fellow, but he is in a position of great difficulty and temptation and unless supported by your presence or directed by your knowledge and experience, it is too much to expect that he can make your farming profitable.

. . . your tenants and neighbours have discovered that you can be cheated and robbed with impunity, and the base Irish nature, cunning and ungrateful, takes advantage of your easy good nature. You would have a fair start elsewhere. At Mullaranny it will now be difficult to bring your people to their bearings, and hateful to live among them. Talk over these matters with Carrie [Caroline]. She is conscientious and sensible and will know as well as yourself that I can have but one object at heart – the welfare and happiness of you both.

In his letter of 29 April 1875 his father is still compelled to take a strong line with Frank:

Thanks for the good account of at least a part of my farm. If I have to stop at Gloucester to buy grass seeds, I shall not arrive for dinner on Saturday, otherwise at 3pm. I should like young Gunter as a cottage tenant very much. He seems a particularly respectable young fellow. I doubt extremely, however if G. Jones will give up the cottage, until he receives regular notice; which would only give possession next March I think. Your occupation of Glen Wye also reduces the cottage accommodation so I am not sure what arrangement will be best. The long letter you mention from Sydney is, I doubt not, some paper respecting your sale of Rosturk, which Reggy had to sign. It will keep perfectly till I arrive . . . As to Thomas Wood, I quite agree with you. Nothing looks more desolate than a wood newly felled. But, if I had not managed my estate to the best advantage, instead of always studying the picturesque, I should not have been able to leave the whole of my hereditary property – improved – with purchases added to it and with a mortgage of £3,800 paid off, to you.

Still less could I have given you £10,000 from the savings and self-denials of 40 years to enable you to marry and settle so happily, as I thank God you have done during my life time.

Perhaps, while doing so much for you, I have hardly been just to others. Even now, what I put by to secure annuities to some of your brothers I intend to go eventually to you and your children. I have, at no time, spent on myself or my establishment, one shilling of the timber I have cut (even of my own planting) though I had every right to do so. I have, indeed, given something to Herbert, who after my life had an undoubted title to it all, and to whose generosity and affection

* The Courtfield estate manager.

you are so much indebted for this position which you hold.

I make these remarks because I have heard from more than one quarter of the comments which you have made. I think, my dear Frank, you will feel that you have less cause for complaint than gratitude. It is well, at all events, that you should understand our relative financial position and know on what principles I have hitherto administered an estate, which I have, now, not many years left to manage. Will you give the enclosed note to Powell. I intended to have up my charger two weeks ago, but it matters little, I shall hardly want him the first 10 days and he very soon gets glossy this time of year. I shall be curious to see the progress at Glen Wye.

By 1876, writing from Dinan in France, John had distanced himself somewhat from Courtfield's affairs:

By sympathy I take pleasure in your shooting and farming, but, I confess that, so near the ordinary limits of human life, I take little interest in anything for myself. Before next summer I shall be able to set aside a few hundreds to spend upon Courtfield on exterior repairs and internal decoration. What may be done it is too soon to say, but candidly, my dear Frank, I would rather hand over my money to you, to expend it as you like, either now or when I am gone, than attempt to make a home again. I feel more strongly every day that I am a 'stranger and a pilgrim and have no lasting city'. My family are all settled and provided for. I am grateful for so many blessings. My interests and pleasures all in my children. We shall proceed with our travels on Monday week and explore many interesting places and pretty litle towns upon the coast. We hear very favourable reports of St. Quay and Pautrieux. One comfort is that wherever we may be we shall find ourselves within a few minutes of Mass and the Blessed Sacrament. Here we have great luxuries in that way. Altogether our stay here has been very pleasant. Mary has cheerful society and I as much as I desire, with plenty of tranquil leisure, which is as attractive to old age, as odious to youth. There is nothing like working hard when we are young. I rejoice that your time is as full.

In 1884 Francis Baynham built the bridge across the Wye at Huntsham at a cost of approximately £3,000, thus making the Huntsham Court farm much more accessible. He put a gate on the bridge but does not seem to have locked it or demanded any toll which turns out to have been shortsighted because although there was little traffic in those days except to the farm, in recent years, since Symonds Yat has become a famous beauty spot, the traffic has enormously increased and a toll would have produced a considerable income.

Of Frank and Caroline Vaughan's six children, the eldest son,

Charles Jerome, inherited the estate and both his brothers became priests: Herbert Joseph, born on 19 November 1874, was educated at the Oratory and Oscott, and died on 17 February 1936 aged sixty-two; Francis John, born on 5 May 1877, was educated at the Oratory and Ushaw, became Bishop of Menevia in 1925 and died on 13 March 1935 aged fifty-seven.

Of the three daughters, Clare, born on 2 July 1872, married in 1902 Leonard Colin Lindsay, FSA, fourth son of the Hon Colin Lindsay of Deer Park, Devon and died on 26 April 1950. She had no children. Alice, born on 12 November 1883, married in July 1913 Wolstan Edward Berkeley, the youngest son of Robert Berkeley of Spetchley, Worcestershire and died on 18 October 1959. She too had no family. The youngest daughter, Mary, born on 16 July 1878, became a Benedictine nun and died on 9 April 1936.

A Match Unmade, 1870

Amongst the Vaughan family papers are two interesting letters from his father to Frank, who was over in Ireland on the Rosturk property. Both are on the delicate subject of a young lady, a Miss Henry, whom Frank clearly wishes to marry. His father is not sure of the wisdom of his choice, as this letter written from Monmouth on 17 September 1870, shows:

My dearest Frank,

The salvation of your soul is the first thing. Worldly wisdom comes afterwards. Your letter this morning surprised, but did not altogether astonish me. I have not much confidence in these sudden ebullitions of feeling, which seldom have a spiritual or even intellectual origin. At the time I will not venture to condemn them. Pray that the grace of God may guide you. Implore your Mother to intercede for you and watch over you in this critical passage of your life. Being unacquainted with the Henrys personally, I speak with diffidence of the proposed match. You know, as well as I do, that fortune and aristocratic connections have their value. As one of a numerous and increasing family I suppose Miss H. has not much and during Herbert's life your income will be small – even after my death. Do not act hastily, but if after due consideration you adhere to your idea, I will not refuse my consent and you shall have a Father's blessing. I will write you again.

Yours vy aff. J. F. Vaughan.

Two days later, back at Courtfield, his father explained exactly why he feared such a match would not make Frank happy:

My dearest Frank,

I had not time to write to you again by the early post yesterday – Sunday – but I prayed very fervently that God would protect and guide you. I told you how I had foreseen that such frequent and intimate intercourse with the Henry family was likely to end. Mrs Henry, probably, with a woman's tact, watched the game and her recent hint to you to stay away was her diplomacy to bring you to the point. I give her credit. No doubt she has studied and knows you well.

But it is not the material manoeuvres, it is your happiness and future welfare that concerns me. You think Miss Henry would become a Catholic. It is probable from what you say. Yet I remember how entirely confident Major Herbert was that his 'Nell' whom he had known so long and well, only waited for her marriage to enter the Church. Young ladies in love are always sympathetic. It does not follow that they have the humility of the Gospel, or the gift of faith, and after the first flush of feeling is over a Mother's influence and prejudice easily reasserts its sway. Remember, my dear Frank, I can only speak in general terms. If I knew Miss Henry, I perhaps might read her character and form a distinct opinion. Beauty of course is a very secondary consideration. Yet a man should consider less the appearance of his wife on her wedding day than what he has to have before his eyes for half a century perhaps. The fair, fresh, blue-eyed girl grows fat and sallow: the attractive, bright brunette gets coarse, repulsive and vulgar looking. Poor human nature! The fact is, Frank, as to appearances a man must judge entirely for himself. 'De qustibus, non.' Only he had better know what he is doing. Religion, in my opinion, is the sine qua non. There is no true, deep happiness, no sacred union of soul, no openess of feeling in all that is most holy and pure in conjugal and parental love, where a chasm of religious difference separates man and wife.

The more they like and love each other, the more they feel the void and the greater source of misery it becomes. I need say very little about money – though important it is secondary. I have no idea of Miss H's fortune. I presume it is much smaller than that of other young ladies you may select.

On this score I should not object, if you are both content to live for some years in narrow means. You will certainly not improve your position in the social scale by marrying into a commercial family and the world will say you have done badly for yourself.

I do not wish to sacrifice happiness to what 'Mrs Grundy says', but look the entire transaction in the face in all its bearings.

Of this I am intimately convinced that your happiness will be mainly dependent on the piety, the faith and religious feelings of your wife. Where these exist, duty, fidelity of affection and that purity of mind which is the greatest charm of woman, are insured. I have written a long letter for I wished you to know my thoughts. I fervently pray that God may direct you to do His will. In these matters man is much in the hands of Providence. Endeavour to please God in what you may do. Trust in Him. Pray to the Holy Family and to those in Heaven who watch over you.

> Your affec. father
> John F. Vaughan.

How lucky Frank was in his father. It would be impossible to write a more diplomatic and kindly letter to a wavering son. His wisdom and understanding ran deep and true, and in this case Frank took his advice for within a year he had met and married Caroline Pope, an interesting match in which providence and the Bishop of Plymouth played their part. The £20,000 marriage portion she brought must also have been a considerable help.

Frank seems to have farmed at Courtfield and led a country gentleman's life with occasional visits to Rome for his papal duties, where he was painted in 1901 by G. Modgillani. We also have a portrait of Caroline Ruth, in a black lace-edged dress, which captures her calm pleasant expression and beautiful blue eyes (which happily have been passed down in the family to my son Oliver). Courtfield and the Welsh marches must have been a tremendous change for this American girl from St Louis and Paris, but she seems to have coped well, brought up a family of three boys and three girls, and become popular with the neighbours. Lord Southwell in a letter to her eldest son Charles on her death in 1919 said:

> I think she was one of the sweetest women I ever met. I remember her so well in the old days at Courtfield when we used to come over; old Peter Lamotte and I to dine . . . how hospitable and kind your mother was to us, how she would put any one of us up at a moment's notice if it were a bad night for going back. How extraordinarily woman-like she was. I remember so well how she hated the rather 'mannish' tendency of the women at the time and was all for womanliness and gentleness. I never forgot it.

Lord Southwell, known as 'Natty', was one of Charles' '10 best friends'. Another letter from Cardinal Merry del Val from Rome, assured Charles, 'I do not forget to pray for your dear Mother, though really she was such a privileged and holy soul that I feel more like praying to her than for her'.

Mrs Pope and her other two daughters Alice and Lilie and her son John O'Fallon Pope often came on visits. Old Jack Gomery liked to tell me stories of the wealth and grandeur of those days – how only the breasts of chicken could be served to Mrs Pope, and Ross station laid out the red carpet for her arrival and were thanked with a scattering of golden guineas. In an old photograph taken outside the back door of Courtfield, the carriage is laden with luggage marked C.P. and at least twelve servants are drawn up around it. Alice Pope died at Courtfield on 26 August 1882, aged twenty-two, and is buried in the family vault.

Lilie Pope's Diaries

In Caroline Vaughan's sister Lilie's diaries for 1885–1905, the summers, which she usually spent at 'beloved Courtfield', sound delightfully friendly with perpetual house parties of regular guests, family and new friends made during her winters abroad.

1897

> On January 2nd the Brother [John O'Fallon Pope] came to Davos and on 7th he received Laetitia Mildmay into the Church. May 17th left Davos and joined Mother and Clare in Paris. London on 18th June and beloved Courtfield on 19th. Herbert came home on July 14th and on 16th a ball was given in our Maybirds honour. During August there were visits from the Coopers, Lily Dormer, Gertrude and Thekla Von Hugel, Bishop Hedley and Maria Merry del Val.

Lilie must have been delicate and her winters were spent at Davos or Biarritz and she was usually ill. The nieces and nephews seem often to have been with her for companionship, and she appears to have been devoted to them all. She and her mother seemed constantly to be travelling between Paris and Rome, where they sometimes wintered, attended by members of the family. But they always gathered at Courtfield from about May to October.

1898–9

Lilie wintered at Biarritz where, her diary tells us, she:

> was soon ill and spent some of the saddest and loneliest hours of my life. But as elsewhere I met with much kindness and made some pleasant acquaintances; Mammie Wolseley was a frequent visitor and Lady

Sullivan and Mrs Fairfax were very kind to me. Teresa Nat Serville, The Pringles, Bye More-Smyth, Miss Owens and the Campbells did much to make my stay a pleasant one. But my chief happiness there was the Dominican Church, all white and gold and very beautiful and the edification and kindness I received from its Fathers.

. . . after spending four days in London I reached Courtfield on 30th May.

June that year seems to have been a quiet month but in July

the boys came home and there were visits from the Clerags, Lubienskies, and Seels and from Agnes Zulietta, and (my great aunt) Bye More-Smyth. In August the Brother came to us and there were visits from Gertrude von Hugel and Daisy Lockwood and Mr Ishenwood. On 16th we made a grand expedition to Tintern, partly by river and partly by road. How beautiful and enjoyable it was! The Glen Trothyites spent the 17th with us, then came a short visit from Irene Throckmorton and on 22nd the Cardinal arrived and spent a few days with us.

1900

In January Charles received a commission in the Army (7th Dragoon Guards) and in the early days of February he went off to South Africa. On March 10th Herbert was ordained Priest at Courtfield by the Cardinal, and on the 12th, the feast of St Gregory, he said his first Mass in the beloved home chapel. At the end of April came the distressing news that Charles was seriously wounded (April 28th) and for some time we were in the greatest anxiety about him. Frank and May then left us and the parting from May was a heart-wrench as a few weeks later, May 23rd the eve of Ascension, she was to leave us for St. Mary's Abbey, East Bergholt. On June 5th we went to London (from Paris) and on 9th to Courtfield. Charles was invalided home to our joy and returned to us on June 15th. Deo Gratias!

We had visits from Alfred Weld-Blundell, Maria Merry del Val, the Brother came on July 21st and on 24th Harry O'Fallon to spend a few days with us. Charlotte Dease was at Courtfield at the same time. The Brother stayed until August 13th and soon after this he was appointed Head of Clarke Hall Oxford a post that greatly pleased us all.

In the second half of August there were visits from Geraldine O'Meara, Bishop Hedley and Mrs Holmes. In October the Cardinal and 'Uncle Edmund' came to Courtfield and on 14th 'our Francis' received the sub-diaconate on the Feast of Our Lady's Maternity. There were visits from American relations, the Millers, Charles O'Fallon, and Anita O'Fallon and her sons William and John; Aunt Carrie, Uncle John and Cousin Lillie, and 'A charming little tea party in the Hall's pretty garden with Mr & Mrs Thompson, old world like people, and Angie Acland and her friends as the guests!'

1903

> Our beloved Francis was ordained Priest as Ushaw on July 5th, came to Courtfield on the 6th, and on 7th said his First Mass in the dear Courtfield Chapel. Leonard Lindsay arrived and proposed and was accepted by our sweet Clare on the Feast of the Guardian Angels, October 2nd and they were married at Courtfield on January 23rd 1902. May was professed at East Bergholt on January 15th. Bessie Cooper came to stay for 12 days also Father Filmer, Mr and Madame Navarro and Father Herbert.

Dear Aunt Lilie! Every sentence breathes love and devotion to the Family, her religion and to Courtfield.

CHARLES VAUGHAN'S EARLY LIFE

Charles Jerome – 'the Squire' – was born on 30 September 1873 and educated at Fort Augustus, the Oratory and Stonyhurst, lord of the manors of Welsh Bicknor and Ruardean, he was Deputy Lieutenant and JP for Herefordshire and Monmouthshire – and High Sheriff of Herefordshire in 1933, exactly a hundred years after his great-grandfather William Vaughan was High Sheriff for Monmouthshire in 1833.

He was sent to Fort Augustus, probably because his Uncle Jerome was Prior and Superior, but in 1887 went on to the Oratory School, Edgbaston, Birmingham when Cardinal Newman was still there, though Charles thought him old and frail. He seems to have enjoyed his schooldays, particularly Fort Augustus where nearly half the boys were his cousins. At the Oratory he started at the bottom but in due course arrived at the top form and was eventually elected Captain of the School. He attributes this to the fact of having won the Athletic Cup to which the boys attached great importance. Father John Norris was headmaster during his time there. The boys loved him and his splendid qualities made it an outstanding epoch for the school.

At that time Catholics were discouraged from going to Oxford and

Cambridge so in 1892 he went as a philosopher* to Stonyhurst which he enjoyed very much.

Charles seems to have been rather lacking in ambition and uncertain what career to pursue. He exchanged several letters with his uncle Herbert, the Cardinal, in 1891 when he was eighteen, asking advice about going into the army or to Oxford or Cambridge, all of which the Cardinal seems to have been against. He wrote to his old headmaster, John Norris, who appears to have disagreed with the Cardinal and recommends the army, and Uncle John, Bishop of Sebastopolis, was also consulted in 1897.

Herbert Vaughan seems to have been fond of his nephew and expected great things of him – as this letter written for his twenty-first birthday on 29 September 1894 shows:

> Archbishops Ho. Westminster

> My dearest Charles,

> As I find it impossible to get to Courtfield to wish you in person the happiest and most joyous of birthdays, I must do so by letter. I hope you may take the great step from boyhood to manhood fully sensible of its increasing duties and responsibilities and with a firm determination to carry on and to hand down the best traditions and the very highest ideals of the race from which you spring.

> In the ordinary course of nature, we must look to you, when our generation has passed away, to represent the family and I trust you will do so with befitting dignity and courage; honour, truth, loyalty to God and country, together with zeal and generosity in the service of that Faith for which our ancestors fought and suffered and bled, and which is the most glorious inheritance of all, are some among the virtues we shall look for and expect to find in you.

Poor Charles! All his relations appeared to expect so much of him. And Aunt Lilie, writing to felicitate him from the Swiss resort of Davos on 26 September, was no exception:

> My darling Charles,

> I wish you a happy birthday and many returns of it. It is, I suppose, the most important birthday of your life, since it is the step

---

* Philosophers were allowed to keep horses and dogs. There were about 2,000 acres of shooting and several miles of fishing. Many good trout were killed from the ponds in front of the college. As the universities are now open to Catholics, Philosophers have been dispensed with.

into manhood – the beginning, in a sense, of a new life. My heart is brimful of high and loving wishes for my darling boy.

I wish for Sunday to be the starting point of a truly noble career, whose aim is the high ideals you have already perceived and grasped and whose motto is 'Loyal in life and in Death to God and to Duty'. This line that I have quoted was the proudest praise that could have been given to your Grandfather, and when you remember his virtues and those of so many generations of Catholic ancestors, whose name you bear, with all it represents of noble traditions, you will remember too, my Charles, the height and the depth and the force of the saying 'Nobless Oblige'.

Oh! I would have you to be like the peerless knights of olden days. 'Sans peur et sans reproche.' With a stainless honour, an interest in every noble cause and a heart attuned to all that is good and true and beautiful. And like them, on the eve of their initiation into Chivalry, I would have you have the high preparation of prayer, with the sanctification of Holy Sacraments and the dedication to the Queen of Heaven – the Protectress and Shield in life and in death.

Perhaps this may sound ambitious, but can love wish for less than the highest and best? Mine can't I know, nor can any other worthy of the name.

Your devoted Aunt Lilie.

I have sent you the gift that I thought would be the most acceptable. I hope it will prove so.

Charles' twenty-first birthday must have been a tremendous occasion. Extremely handsome, well endowed and with a host of adoring relations, his uncles princes of the Church and all his family moving in the highest society.

By 1897, at least one of his family felt their high expectations for Charles were not being fulfilled. In October his uncle John Vaughan wrote severely in reply to a letter from his nephew, asking for guidance:

You ask me for my candid opinion as regards your present position and occupation. Now, in answering you please to bear in mind that I am expressing merely my own views, and secondly, that I am quite prepared to believe that such views, tho' theoretically sound and good, may yet be in your case impracticable.

In the first place then; I don't think you have half enough to do. I speak, remember of real, honest, downright work. Of course one may always fill up the day and be killing time with trivialities. But, for a serious-minded man, for a man who can look right thro'

135

time into eternity, and who can (in some measure at least) weigh the responsibilities of life, it appears to me that to pass one's days in mere shooting and fishing and riding and dining out, and dancing, etc., must be most unsatisfactory.

Such things, it appears to me are life's pastimes and recreations – not its real business. They in no way help to discipline one's character, to strengthen and steady one's will, or even to form in one habits of self-restraint and of self-reliance; nor are they calculated to bring out one's best and noblest qualities. Your Father is still in the prime of life, he may very likely, with ordinary care, live another twenty or five and twenty years. Now, if instead of your living on at Courtfield during these twenty years, *doing nothing in particular*, and with no fixed and determinate object in life, you were to devote your time and attention and energies to some special profession, whether it be engineering, or land agency or electricity or brewing or 'squatting' or gaining experience in the colonies, etc., what advantages it would give you. I will point out some of the more obvious:

1) You would be provided with certain definite occupation, you would have the satisfaction of feeling that you possessed a definite object in life – that you were a 'worker' in the great human hive, and not a mere 'drone'.
2) You would have something on which to exercise your energies and mental faculties, which by an inexorable law of nature, develop and strengthen by use and rust and decay by disuse.
3) You would be obliging yourself to submit to the restraints and self discipline that regular work (of whatever kind) always entails and must entail if conscientiously carried out.
4) The practice of a profession would teach you tact, method, order, application, care, industry and the value of time and how to distribute it economically.
5) Your interests would multiply, your general knowledge of men and of the world would extend, your faculties would brighten and you would be a real influence for good in the world.
6) Then, when you are called upon at last to take your Father's place and to settle down as the squire of Courtfield, you would bring to the task a mind and a heart far better fitted – brighter, keener and well disciplined. The experience gained would be invaluable and of the greatest possible service and your memory well stored with a practical knowledge of men and things, would make you a much more valuable member of society.

You may, of course, fancy you have now plenty of serious work. But if you do think so, it can be only because you have never known what real work is. To pay a few men their weekly or monthly wage, or to walk over the farm now and again just to see what the men are about, and so on, does not fill any life – does not set all one's soul and dormant energies in motion.

Of course people are so differently constructed, and I have no right to judge you, by myself; but were I in your place, with your opportunities and prospects, I could no more dream away my time as you seem content to do, than I could fly. A holiday is all very well and no one so enjoys a few weeks recreation as those whose lives are spent in toil. But to make of life one long holiday, to have no settled work or task to do, is what I should find extremely difficult to assent to.

Now, my dear old Charles, I have done what you asked me. So don't now be angry with me for having had my say. I dare say you would gladly do more if you had more encouragement, and if circumstances were different. I am not blaming you, some persons find circumstances too strong for them. Others are so strong in will and character that they rise and struggle and force their way in spite of every obstacle and difficulty. Even tho' my words may produce no radical change in your life – and I do not expect they will – still they may do you some good, and make you think and perhaps even induce you to devote more of your time to what is serious and profitable.

I have not written so long a letter for ages. Fancy 20 pages!! I am sure you will not expect to hear from me again this side of Xmas! Eh?

Ever your affectionate uncle,
John S. Vaughan.

Clearly John Vaughan considered Charles to be leading an indolent and useless life, but one wonders what the difficult circumstances implied can be for Charles' own account of this time of his life gives no hint of them. Quite otherwise: in an article on 'Life at Courtfield' by F. O. Blundell, which he supplied the material for, he states, 'My Father's great enjoyment in life was travel and so I was at Courtfield alone with my Mother for five years, my occupation being the farming of the Home Farm and looking after the gardens and stables. I had fifteen men under me. I did a lot of shooting and hunting and some racing and fishing, but I was also fond of music and reading. I think these were the five happiest years of my life.'

They had a resident chaplain who said daily Mass at Courtfield at 8.30am but he always went up to the farm before Mass and had a good appetite for breakfast at 9.15.

At any event, perhaps it was partly as a result of his uncle's letter that Charles set off on his travels to America and Mexico in 1898 to see the world and get a broader view.

Charles Vaughan's American Tour, 1898–9

In November 1898 Charles went on a most interesting tour of America and Mexico. Luckily he kept a journal, which makes very detailed and excellent reading. He sailed from Liverpool on Sunday 13 November 1898 on the RMS *Lucamia*, a very comfortable ship, and met a friend on board, Peter Fogarty, going to America for the winter. Also on board was Dame Nellie Melba, de Lussan the renowned vocalist, and Tod Sloan the famous American jockey, pioneer of the 'short' style of riding. He was introduced to a Mr Sands of New York who asked him if Cardinal Vaughan was his father! Charles remarks that Mr Sands does not seem to know much about the celibacy of the clergy.

Arriving in New York on 19 November 1898, a day late owing to rough weather, he took the Pennsylvanian Route and got to St Louis on 20 November, where he was met by Charles O'Fallon and drove in a buggy to his house, 3651 Washington Boulevard. There he was greeted by Uncle John and Aunt Carrie and Cousin Lilie Mastyn. He met quite a dozen relations in St Louis and was introduced to scores of people all of whom he found excessively kind. Dinners and lunches were held every day during his fortnight's stay, and he was made an honorary member of several clubs. He observed: 'Fine large houses in Westmorland and Portland Place. Most have electric light, electric bells and a telephone. Everyone in St Louis works. A boy directly he leaves school or college goes into some business or other. Very few indeed do absolutely nothing – all the men have a nominal occupation, hence St Louis is a very busy town.'

Charles did a lot of riding and driving, and spent a few days as a guest of Mr R. S. Bookings at Selma Hall – a picturesque, castellated house on the banks of the Mississippi, where he shot his first quail. Altogether he had a lovely time. He went on to San Antonio in Texas where he ran into Pat Milmo, an old Stonyhurst pal, and they had dinner together. Another friend, Gervase Scrope, came to meet him and they left for his ranch next day, travelling on the Southern Pacific through the arid plains of Texas to Eagles Pass and on to Allende. At C. P. Diaz he had difficulty getting his guns out of bond. He found it a very dirty town inhabited by Greeks, Turks and all nations under the sun: 'the cowboys come in and spend their month's earnings lavishly. They are a tough lot however.'

At Allende, Charles and his party were surrounded by Mexicans and had to show the officials the contents of their bags and trunks, but luckily Gervase Scrope was known to them which helped. At

9pm they got into their buggy and started on their midnight drive to the ranch – a distance of thirty miles. The ranch, El Pensamiento, is about one hundred thousand acres and has eighty-five miles of four-strand barbed-wire fencing. The San Antonio river runs through the property for twenty-five miles and provides excellent bass fishing and duck shooting in the winter, and all sorts of game abound. There are also poisonous snakes, scorpions, tarantulas and rats. His notes about the sheep, cross-breeding, the value of wool and general management, and the men's wages are all interesting. He had his first experience of rounding up and branding wild horses, and was greatly impressed by the skill with which the cowboys handled their lassoos. Three of them went on a shooting expedition in the mountains expecting to kill deer, bear, mountain lion and wild turkey, but in this they were disappointed. However, he enjoyed the wild, deserted and destitute surroundings, tramping up canyons unvisited by white man, and sleeping out under the stars. They did this for ten days in January 1899. The weather was delightful though cold at night.

This seems to have been a time when settlers took up vast tracts of land which could be bought for from three pence to six shillings an acre from the government. After two months with Gervase Scrope Charles moved on to other ranches including a visit to Don Patricio Milmo, a remarkable man who had arrived from Ireland in 1847 with 80 dollars in his pocket and was now said to be worth $27 million, with 1,980,000 acres, 107 ranch houses and 1,500 miles of four-strand barbed-wire fencing.

Charles gave a list of his stock:

147,000 head of sheep
70,000 head of goats
43,000 head of cattle
12,000 head of horses
2,000 head of donkeys
500 head of mules

And added:

He is old now [he died two days later and both Charles and Gervase attended the funeral] and though not personally managing, he inspects all the books, goes through everything and all is carried out under his direction. It is calculated that from wool alone he makes about £8,000 a year.

He stayed on Mr Clobe's ranch where he enjoyed splendid quail shooting and was delighted to see Hereford cattle which Mr Clobe had introduced to cross with the native cattle. Clobe was enormously wealthy and owned over two million acres. Besides horses, sheep and cattle, there were a great many very well-bred donkeys and mules produced here. Water was of the utmost importance on these ranches. They went hunting with three couple of hounds – a kind of bloodhound – who went after wild cat, lion, coyote, fox and deer. Dick Marshall, the manager, hunted them well – the music of his horn reminded Charles of the happy days he'd had hunting in England – and they had one or two excellent runs.

Of the churches he noted that they are very fine and invariably the largest building in the town. Children and dogs ran in and out and no one took the slightest notice. They were frequently magnificently ornamented inside with gold and silver. He was surprised one Sunday when attending Mass at a town called Saltillo to find the organist playing valse (waltz) music. They stayed for a time in Monterey, a rapidly growing town, with mining, smelting, brewing and the railway built by an English firm.

Charles had really enjoyed his three months in Mexico and was very sad at parting from his friend Gervase Scrope. He went back to his relations in St Louis, where he was again lavishly entertained and fêted. He was struck by the large number who started from nothing and were now millionaires: 'The one great standard they all go by is the almighty dollar'. He found American girls generally good-looking, bright, clever and exquisitely dressed à la Parisienne', full of animation and self-assurance and completely unaffected. All the men showed the greatest respect for women – 'If a girl wants a good time from a girl's point of view only let her go to America and she will find herself a queen', he observed. Of the men he said, quoting Max O'Rill, 'the typical American does not exist. There are Americans in plenty but *the* American has not made his appearance yet! The type existed a hundred years ago in New England. He is still there but he is not now a national type, he is only a local one.'

Writing about religion in America, Charles remarked that Episcopalians and Methodists flourish to a great extent, though the Catholic church was strong too, but the different forms of Protestantism had got a certain hold on the American people, whose attitude was 'we have all got to get across the stream so what does it matter how you go?'. To which Charles' reply was that they *may* get across by other means but he prefers the *certainty* of the Catholic church if only we do as she tells us.

After this most interesting trip Charles returned to Courtfield in April 1899 and resumed life as an English country gentleman.

He did his training with the Royal Monmouthshire Royal Engineers for three months, sat on various committees, councils, etc., and supported horse shows, flower shows, racing, cricket, etc., until all this was changed by the outbreak of the Boer War. Charles had served in the RMRE for four years as a subaltern and two years as a captain when just before the Boer War he joined the 7th Dragoon Guards as a 2nd Lieutenant at Aldershot, and shortly afterwards they all went out to South Africa taking their horses with them. They left Southampton on the SS *Armenian* on 9 February 1900 and there are many letters from Charles describing the discomforts of the voyage and the many deaths suffered by troops and horses. Mermaid, his own horse, seems to have travelled well, but caught a cold after arrival at the Cape in early March. Charles himself had not been there long before he was dangerously wounded and sent back to England. When he recovered he was posted to the 3rd Provisional Regiment of Dragoons, consisting of the reserve squadron of the Royals and the 7th Dragoon Guards quartered at Shorncliffe. And then,

> When the Boer War was well over, instead of rejoining my regiment I resigned my commission and rejoined the RMRE as Junior Captain. Before doing so, however, I had the honour of being made Adjutant to four regiments of cavalry for the Coronation of King Edward VII. They consisted of a squadron from the Royals, Greys, Bays and Black Horse and we assembled at Hounslow.

· 6 ·

The Twentieth Century

IN SEPTEMBER 1907 Charles Vaughan was offered a post as Extra
aide-de-camp to the Governor of Tasmania. He replied that he felt
certain he would like it but as His Excellency, Sir George Strickland,
would shortly be returning to England on six months' leave, it was
thought best for Charles to wait and join him in Hobart on his return
early in November 1908.

CHARLES VAUGHAN, SQUIRE OF COURTFIELD

In the meantime Charles received the following letter from his
grandmother, Mrs Pope:

Hotel d'Able
Avenue de l'Alma
Paris

30th November 1907

My darling Charles,

I am writing to entreat you not to go to Tasmania. It would
break the hearts of your Mother and your old Grannie if you were
to go. Your Father is in an uncertain state of health. Alice is delicate,
and both Herbert and Francis are not well. You are the only one
to whom your Mother can turn in case of need. Stay with us my
beloved Charles – do not refuse the entreaty of your most loving
Grannie.

Perhaps it was a pity he was not allowed to go, for shortly after
he received a fateful few letters from Miss Florence Lister-Kaye,
youngest daughter of Sir Cecil and Lady Beatrice Lister-Kaye, who
lived with her grandmother at The Oaks, Woodford Wells, in Essex:

20th December 1907

Do write and give me some information as to what is going on. I am utterly wretched and can get no information. Fr. Bernard has taken the law into his own hands and until I hear from him I am not supposed to write to you, but *must* hear something as to how things are going. It is utterly ridiculous and I am beginning to get rebellious! Don't give me away and say I have written or there will be a row, but I can occasionally be awfully obstinate and I *won't* submit much longer not to be allowed to see you.

I'm simply dying to have a talk with you – but will say no more for fear of giving myself away altogether. I can only repeat 'Nil Desperandum' and *do* write.

This letter is not signed, but it seems the lady wanted him. One wonders why Father Bernard was hanging back? Perhaps getting cold feet? He must have known Florence better than Charles did at that stage. She wrote again on 2 January 1908, also from the Oaks:

Thanks awfully for your letter. I have a lovely piece of news. Grannie has allowed me to write and ask you to come here on Saturday next 4th until Monday when we return to London.

It's simply splendid you are to come and talk over ways and means with her, so be sure of your facts and if only we can scrape enough money, no objection will be raised as she is most anxious to help us and would like nothing better, therefore be sure and come. Most of the people will have gone so you needn't be alarmed, there will only be two or three left. Now the station is Woodford and you have to go to Liverpool Street station. There are trains about every ten minutes or so. I expect you would not catch one before 5.36 which is a good one and gets to Woodford at 5.56 and there are plenty of cabs and the house is about 10 minutes from the station. I think now you won't lose your way! I'm so excited. Once you get hold of Grannie I'm sure all will be well. She really is such a darling and would give anything to make me happy.

Yours ever,

Christine* Lister-Kaye.

In the days before film stars the glamour of the military man had to suffice – the shop girls of Monmouth would crowd the parade ground to watch Charles on duty. He was said to be the best-looking officer in the RMRE at that time. No doubt Chris was equally smitten,

* She preferred to call herself Christine or 'Chris'. Henceforth the text will refer to her by this name.

and as a recent convert would have found his exalted Catholic connections an additional attraction. From the Vaughan point of view, the granddaughter of a rich duke must have seemed an excellent catch. So, on his first visit to Woodford, Charles' fate was sealed. They were soon engaged and Chris began planning their wedding.

Did no one see the rocks ahead? Perhaps Father Bernard may have had doubts when he forbade her to write (one wonders what his reason was?) but, as we have seen, Chris was not allowing this to stand in her way. Clearly she was always difficult, but she also possessed a quite extraordinary charm and magnetism* when she chose to exert it, and many people came under her spell.

Charles was set on this marriage to the Duchess'** granddaughter, whom he had probably met through his Uncle Bernard, at that time at the height of his powers and famous throughout London. His sermons on the 'Sins of Society' crammed the church on Sunday and he was equally well known in the East End and among the 'coasters'. The Dowager Duchess, then twice widowed, was a great friend of his. Father Bernard had received her into the Church about sixteen years previously. She took a tremendous interest in helping with his settlements and work among the poor of the East End. Florence – or, as she preferred it, Christine – was the Duchess' favourite grandchild. When she too became a Catholic she quarrelled with her parents and went to live with her. She soon tired of the artificiality of the 'London Season' and became interested in helping the Duchess with her work among the East End poor. A lot of these poor people were allocated seats for her enormous wedding on 3 March 1908 when about 2,000 people filled Westminster Cathedral for the society wedding of the year. Her estranged parents did not attend, so she drove to the great door with the Dowager Duchess

---

* I experienced this briefly when we first met and she expressed the hope that her son Joe and I would marry: directly we did, however, her attitude completely changed.

** The Dowager Duchess of Newcastle – Henrietta Adela, daughter and heiress of Henry Hope of Deepdene, Surrey. She married on 11 February 1861, Henry Pelham Alexander, 6th Duke of Newcastle (died 22 February 1879). Married secondly, on 7 April 1880, Thomas Theobald Hohler, son of Rev. F. W. Hohler, Rector of Winstone and of Colisbourne, Gloucestershire. She died on 8 May 1913. From the Newcastle marriage she had two sons, Henry Pelham Archibald Douglas, 7th Duke (1864–1928), Henry Francis Hope Pelham Clinton Hope, 8th Duke (1866–1941) and three daughters: Beatrice Adeline (1862–1935), who married, in 1880, Sir Cecil Edmund Lister-Kaye, 4th Baronet; Emily Augusta Mary (1863–1919), who married in 1882 Prince Doria Pamphilj of Rome, and Florence Josephine (1868–1935).

of Newcastle, where she was met and escorted up the aisle by her Uncle Sir John Lister-Kaye who also gave her away. Four Vaughans, two brothers and two uncles of the bridegroom, conducted the ceremony. Charles' brother Herbert married them, assisted by his other brother Francis and Uncle Kenelm; Uncle Bernard gave the address on the sanctity and mystery of marriage and also read the special telegram of blessing from the Pope. Mr John Trappes-Lomax was best man.

The tall bride was described as looking very pretty in a robe of exquisite white satin with full court train of silver brocade trimmed with antique lace. Her veil, a present from the Duchess, a family heirloom which had been in the Newcastle family for five generations, covered a tiara of orange blossom and she wore a magnificent pearl-and-diamond dog-collar of twenty-one rows, the gift of Prince and Princess Doria (her aunt) and a pearl-and-diamond brooch from Sir John and Lady Lister-Kaye. Eight bridesmaids in dresses of white ninon-de-soir over deep satin hems, and sashes of pale blue ribbon, with charmingly becoming hats of light white straw trimmed with clusters of pale pink La France roses and blue satin ribbons, accompanied her. There were also two little pages – Viscount Encombe, the eight-year-old grandson of Lord Eldon, and the Hon Robert Southwell, eldest son of Viscount Southwell – dressed in pale blue satin cavalier suits with lace collars and cuffs, and slung capes of blue satin lined with white. Masses of white flowers and tall palms decorated the cathedral, and the beautiful nuptial Mass, exquisitely rendered by a choir of picked voices under the directorship of Mr Terry, was a feature of the service and included the Lohengrin Bridal March, Gounod's 'Ave Maria', Waddington's 'Salve Regina' and Neidermeyer's 'Paternoster'. Only the bridal couple received Holy Communion.

After the ceremony the Duchess gave a reception and wedding breakfast for about 450 guests at the Ritz Hotel, and the wedding presents, which numbered over 500, were on display. Scores of newspapers up and down the country and in Ireland reported the event:

> One of the most important pre-Lenten weddings took place on Shrove Tuesday at the new Westminster Cathedral when Miss Florence Lister-Kaye of Denby Grange, Wakefield, a granddaughter of the Duke of Newcastle of Clumber, Notts., was married to Captain Charles Vaughan late of the 7th Dragoon Guards and private Chamberlain to the Pope; eldest son of Colonel and Mrs Vaughan of Courtfield, Herefordshire and nephew of the late Cardinal Vaughan.

One would like to think that this brilliant wedding led to happiness, but alas it was not so. Even on the honeymoon, spent on the Italian lakes and in Rome, there were reports of tears and tantrums which grew steadily worse as the years went on. They were totally unsuited to each other: Charles, prosaic, pious, and patient, was no match for this semi-intellectual virago he had married.

Charles duly took his place in Herefordshire as the ideal squire – a son of the soil deeply interested in his estate, with a fatherly care for all who worked on it. He also enjoyed music, playing the piano and the church organ, reading and the arts. He used to say if a book was worth reading, it was worth buying, and so helped to build up a good library at Courtfield. He was an excellent shot, a good fisherman and in his younger days fond of hunting. Very kind and jolly with a keen sense of humour, he was a man of firm faith whose religion entered into his daily life and was reflected in his conduct. He often proved a tower of strength to friends and acquaintances.

He was in demand as patron of local agricultural shows and festivities, as can be seen in a letter from Mr Knaggs, honorary secretary of the Goodrich Horticultural Society in 1920, which said: 'The feeling of the meeting was that your sporting qualities, and your regard to the welfare of the district would appeal to the whole countryside. There is no one more popular or better liked in the neighbourhood and your assumption of President would create the greatest satisfaction.' Charles' reply, pencilled on the back of this letter, is characteristic:

Dear Sir,

Your all too flattering remarks about my personality fill me with confusion and I feel that there must be some exaggeration. I am intensely honoured that a unanimous vote should have been recorded electing me as President of the Goodrich and District Horticultural Society, which I have the greatest pleasure in accepting.

He is also thanked for unveiling the village war memorial:

Goodrich Court

May 5th

My Dear Charles,

I want you to know how immensely appreciated your address has been, indeed nothing could have been nicer. Your touching reference to the bravery of the fallen, your sympathetic words to the relations and praise for those who served, all spoken with such dignity and

146

feeling. It was all delightfully done and I thank you very warmly for kindly consenting to unveil the memorial. With love and hope you will have good sport and an enjoyable time in Scotland,

Yours affectly,
Blanche Moffatt.

As well as these pleasant rural duties, Charles was also prominent in ecclesiastical circles and was founder and chairman of the Political Court Club.

He went to Rome regularly to perform his papal duties, having been Privy Chamberlain to four Popes: Pius X, whom he called his greatest hero in real life, Benedict XV, Pius XI and Pius XII. In 1939 when Cardinal Hinsley led the British delegation to the General Meeting of all Nationalities at the Budapest Eucharistic Congress, before a vast gathering of thousands of people of all nations, Charles, resplendent in his papal uniform, spoke with such verve and eloquence that he was acclaimed the hero of the hour.

He was also Gold Staff Officer at three Coronations: King Edward VII, George V and George VI. He was mentioned in dispatches three times and awarded an OBE and also given the Order of St Maurice and St Lazarus for his work during the 1914–18 war on the staff in Italy as DAQMG – this was not a papal order but conferred by the King of Italy and Charles was very proud of it. In 1938 he was made Lt-Colonel of the Royal Monmouthshire Royal Engineers, as his father and grandfather had been before him. He was High Sheriff of Herefordshire in 1933, a Deputy Lieutenant for Monmouthshire and JP for Monmouthshire and Herefordshire.

Coming from such an extraordinarily 'priestly' family, Charles may not have had a great understanding of women, but he really was the stuff that England's country gentlemen are made of. To someone kind and helpful he would have been a marvellous husband. What an unbalanced, foolish woman his wife was, cruel and selfish, and what a legacy of pain she bequeathed. These lines from Yeats' lovely poem 'A Prayer for My Daughter' perhaps fit her best:

> An intellectual hatred is the worst,
> So let her think opinions are accursed.
> Have I not seen the loveliest woman born
> Out of the mouth of Plenty's horn,
> Because of her opinionated mind
> Barter that horn and every good
> Be quiet natures understood
> For an old bellows full of angry wind?

They had two children, Henrietta (Rita) and Joseph Herbert (Joe). Henrietta Mary Christine, named after the Duchess, was born on 24 December 1908 and Joseph fifteen months later on 15 March 1910. Rita died when she was ten years old on 23 October 1918, of the dreadful Spanish 'flu that ravaged the country towards the end of the First World War. It very nearly killed Joe too. Both children were at school at Bath Convent. Their mother was over in Ireland staying with her sister, the Countess of Rosse, at Birr Castle and did not realise how serious their illness was. She was completely shattered when she heard of her daughter's death. Rita died at the convent and was buried in Bath and later transferred to Courtfield to that lovely peaceful spot called the Hermitage – the first Vaughan to lie there. A fine stained-glass window was erected in the Hermitage to her memory and the following verses were on her memorial card:

Rita Vaughan
Born December 24th 1908
Died October 23rd 1918

Gone from a world of clouds and pain
To a land where sunbeams ever reign
Gone in the flush of her childhood's prime
With a spirit unscarred by the touch of time.

At rest, though the day was yet so young,
But alas! Our hearts with grief were wrung:
At rest for her portioned task was o'er
And the Master had knocked on his Servant's door.

He found her watching in innocence sweet
Awaiting the summons her Lord to greet:
She passed from this earth of griefs and sighs
To enter the gates of Paradise.

Thus has she left us: Oh, would we fain
Bring her glorious spirit to earth again!
But no! Though 'twas cruel to breathe farewell,
Hope was the note of her funeral knell.

For we know she is safe through the narrow way
That leads to the realms of endless day;
And again we shall see her and clasp her hand
As we stand at the gates of the Promised Land.

There's a new made grave in Courtfield Shrine
Where dwelleth the shadow of Peace Divine;
And here what is mortal of her doth rest
With lilies growing above her breast.

But the humble Cross that marks her head
Points the way her spirit fled
As she soared aloft and severed apart
The links that bound us heart to heart.

Hid from mortals but safe with Thee
Are garnered fruits we cannot see:
We have no doubt but our little one
Was welcomed with the words 'Well Done'.

Master Divine, who in all our grief
Can soothe with the balm of a grand relief,
We bow to Thy Will and our hearts resign
With no wish to claim what was always Thine.

Thou, who didst weep in the days of old,
As John has the beautiful story told
For Lazarus dead, will not blame our tears
But will change them to smiles in the endless years.

These touching verses were, according to Joseph, written by a
gardener at Courtfield.

From her portrait and photographs, Rita appears to have been a
lovely child with long fair hair, pink cheeks and blue eyes. She and
Joseph, who was fifteen months her junior, did everything together
and were devoted to each other. Her death in fact seemed to cause a sort
of mental block and he found difficulty in recalling much about her,
though he was eight at the time and very nearly died too. He used
to tell me that he hated Bath Convent where he was sent when only
five years old, wearing a little top hat! It is difficult to understand
why these children were sent to boarding school so young, especially
in an age when it was quite easy to get governesses.

For the two years previous to her marriage, Chris had lived with
her grandmother at 15 Mount Street, or in her Essex home, The Oaks.
Soon after they married, Charles was found a job there as agent and
it seems the three lived together in this house. The Duchess, at the
instigation of Cardinal Vaughan, had purchased this property in
1894 and built a church, friary and schools for the Franciscan Order,
and the house for herself. She spent a lot of money doing all this,

but unfortunately there was misunderstanding between French and English Franciscans which caused her much trouble and unhappiness. She died an 8 May 1913, leaving most of her possessions to Chris and Charles.

At the start of the 1914–18 war Charles joined his regiment as a major and was soon sent to France in command of a company of the RMRE consisting of a captain, four subalterns and 250 men. They landed at Le Havre and went on to St Omer and Ypres. Later he was given a staff appointment and was sent to Italy as DAQMC, where he remained until the end of the War. He was mentioned in dispatches three times and given an OBE. During the War they rented houses in Broadway and Kemerton where Charles was sometimes able to come home on leave. His wife wrote to him daily, letters full of complaints about one thing or another and stressing how desperately she was missing him and needing him. She appears to have been a highly neurotic and hysterical woman, often suffering from deep depression and given to endless crazes which occupied her for a very short while: learning Latin, Braille, priest's office, gardening, altering houses, playing Lady Bountiful at Courtfield, psychology, typing, and even prison work. It seems nothing lasted long, with the sole exception of her religion which she appears to have clung to. In her often most disagreeable letters to Charles she frequently stresses that praying before the Blessed Sacrament is the only comfort she can find.

She quarrelled with everyone including Charles' parents as well as her own, and eventually there was hardly anyone in Broadway she was on speaking terms with.

In 1920, when the political situation in Ireland was exceptionally difficult, Archbishop Mannix of Australia decided to visit Terrance Macswiney, the hunger-striking Lord Mayor of Cork. Mannix was a fanatical Irishman intent on stirring up trouble, and his recent campaign against England in the United States had caused the British government to take the grave step of banning his projected visit to Ireland. Something of a sensation was caused when a gun-boat was sent out to take this firebrand off his ship at Dover. The incident was widely reported in the press, as was the fact that Dr Mannix was subsequently invited to stay at Courtfield with such a distinguished Catholic family as the Vaughans. It is difficult to imagine that Charles would have been greatly interested, but the situation had tremendous appeal for Chris and gave her a splendid opportunity to exercise her volatile and quirky 'do-goodery' regardless of consequences. Doubtless she relished the excitement and disapproval generated in the district, but Charles as head of the family had the unpleasant experience of being cut by his neighbours and in his club. This postcard was just one example of the kind of bad feeling Chris' action stirred up:

> A very nice guest too! A hater of England, a stirrer up of strife wherever he goes. Yet he stays in an English gentleman's house because he's an R.C. prelate! So with you creed comes before loyalty. It is to be hoped that your neighbourhood is unhealthy.

Poor Charles, the soul of loyalty, must have been dreadfully hurt by the opprobrium caused by this indiscretion.

Chris at this stage seems to have been taken up with the wrongs and injustices suffered by Ireland. In a later letter to her son Joe, written in 1935, about the political situation in Europe and the follies she considers the British Government are perpetrating, she said, 'I feel today as I felt many years ago when I stood alone fighting violently for Ireland. I thought, and said then, that the crimes England had committed against Ireland cried to Heaven for vengeance. Now I think her crimes against the civilized world scream for vengeance!' And in another letter of December the same year, she wrote:

> In the long, long ago when I fought for Ireland, I remember, at some public gathering, refusing to stand up for 'God save the King', so strong were my feelings. Today I feel even stronger, and should like to do something even more dire! as a gesture of course. But you see I can't change and even my immense old age hasn't tamed me. But I must always be alone I suppose. I had hopes of you once, but not after you were 9 years old!

At this period there are many letters urging Joe to join the Fascists, one of these telling him: 'Sorry you won't take my suggestion of becoming a full blown Fascist seriously! Later on you will be sorry.' It is easy to see how this attitude led to the Mannix affair which cast such a slur on the family.

One wonders if they would have been happier if Charles had allowed the separation she appears to want. But, presumably, the rigid Catholicism of Charles' upbringing and way of thinking may have made this impossible for him to contemplate. For him the sacrament of marriage was sacred and could only be broken by death – though he must have known that the Church allowed separation in exceptional cases, if never remarriage. But very likely also he was deeply in love with his wife. A touching memento of their early

151

married life is a little book he wrote for her twenty-fifth birthday entitled *New Year's Day Thoughts,* a counsel of perfection of such a spiritual nature that one imagines them both becoming saints.

An Unhappy Marriage, and an Unfortunate Affair

The War over, Frank having died in 1919, and Carrie removed to a small house in Kemerton, Charles and Chris came to live at Courtfield, celebrating the event with a two-day sale of most of the furniture to make room for that which the Duchess had left them.

Chris soon found that her Herefordshire neighbours bored her and refused either to receive or return their calls. She had a nine-hole golf course laid out in the park and there was also a tennis court where she used to entertain her friends, mostly from London or abroad, while ignoring her local neighbours. She was not sporting and especially disliked shooting parties so Charles had to carry on with these alone, as indeed he had to do with neighbouring dinner parties and the usual functions of country life. Understandably, Herefordshire people did not care for her and she became increasingly disenchanted with life at Courtfield which she found exceedingly dull. She much preferred London where they usually had a house, and where she spent most of her time.

Chris's liking for dabbling in politics and literature probably led to her friendship with Don Gregory. She was seeking intellectual companionship which she thought she had found in Don Gregory whom she came to regard as the love of her life. Gregory had a distinguished career at the Foreign Office and became Assistant Under-Secretary in 1925. However, he had to resign his post in 1928 because of the enquiries into the 'francs case', when it was discovered that he and other FO officials had been speculating in French francs. His own marriage also seems to have been under strain and in 1929 he went to live abroad. He had already written a book of reminiscences called *On the Edge of Diplomacy*, and wanted to write a life of Engelbert Dollfuss, the Austrian politician and Chancellor.

A great scandal was created in Catholic circles when in the autumn of 1929 Chris went off to join Gregory abroad. Charles was devastated by her desertion, and their son Joe, then nineteen and up at Christ Church, Oxford, dreadfully hurt and angry – he refused to have any communication with her for several years, although eventually she wore him down.

Here are two letters Chris sent to Charles at the time of her leaving him:

Kasturmanbaum. 7.9.29.

My dear old Charles,

I wish I could expect you to believe how *desperately* sorry I am to hear that you have been so ill and that I have dealt you so bitter a blow. Will you try to believe that I did what I did because I really love D so desperately that I could not give him up and it seemed cleaner and better to go? Also that life had been so utterly impossible at home that I felt I must go or go mad? Also that over and over again I asked you to let me separate because we could not get on. Entirely my fault of course. Also that *I could not believe* you really cared much for me and that I quite honestly thought that on the whole you would be relieved if I left? And you *will* be, too, I am sure. Just think how horrible I am really and how quite unsuited to your life? There is the wild, gypsy tramp life of freedom which has always called, and for years I have stifled and chaffed and cried with misery.

And I feel truly – *please, please,* do try and believe this – that I was personally of little or no value either to you or Joe or anybody else of your world because, somehow to me, it wasn't real, and I was an outsider.

Religion, life as we lived it, or as I tried to live it with you, was killing me by inches and I should have done worse had I remained.

There is so much of the divine spark in you that I believe you may dimly understand and, some day, forgive my seeming inhumanity and defiance of all tradition and laws.

One thing I beg of you to stop Ivo talking violence and try to prevent him interfering in any way. I have wronged you and Joe – the others only in the conventional way and they have never cared. Any violence only embitters relationships all around. And I alone am to blame.

If you can bring yourself to, will you send me a few lines? even angry ones, and just tell me how you are? If you don't I shall quite understand.

Bless you, dear, always,
your Wife.

In a second letter to Charles, dated 21 September, she says:

By this time you will have got my letter from Paris telling you that at the end of my tether and utterly nerve-shattered, I have made off abroad. I told you I had gone with friends, but you will no doubt have guessed who I meant. You have long since known the attachment that has grown up in me for a particular individual during the last few months, and it is only fair that you should know that it has not been a wholly platonic one.

Although I recognise to the full all that you are in the way of goodness and patience and moral worth, I have for years and years, as you all know, been utterly miserable and starving for intellectual companionship. It was a choice of continuing with you as a nervous wreck, who could be of no earthly use to either of you, or leaving you to lead a life of your own, untroubled and unharassed by my filthy tempers and impatience. I have pondered over this for weeks and weeks – and at last I reached the conclusion that the only chance for both of us (and Joe – who after all must make his own life now) was to lead an existence of our own.

There was another alternative – a life of camouflage, deception and concealment – which the majority of married people who are not at one habitually lead.

I cannot and will not do anything so dishonest any longer. It is unfair to you and degrading to me. The only straight course is to come out into the open. I cannot and will not give up an attachment which means more than my life to me, and which alone has made my life possible with you lately. You know how often in past years I have longed to make an end of it all.

It is brutal of me but I make no excuse whatsoever. I do not expect you to forgive me – only to understand that with my highly strung nature I am not like other people, and that another few weeks of the unnatural life we were trying to live together would have ended in such a ghastly row that we should have parted in bitterness such as could never have been healed.

I have naturally not failed to weigh up the consequences, above all the scandal that my departure will cause.

I suggest that at first, it may be possible to let it be known that I have gone abroad for some months to go on with my writing – which is literally true – that my literary partnership is essential to its success – or if you like that I am quite mad.

But the scandal of a continuance of a bickering domestic existence would in my mind be infinitely greater, and at least I must be given credit of the courage of my convictions in having chosen the more straightforward course abominable and unpalatable though it may seem, just as it is *final* and *irrevocable*.

Naturally, it gives me a heartache to deal this blow to you and Joe – but as a half-dead person, I should be useless to both of you – I am enclosing you a letter for him which please give him on his return, and I shall try to prove to him that I am not really the criminal many people will take me to be since in sacrificing comforts and worldly position for an exceedingly financially precarious existence, I can hardly be accused of lack of idealism.

I cannot hope that he is old enough yet to understand that there are values in life other than those on which the conventional world lives and thrives – but if he is to grow up any sort of a man, he must

154

realise that the great world is not shelter and Courtfield, but a vast rough and tumble and exquisite suffering.

I do want you to realise that the irrevocable step which I have taken, has not been done in haste or with any undue influence – rather the contrary – he has begged me over and over again and even to the last moment to consider well what I am giving up and the possibility of hardship. I have chosen.

Forgive me if you can and anyhow do not think too harshly of me.

Will you write to Poste Restante, Lucerne. I have arranged for letters to be forwarded. As for the next few months we are going up into the mountains.

From your Wife.

His brother Francis – then Bishop of Menevia – rushed to Charles's side. After staying a little with him and Joe at Courtfield, he wrote to console and fortify as best he could:

Bishops House,
Wrexham,

October 9th 1929

Dearest James,*

I can't tell you in words how deeply I feel for you, and with you in the terrible cross that has fallen upon you. I really don't think it could be a heavier one. It is not of your choosing, so all you can do is bow to the most adorable will of God, and ask Him for the grace and strength and courage to bear it. A cross can crush us or lift us up. This one will lift you up and bear you to Heaven. Don't brood too much, James, on it all. It can do you no good. Pray and keep close to God – as I know you are doing, and He will help you in a way you don't know now.

I felt terribly stunned at it all whilst at Courtfield and tried to keep up a stout heart. I hope prayer will bring her to her senses. Of course it will never be the same, still it will steady you. It will calm you in all your dealings with her. Try and eat and sleep, both important factors when one's nerves are shattered and one is generally unhinged. Easier said than done.

All this is not your doing and that should give you peace of soul. You have been gentle and quiet with her. That is your nature. I did enjoy myself with you and Joe, and I hope it was a wee bit of a comfort.

Your devoted brother,
Francis

* Charles and his brother seem to have always called each other James.

Various friends and relations went after her to Switzerland and further up the Alps, endeavouring to persuade her to return, and Charles had a meeting with her in Munich and promised to 'forgive and forget' if she would give up Gregory and return to him, but this she would not do: 'She was assisting Don with his writing and could not possibly let him down'. His book *Dolfuss and his Times* was published in 1935 but he did not turn out to be the world-shattering genius Chris imagined him to be.

From her many letters to Joe, the couple seem to have been constantly moving around in Switzerland, Austria and Italy – where they lived at Assisi for a time – and appear to have led a rather hand-to-mouth existence, usually short of money. She often asks Joe to sell various possessions of hers and then send the money.

Chris was beautiful, tall and slender with masses of Titian-red hair and a very white skin, but her tawny eyes were glittering and cruel. I think she exuded a sort of animal magnetism and perhaps enjoyed being cruel – in one letter to her son she writes, 'if you can't make people love you then at least make them fear you'. She had tremendous vitality and was extremely plausible with little regard for truth, which made her very difficult to cope with. There is a revealing letter from her sister Adeline to Joe, written on 27 December 1929 soon after she had gone off:

> Would you send me a line to tell me if all correspondence is now over between the family and your ex-Mother! – in my solitary opinion I would accept her condition of a weekly letter. Knowing her instability I would gamble on it as not continuing for very long. By her return, appearances would be saved, also the social structure, family, etc: Scandal would be avoided. And she will probably have to be taken back later, so why not at once?
>
> But if everything is over – but only then – I want my brief say: that I am delighted she has behaved as she has, as it proves what I have always known her to be. A quite heartless, shallow, selfish, vain woman. My remarks will probably make her so angry that she will return [on] the next boat to prove me wrong! There are occasions when one is delighted to be wrong. I consider it essential that she should return.

It seems the sisters did not have much time for each other. Perhaps the roots of Chris' difficult nature lay in her early upbringing and family life?

In a letter to Joe dated 15 August 1930, Charles was perhaps equally revealing:

When your Mother went away and left me I altered my Will. I had left everything to her but her cruel behaviour forced me to change my Will in your favour. She has the jointure from Courtfield – that must always remain – but what I want to emphasize is that you must never let your Mother suffer from poverty or want of money. She has caused me no end of pain, suffering, even agony, but my love for her has not, and I suppose never will be exterminated.

Chris did not come back, but spent the next ten years roving around Europe with Don Gregory, leaving her husband and son to carry on without her both at Courtfield and in London. In 1939 World War II brought them back to England where for a time they stayed with Gregory's elder daughter, Barbara, who had married Sir Oliver Welby and lived at Newton Hall, Sleaford, Lincs., and eventually took a house, perhaps aptly called Folly Farm, at Oasby, near Grantham.

Before long, in the middle of April 1940, a registered express letter was sent to Charles suggesting a meeting at his London house. This was apparently the first communication with her husband since leaving him for Don Gregory ten years previously. The romantic idyll was over – Chris was now ready to come home. Included here is this letter, and two others negotiating her return to her husband. They illustrate graphically her skill in manoeuvring Charles exactly where she wanted him:

> Folly Farm,
> Oasby,
> GRANTHAM.

14.IV.40

> Tel. Culverthorpe 60

My Dear Charles,

I expected and hoped that when the present world catastrophe fell on us all, and still more when Joe went to the Front, that you would get into touch with me and I was, of course, under the tragic circumstances, most ready to respond.

I thought again that you would return when you heard that I was back in England and very ill.

Seven months have elapsed since the first, and four since the latter. It seems therefore that you must be waiting for me to heal the silence – because I cannot believe that you are indifferent to our common anxiety – which surely should be that God sent means to try, anyhow, to find a way to be in touch with each other and let all bitterness between us cease.

I therefore affectionately suggest that we should meet as soon

as possible and talk the whole situation over calmly and reasonably.

Would you come to London therefore, as soon as convenient to you
and invite me to lunch with you in Spanish Place – and lots to drink
please!!!

Perhaps you will bring Kitty too – the old Nanny would I know as
much like to see me as I would her.

> My love to you
> Affectionately yours,
> Chris

P.S. I must ask you for technical reasons – which Joe knows of and
approves – I will explain it all when we meet, to address me as Mrs
Gregory.

She immediately tries to put Charles in the wrong for not having
written, and clearly she is now determined on returning to the
comforts of Courtfield. Her PS shows that his feelings are in no way
being considered. Four days later she wrote again:

> Folly Farm,
> Oasby, GRANTHAM.

18.IV.40

> Tel. Culverthorpe 60

My Dear Charles,

Thank you very much for your exceedingly nice letter which has
much relieved my mind, because I feel more than ever that in these
ghastly times through which we are living, all personal bitternesses
should cease.

I shall be delighted to lunch with you on Wednesday 24th I shall
be coming up for the day and arrive at King's Cross at 12.15. Would
you care to meet me? If not, I shall come straight on to Spanish Place.
There is a train back at 5.30, so we shall have plenty of time.

Yes, Joe writes to me too, that he's well and contented and very
busy and I think we must be very thankful that he has such a good
job and *is* busy all the time. I do so pity those who mostly have to
wait for something to do.

Tell Kitty I shall much look forward to her excellent lunch! It
is certainly wonderful that she has learned to cook so well. She
must have a natural aptitude. I unfortunately have none, and hate it
anyway!

> My love to you
> Ever your affectionate
> Chris

P.S. I feel sure that you will not have told anybody except Kitty, of course, that I have written to you – until afterwards.

This second letter shows her relief, but she is not quite sure of him yet, so no one must know that she has written, until afterwards – a complete giveaway. Her third, written some weeks later, shows just how much progress she has made with Charles – and her objectives – in the interim:

Folly Farm,
Oasby,
GRANTHAM.

27.V.40

Tel. Culverthorpe 60

My Darling,

I must write you a few lines to tell you how very much touched I am by your generosity and understanding. Indeed I will not fail to respond, and we shall, and can be, very loving companions, and I will do all I can to make up to you for the years of loneliness – but con amore now, and not from a sense of duty.

I think you will understand what I mean, but if I am obscure you can ask me on Monday!

I am so used to writing in parables and being not quite sure which language I am using, that you will have to get used to it – and just ask quite simply what the devil I mean!

The news from Norway* is not encouraging this morning, but we must have patience.

Do order the *Daily Telegraph* because it really is the best daily now and unless you order a newspaper you can not get them nowadays.

Excuse a rather worse scrawl than usual, but I'm writing on my knee which is not easy.

Do find me a puppy.

Very much love and on Wednesday,

Ever yours,
Chris

The third letter appears to have been written a month later. Things seem to have been arranged to her satisfaction and no doubt she would have the *Daily Telegraph* and the puppy too before long! She would soon be back in the comforts of Courtfield, with Kitty,

---

* The order had just gone out for the evacuation of British troops from northern Norway.

Lily and Rose, the best cook in England, to minister to her! But her protestations of love and affection for Charles blew away with the wind and soon she was abusing and taunting him as only she knew how.

Quite soon after her return Chris captivated a spinster lady who had a charming house near Monmouth, converted her to Roman Catholicism and installed her in a house on the Courtfield estate, thereby ensuring she had a trusty dogsbody for her every need. Later, when she decided to live in London, this completely country lady could be seen stumping up and down Queen's Gate exercising Chris's dog, and acting as chauffeur and messenger for all her whims. When she died suddenly from a heart attack some years later Chris no doubt missed her ministrations, but everyone was shocked that she did not even attend her funeral down there.

Charles referred to his wife as 'The Disturbing Element' and, as sailors do in dirty shaggy weather, he close-hauled, kept his head down and seldom attempted to stand up to her. He regarded love and marriage as sacred and felt he had done right in taking her back, a view which the letters from his many friends confirm. Completely brazen, showing none of that contrition which might have been seemly in an erring wife, she tore around the place in navy-blue trousers or her WVS uniform bossing everyone and creating trouble and discord wherever possible. After the War was over she often took flats in London which Charles paid for. Eventually he protested, whereupon she sold most of the Courtfield furniture claiming it was hers, though Charles maintained the Duchess had left it to them jointly. He was very sad, wrung his hands and said, 'it's all wrong', but he was quite unable to stop her; so two large pantechnicons of valuable furniture and china went off to a Herefordshire antique dealer.*

Don Gregory was probably a far more suitable man for her than Charles. One wonders why they did not stay together? Perhaps their ten years abroad had been more than enough for him and he may well have been mightily relieved when she went back to her husband. She would have been a most difficult woman for any man to live with. A letter written to Charles when she left him in 1929 by a Jesuit priest at Mount Street, who seems to have known them well,

---

* We had to buy furniture for the house after this, which may have sown the seeds whereby I eventually became an antiques dealer and opened my shop, White Horses Antiques, Ross-on-Wye, which I started in 1960 and ran for twenty-three years with pleasure and profit.

indicates that Gregory did not want Chris following him abroad: 'What you have to be sure of is, that while that man is a scoundrel in one way, he is a fool in more ways, and I have told him so very clearly indeed. I do not believe that he wants the situation at all.' After their parting Don Gregory lived in Ashburton near Buckfast Abbey where he went to Mass and attended discussion groups. He had many friends and was well liked by the village. Monsignor Croft-Fraser lived with him there for years. He used to visit his wife once a year and she is buried beside him at Buckfast Abbey.

MYSELF, AND JOE VAUGHAN

I would like to begin by describing my early life and the kind of religion I grew up with at my Irish home, Ballynatray. Templemichael, with its ruins of an old Knights Templar Castle on the banks of the beautiful Blackwater, had an enchanting view back across the river towards Ballynatray, and it was here that we went to church on Sundays. My father, Captain Rowland Holroyd-Smith, was a staunch churchman and family attendance was compulsory. Usually we walked or sometimes he drove us the mile-and-a-half in the pony trap, and the pony had to be carefully tied to a tree while we were at church. Low-church Irish services seemed unremittingly long and dull, occasionally shortened when my parents told the clergyman to cut the sermon as they were having a lunch party.

We were about the only people there apart from the clergyman and his driver who came from Ardmore eight miles away. We sat in our family box pew – the purple curtains had long since disintegrated though the iron railings were still there. In winter there was a small coal fire in the pretty Regency hob grate which we were glad of, and it also helped dissipate the horrid musty smell. Around the walls were splendid marble memorials to our ancestors which I enjoyed reading, my favourite being an ornate pink and white marble affair to Penelope Caroline, Princess of Capua.*

We never discussed religion at home – it was like sex, a taboo

---

* When the church was deconsecrated and falling down in 1973, my brother, Oliver, had these moved into St Mary's Collegiate Church in Youghal where they have been re-erected. And this reminds me of an occasion when another brother Horace was taking visitors to a Sunday train in Youghal and, finding he could not be back in time, went to St Mary's, thereby earning a stern rebuke from his father who considered he should only attend our own church. I wondered if he thought God dwelt exclusively at Templemichael!

subject, though we were conscious of the suspicion and hostility with which the Catholic religion was regarded. I used to wonder about this for it seemed to me that our servants, tenants and the country people had a far greater belief and love of God, and a lot more life in their chapel at Glendyne. Sometimes I said that if I ever needed religion, I'd have to be a Catholic. (And so it happened – changing my faith was to be the best move of my life; it would open my mind to the love of God, enlightenment, and encouragement.)

My first marriage was more of a partnership based on love of horses. Children were ruled out and we agreed to go our separate ways should we ever wish to. We had met hunting in Leicestershire in 1931. He was half-American, most amusing, had knocked about a lot, was completely amoral, and as it turned out a bit of a scoundrel. He came to Ballynatray, admired my horsemanship, and really did – I believe – fall in love with me. After my restricted and emotionally starved home life I greatly enjoyed his amusing and cheerful company, but my parents were furious when he told them we were engaged. My father, who had just leased him his best racehorse, exploded, 'You can't come here and take my horse and my daughter', to which he got the suave reply, 'Oh well!, I'll have the daughter then'. Certainly he was an exciting and ardent suitor. Once he saw my mother and me off on the Irish mail from Paddington; as the train drew to its first stop at Reading, there he was on the platform with a lovely bunch of roses! He'd raced the train in his silver Alvis. Even my mother was impressed.

I often had qualms about marrying him and once broke off our engagement, but his dramatic threats of suicide, coupled with the real distress caused to his invalid mother, caused me to go on with it. Our life centred around horses and hunting and became a fast, amusing, reckless sort of gallop, with quarrels and infidelities on both sides. We were very successful with our beautiful horses, winning prizes at all the major shows. Our best day was at the Royal in 1937 where we took a show hack and a heavyweight cob who won all their classes: three firsts, a championship and reserve champion. The Duchess of Gloucester presented me with a fine silver cup and it was indeed a happy day. I also rode my one and only point-to-point in the 1938 South Oxfordshire Adjacent Hunts ladies' race. There were six runners and once the field had got into its stride, Hanum, a winner of two hurdle races, and my mare, Keene Head, went out in front and fought out a very fast race all the way, three-and-a-half miles over twenty-three fences. A few days previously we'd been at Reg Hobbs' stables seeing his beautiful little horse Battleship who had just won the Grand National ridden by his son Bruce, the youngest jockey ever to win the National. He was kind enough to give me a few hints on race riding, and coming to the last I had remembered his words, 'if you're there with a chance go for it as if it wasn't there'. So I drove her into it for all I was worth, she responded with a tremendous jump, gaining several lengths, and just managed to hang on and win by a head. It was a wonderful moment. I was riding side-saddle and felt exhausted after the race, so decided after that to stick to hunting and showing. Keene Head was a bold and brilliant huntress and also won me several good hack classes. She was 15.2 hands, a thoroughbred mare, bay with black points and a good set of limbs. Seldom sick or sorry, I had some wonderful hunts on her. Though she pulled hard in a racing snaffle, she understood the difference in the show ring and had a lovely head carriage and easy mouth in a short-cheeked double bridle. I've ridden many good horses, but she was one of the best and bravest and I loved her dearly.

I was also fond of poetry and reading and occasionally felt there should be more in life than this round of hunting, racing, showing, pubs and parties with brittle friends – a bit like a Noël Coward play. I knew little of God or marriage, but sometimes inwardly had the conviction that it was not marriage in the sight of God. And I did throw away my wedding ring. Finally I divorced him because of a girl I'd been at school with: she had left her husband and told me they were crazy about each other. Subsequently, they married, had two children and divorced. He was never marriageable material.

About this time I'd also fallen in love with an Oxford under-graduate, a Scotsman, several years younger than I, and this was his first serious love affair. But the War came, he was just starting his career as an officer in the Scots Guards, and somehow it did not work out. But the agony I suffered at the time set me searching for God which ultimately led me to the rock of the Catholic Church and the ever-loving arms of Our Lady. How lucky I was eventually to be instructed by such a perceptive priest as Father Anderson, himself a convert. I enjoyed our many interesting conversations and the kindness and understanding he invariably showed me. I'd been living in a dark room and now the blinds were pulled up and blessed light and sunshine flowing in. Interestingly, I'd got to know him through my Aunt Bye More Smyth, whom Aunt Lilie mentions in her diary as a visitor to Courtfield in the happy houseparty days (see page 132).

When I became a Catholic and, under instruction, learnt what marriage really entailed, I knew with complete certainty that I was entitled to an annulment. Unfortunately this was a long process that had to be proved to the satisfaction of the ecclesiastical courts whose wheels turn slowly, and I think it took about two or three years.

Joe Vaughan and I first met in 1937, at Islington horse show where I was showing a nice three-year-old who came second in a strong class of twenty-three. A mutual barrister friend introduced us. I didn't really remember Joe as I was busy with my horse and did not take much notice. However, we all met again at dinner that evening. I was wearing a lovely dress of patterned old Irish poplin (made from one of my mother's court trains) which everyone greatly admired. We had a pleasant evening, went on to a night club and in the small hours Joe took me back to my hotel, stopping first at 1 Spanish Place, his London home, where we had a drink and talked – all very proper. Our next meeting was not until 1940. I was dining with a friend at the Berkeley and as we were leaving passed a table with several officers obviously celebrating their return from Dunkirk, one of whom sprang up and addressed me by name. I replied, 'You look very nice, but I'm afraid I can't remember . . .' When he told me he was Joe Vaughan I was delighted and suggested he joined us at the club we were going to. He telephoned there and got my address and soon we were going out together, doing our courting during the worst of the Blitz.

He maintained that he had fallen in love with me in my 'battered green hat' at Islington. But as I was married had done nothing about it. He was stationed at Highgate with the RMRE and I was an ambulance driver in Chelsea. We had many happy and sometimes bizarre evenings together – once, dancing in the rain at the night club where the roof was damaged, we simply put on our mackintoshes and carried on! Another evening at the Berkeley the restaurant was rocked by a stick of bombs, and people quickly disappeared to the shelter, leaving a few like ourselves to go on with dinner, calmly served by an elderly waiter wearing a long row of World War I medals.

Our mutual attraction soon ripened into love and we talked of marriage but came up against a difficulty: I was under instruction in the Catholic faith with Father Anderson at St Mary's, Cadogan Place, and was indeed received into the Church the following year, on 12 April 1941. However, as it was wartime and Joe was expecting to be sent overseas, we decided to go ahead, and got married. We could not have the Church's blessing, so on St Swithun's Day went to Mass and Holy Communion in the Lady Chapel of Westminster Cathedral and there married each other, followed by a civil ceremony at Chelsea register office on 15 July 1942. It was all rather different from Joe's parents' tremendous wedding in 1908. We snatched a few days' honeymoon in the Lake District, during which Joe took me on the longest walk of my life, from Ullswater to Windermere and back, over the Kirkstone Pass, twenty-five long miles in pouring rain all the way – perhaps he was testing my staying power. When we got to Largs, where the Army was assembling for the invasion of North Africa, the whole place was chock-a-block with troops. Joe had a billet with his unit, but I had to make do with the dining-room floor of some lodging-house and spent several days searching for accommodation, which we eventually found in a house belonging to a nice Scottish couple, the Dominies, with whom we sometimes had jolly 'conversaziones' in the evening.

The invasion force set out in early October and I saw Joe off at 3.30 one morning, looking like a Christmas tree weighed down with all his kit. I asked if he had his sword, which made him laugh. It was an emotional parting, we both kept stiff upper lips, but I felt dreadfully sad as he marched off into the night and I crept back to bed to await the dawn and the train journey back to Courtfield with his dog and belongings. I did not see him again for two-and-a-half years.

On the crowded train from Glasgow, I noticed the soldier opposite had no sandwiches and was wearing a curious assortment of clothes. I shared my lunch with him and he told me he was on leave after being shipwrecked, hence his odd uniform. It turned out he was Robin Snead-Cox, a Herefordshire neighbour who knew my husband and in fact had been at Downside with him; it was his father who had written the life of Cardinal Vaughan. This happy chance meeting passed the journey pleasantly for us both and he helped me with my luggage at Gloucester and came on to Ross with me as of course there were no porters.

Joe was with the Central Mediterranean Force in North Africa for a year or so, and then went on up through Italy. He met my brother John in Rome and took him to visit the Dorias, his mother's relations. He did not I think see much fighting. The worst part of his war was earlier, in France, and the Dunkirk retreat which he came through unscathed.

Patrick Charles More, our firstborn, arrived on Monday 31 May 1943 at 6.20 p.m. at the Savernake cottage hospital. I'd been in labour since early morning and was very tired. At this time I was a paying guest in a house near Marlborough, as it seemed safer than London under bombardment. I did not know the district or have any friends so it was a lonely time. The hospital sent a cable for me telling Joe the good news, but he never received it, wartime communications being extraordinarily difficult. Eventually a brother officer brought him the news some weeks later.

As I knew nothing about babies I had engaged a hospital nurse for a month, hoping to learn from her. She had rigid ideas about feeding and as Patrick was over 7½ pounds would not feed him during the night. The result was a lot of crying for he was a large and hungry baby and I was too ignorant to insist on him being fed.

As we had no home Joe would have liked us to stay at Courtfield, but his mother made it abundantly clear that I was *persona non grata*. Hotels under wartime conditions did not care to take babies, so after a good deal of moving around it was with considerable relief that I managed to buy a cottage in Tewkesbury for £1,000, No. 4 St Mary's Lane. Patrick and I had a home at last and we found many kind, friendly people in lovely old Tewkesbury. My father-in-law sent me beds and useful bits and pieces from Courtfield, and he also helped me about getting a mortgage. I went to local sales and bought some quite nice furniture very cheaply.

The Purefoys – he was the vicar of the Abbey – were very kind, allowing me to push the pram around their lovely garden and the Abbey grounds; and we had the ham – a hundred-acre meadow – down by the Severn, and many other lovely walks. Really our cottage proved a great success.

When my brother Oliver returned after three-and-a-half years as a prisoner of war he was in a bad way. He came to stay with me and I was glad to be able to look after him. Food was still very scarce, and poor Oliver, who had been starved for years, would eat up our week's ration in one meal! Kind friends often brought one egg (a great luxury) or a tiny bit of butter or a rasher of bacon to help feed him. Our grocer also was sympathetic and when his shop was empty often produced a surprise from under the counter.

Best of all, there was a home for Joe to come to when the War ended in 1945. Our second son, Oliver John, was born there on Sunday 28 July 1946. I was in labour most of the night and about 6.30 in the morning Joe fetched the district nurse and then took himself off to Mass to pray for us. The baby arrived at 8.20 while he was away. A beautiful pink-and-white baby, he was always so good, sleeping the clock round, and not crying at all. Patrick, then three, amused our friends who came to enquire if he had a baby brother. 'No', he would say. 'Oh, a little sister then?' 'No.' A wondering pause, then, 'We have an Oliver John'.

At his father's invitation Joe and I and our two small sons came to live at Courtfield in 1947 and stayed there for three years. The house divided very pleasantly: we had the Georgian front consisting of hall, drawing-room and dining-room. Charles, who was then starting to have trouble with his legs, had his bed moved downstairs to his 'den', and Chris had the octagon hall, small drawing-room and library. We used to visit each other in the evenings and Charles seemed greatly to enjoy the children. He often said to me, 'two things make me happy in my old age. One is that Patrick is a boy, and the other that you like this place.'

Joe set up in practice as a barrister on the Oxford circuit with chambers in Gloucester, where he went daily. I am very glad now that I had the opportunity of getting to know my father-in-law a little during the last year of his life. He could so easily have been unpleasant to me, who, until my annulment came through, can hardly have been his ideal of a daughter-in-law. On the contrary he was most kind and we genuinely liked and respected each other.

Eventually, as his legs got worse, we prevailed on Charles to get an invalid chair in which Joe often pushed him around the garden or along the drive. He was a kindly, sweet old man and we were all very sorry when he caught a chill in church on a bitterly cold Sunday in January 1948 and died a week later, on the 30th. Some Blue Nuns from London came to nurse him and assured us that it was only because they were nuns, that the devoted Kitty, Lily and Rose would allow them near him! Chris was away in London, but came down for his funeral, and his burial, beside Rita, in the Hermitage. She was furious when she found he had left her only £5,000 in his will and even got her sister to write a rude letter to Joe about it, affirming that 'they blushed at the name of Vaughan'.

Our twins, Richard Herbert and Thomas Francis, were born just a few months later at Courtfield, on Friday 28 May 1948. Richard arrived without much trouble at 10.30 a.m., but Tommy, owing to his exceptionally large head, was very difficult and was not born until 1 p.m. Joe was again absent, having gone to his chambers in Gloucester. He was, I think, unable to face the big moments of life and spent a long time on the bottle at this particular juncture, which should have been a very happy occasion. But I was fortunate in other ways: for one, I had a splendid monthly nurse, Sister Paterson, who went the rounds of old Catholic families. She ruled with a rod of iron, often would not allow Joe in, but took the greatest care of me and the babies, never leaving them for the first forty-eight hours as Tommy needed continual attention.

My troubles really began that year – or perhaps even the day – of Charles' death: Joe, always a hearty drinker, took a most alarming turn. For days he neither dressed nor shaved, wandering about the house day and night in his grandfather's long blue greatcoat, making rambling incoherent speeches and remarks. Gradually, I noticed a dirty track forming across the carpet in the hall that led to the cellar door; he was up and down the dusty cellar stone steps drinking his way through his father's considerable cellar. Too impatient to pull corks, he took to cracking the tops off the bottles and pouring the wine down his throat. His father had been a restraining influence and now he was gone – Joe had the bit between his teeth and was determined to kick over the traces. It was a nightmare. Alcoholism is a terrible disease. The most difficult thing is to get people, the sufferer included, to recognise this. There is some similarity to diabetes in which the body is unable to deal with sugar; in dipsomania it is unable to deal with alcohol. The Jekyll-and-Hyde situation which develops, causing complete personality changes, is one of the most frightening aspects of all. Joe's doctors were not told the truth and usually he could persuade them and his 'friends' that I was impossible, 'a jumped-up jade', and there was nothing wrong with him. He would not admit to being an alcoholic and assured himself, and those of our friends whose help I sought, that I was making a fuss about nothing and that he could perfectly well control his drinking – which of course he was totally unable to do.

There really is no cure for alcoholism except complete abstinence and this Joe could not face. He did go to expensive clinics and have different treatments from time to time, but had no real intention of giving up drink. It was during a stay in one of these places, having treatment from Dr Joshua Bierer, that he wrote to me saying he was thinking of selling Courtfield – he probably got the idea from his mother who was always saying how much she disliked the place. For my part I was ready to acquiesce to anything that might do him good. Finally he sold it to the Mill Hill Missionary Society which his great-uncle the Cardinal had founded in 1866. It seemed like the spiritual side of the family taking over. They bought the house, church, park and a few cottages for £14,000. We kept the land. In some ways Joe was very sad to sell. He told me he cried one day driving down Cats Hill and looking across the river to Courtfield.

We moved to Bourton-on-the-Water, but things, alas, were no better. After two years we moved again to London where we bought No. 2 Cambridge Place, just off Victoria Road, in Kensington. Patrick and Oliver first went to Hill House, Knightsbridge, a small school

168

run by Colonel Stuart Townsend, where Prince Charles later went, and subsequently to St Philip's, a Catholic day school in Hereford Square; the twins went to Lady Eden's School just down the road from where we lived.

Joe inherited a lot of money under the Pope family settlement when his Aunt Clare died in 1950 and happily set to, drinking and gambling his way through this, helped by friends and spongers who were one of the greatest difficulties I had to contend with. His mother was another – visiting her usually triggered off a bout. He became increasingly bitter towards me and moved out to a flat in 109 Onslow Square and we saw little of him. Cruises, trips abroad and such diversions recommended by his mother and different doctors did him no good. I once got telegrams from the hospital at St Helena telling me he was dangerously ill with alcoholic poisoning. His iron constitution as usual pulled him through. The children and I were left to get on as best we could on the very small income allowed us. Once, in a dream, my mother-in-law said to me, 'Do the best you can with what you've got, and let God take care of the rest'. In real life she never said anything of the sort! Only prayer, the help of God, and the love of my darling children enabled me to survive this most difficult time.

GLEN WYE

At last my good solicitor advised a legal separation in order to make some financial settlement for me and the children and to try to safeguard the next fortune Joe would inherit when his Aunt Alice died. This also enabled me to buy Glen Wye from the trustees – the second best move I've made in my life – and to re-establish the family there in 1955. We were much helped by Miss Helen MacMahon, 'Mackie', a tall, distinguished-looking Irish lady who came as a mother's help and became a valued friend and counsellor – thus does God dispose things in the tapestry of life.

Dear old Rose came out of retirement to cook for us, so we had delicious food – and Nanny Biddy from Youghal, who had known me as a child, looked after Patrick and Oliver. She was our nanny for several years, a kind good person and a most devout Catholic. She adored the twins and was probably even better with babies than older children. She loved taking them all for frequent little visits to the Blessed Sacrament. We sorely missed her when she had to leave suddenly for a serious operation. Years later, she and her sister came to live in the flat over my antiques shop in Ross and enjoyed helping with that until they both got too old and had to retire to Nazareth House.

Glen Wye, when we came to live there in 1955, was dreadfully dilapidated inside and out. There was no garden and we spent our first year clearing brambles and scrub, cutting useless sycamore trees and clearing a muddy swamp to make a paddling pool for the children. Old Jack Gomery, who worked all his life on the estate – as had his father before him – did most of this. Digging out the swamp was exceptionally hard and dirty work which occasioned some of his choicest language – and he was famous for his vocabulary. (Later, as the children grew, we turned this into a pretty little swimming-pool which gives us all, grandchildren included now, a lot of pleasure.) Jack was a great character and well known in the neighbourhood. In his younger days he was given to fisticuffs and frequent overindulgence in 'scrumpy' and his language could be pretty lurid when annoyed. I do remember a tutor staying here for my sons' holidays who overheard an early morning serenade below his window when Jack must have run into some snag while digging out the old swamp to make the pool, which caused him to say at breakfast 'I don't think you should allow the boys to associate with that man – you can have no idea of the language he uses'. I assured him I did know, but added that I also knew Jack would willingly lay down his life for any one of my children. Such characters, always rare, no longer exist today. He loved the family and was a great worker who had no time for 'them scampers' as he called fellows who dodged their work. He had a colourful turn of phrase and once told me he was as 'independent as an elf'! He drove an ancient and evil-tempered donkey – usually at full gallop – in a small, green spring cart and always in a curious kneeling, crouching position. This donkey, Benjamin, used to bring him to work, take him up and down Coppit Hill to Goodrich, occasionally to Ross, and usually got him safely home when the scrumpy had proved too much! Once, when a pretty girl of whom Jack approved because she sometimes went out ferreting with him, got engaged and brought her fiancé to stay, he was heard muttering, 'An' what are our boys about letting a nice girl like that slip through their fingers?' Alas, they are both now dead. Jack was found in his cottage among his beloved dogs, having apparently suffered a heart attack as he had been perfectly well the day before; and the lovely girl we were all so fond of was tragically killed in a train crash in Mexico.

We were lucky enough to find a wonderful and truly artistic

German stonemason, Hans Franzen, a prisoner of war who settled in this country and for twenty years came to us for a month or two every year and so gradually built up an architecturally beautiful garden. He came originally from the stone quarries in Germany and certainly was a genius with stone who could copy any plan I drew and often improve on it. He was a joy to work with and used smilingly to say, 'you're the head and I'm the hans'.

The children went to our local Goodrich village school until old enough to go on to their preparatory schools. They learnt nothing but good from Miss Evans, the small, forceful Welsh headmistress, who ruled strictly and was by no means popular with all the parents; but she taught her charges a decent standard of behaviour and a love of music, drama and singing. A most perceptive and humorous person, she often helped me by having the twins to stay when I had to cope with difficulties with Joe. I was very fond of and owe a great deal to her. May she rest in peace.

Our priest at Courtfield was not pleased that I allowed my children to join in the daily prayers at school, which consisted of the Lord's Prayer, a prayer for their daily work and singing a hymn. He came to see me and threatened me with excommunication, shouting, 'They'll lose their Faith, they'll lose their Faith'. I replied that if the Faith was so easily lost, it would not be worth having. He was very angry, but I felt it was much better not to single them out by segregation to the playground where they would only tell each other dirty stories while prayers were going on!

Patrick and Oliver went on to Farleigh House in Hampshire, a Catholic preparatory school run by Jocelyn Trappes-Lomax who proved a good friend. Patrick went on to Stonyhurst and was the sixth generation of his family to be educated there. He was good at sports and won the long jump and Victor Ludorum for juniors in 1959. Oliver and the twins were sent to the Dominican junior school at Llanarth, an old Herbert home in Monmouthshire, where they were very happy. Tommy was Head Boy towards the end of his time there. As the school was only twenty miles away it was easy to have them home at half-term and they often brought friends with them. Later they went on to Laxton, the Dominican senior school in Northamptonshire.

The children and I never ceased to pray for Joe's recovery, though most people thought it hopeless. A doctor who treated him for several years told me that only a miracle could cure him, but I never quite gave up hope. In Dublin once I took a tram out to Glasnevan and prayed earnestly at Mat Talbot's grave – he had conquered this terrible affliction. I also prayed to St Rita of Cascia who knew all about it as she had had a husband with the same trouble. No one who has not loved and tried to live with an alcoholic can possibly know the heartbreak and horror of it. And, of course, we prayed to Eliza and all the good and holy Vaughans. Eventually, the 'miracle' happened. Joe dropped all doctors and cures and, to his everlasting credit, never touched a drink for the last fifteen years of his life.

Re-creating Glen Wye, house and garden, proved an absorbing interest for us all. The boys loved it and spent a happy childhood on their ancestral acres – something they could not have had anywhere else in the world. Perhaps also, in some mysterious, unknown way, it contributed to Joe's recovery. The spirit of his forebears must have helped him in what was surely a heroic exercise of will. He became a kind, companionable husband and a wonderful father to our sons, able to romp and play and enter into their amusements.

We travelled extensively, motoring all over Europe; Joe was an excellent driver and the ideal travelling companion; we saw many countries – Mexico, Morocco, Malta, Greece, Turkey and the lovely islands of the Aegean Sea – yet we always returned with joy to our beloved Glen Wye and found it more beautiful and satisfying than anywhere else. From time to time we took some of the children with us.

In these years we altered the house considerably, literally turning it back to front: building a Regency porch and a garden veranda; enlarging existing rooms and moving the staircase to make a hall; and all the time the garden was becoming more beautiful and the trees and shrubs we'd planted, like our children, were growing up. Joe took a keen interest in improving the place and was happy to be back at Courtfield. He really was a very 'good' man. Perhaps unfortunate influences in early life had contributed to his terrible disease, and as he told me was often badly advised. He was kind and affectionate and we had happy times together. He probably suffered from the cloistral weight of family tradition and an over-strict Catholic upbringing. I sometimes said to him, 'you swallowed the whole thing, hook, line and sinker, and it's given you indigestion ever since!'.

His mother's defection undoubtedly had a devastating effect on Joe. He had adored her. Knowing this, there is a rather tragic irony to these optimistic verses by Kate Riley, the author of *Tales of Old Ross*.

They were written for his twenty-first birthday, not so long after her flight from his life:

To Joseph Herbert Vaughan of Courtfield, March 15th 1931

Across the vale, the happy bells are ringing,
The hills are flushing with the touch of spring,
The river smiles – so gladsome in its flowing –
And in our hearts a joyous song we sing!

For with the Spring new life for you is dawning,
Upon your way you reach another state,
And those who love you stand with eyes of yearning
To watch you step with hope into your heritage.

Your waking hours you'll spend 'mid scenes of beauty
Where peace and sweet content together dwell,
(The homeland you have learnt to prize so dearly)
With faithful hearts to guard and serve you well.

Where royal Henry's infant head once rested
Your nights will pass in dreams of happy days,
And his brave soul will pour a benediction
To give you faith and courage, and your strength to raise.

So firmly stand and face the years before you,
And live a life as valiant and as true,
As did your forebears – holding up their banner –
For 'Duw a Digon' surely speaks through them to you.

Joe was never really free of his mother's influence – though one could not say that he loved her, he burnt her portrait in one of his drunken fits – and their relationship always struck me as unhealthy. For her part he was an extension of herself – she was determined never to let him go and she did not, until her death on 19 October 1961. She would, I believe, have hated whoever he married – and she had a very deadly hatred.

This could account for Joe's unkindness to me and the children; he kept us very short of money when we lived in London. I frequently had to sell things to buy food and clothes for the boys. Later, when I asked him about this, all he would say was that he had been badly advised. The mainspring of his life had been broken when his adored mother went off, and ever afterwards he was incomplete. Kitty, who nursed him through a delirium in 1930 following appendicitis, not long after Chris' defection with Don Gregory, told me he used to cry out, 'I want to die, my Mother's left me'. After he gave up drinking and came to live with me and the children at Glen Wye he certainly became calmer and happier and, as I said, started to take an interest in creating the garden and looking after the estate, especially the woodlands, some of which he leased to the Forestry Commission; and Thomas Wood and the Windells he cut and replanted. Very fond of racing, he was a member of Cheltenham and Chepstow and we went to every meeting; we also played a lot of bridge and entertained a good deal.

Joe took his place on local councils and committees, became President of our Goodrich branch of the Conservative party, and attended all the Wye Fishery Board meetings. He was also an active member of the Country Landowners Association, as a letter from the Regional Secretary, Mr Dent, dated 24 June 1968 shows:

Dear Major Vaughan,

I cannot let your retirement from the C.L.A. Council pass without a personal word of thanks for all that you have done for the Branch during the past twenty years. During that time you have been a most regular attender at meetings and your reports have always been comprehensive and lucid.

Although your retirement was not marked by any ceremony I do just want you to know that your valuable contribution has been greatly appreciated, not only by myself but by all our members in Herefordshire.

Yours sincerely,
Vernon Dent

Occasionally Joe spoke of dying and said how he would hate to have a long illness, but would like a day or two to prepare himself for death. He also said that, should I die before him, he'd move to Cheltenham, into a suite at the Queens Hotel from which he could amble down to the bridge club, see his friends, and go racing.

As it turned out he had a sudden death in bed after a beautiful summer Sunday here with Mass and Holy Communion in the morning, friends to lunch, and the evening spent planning our trip to America, to start a week hence. He had arranged that we should fly out and pay visits to some of his American relations, returning by sea on the SS *France*, and he was particularly looking forward to enjoying the excellent French cooking on board.

When he came to bed he remarked what a delightful day we'd had and how he'd appreciated our friends' enjoyment of the garden and Glen Wye. A fence in the reservoir paddock needed mending and he asked me to remind him to ring Jeremy (our agent) about it in the morning. These were his last words: about 4 a.m. he gave a convulsive jump which woke me and I put my hand out and asked if he was all right. Getting no reply, I switched on the light and saw him with his head thrown back and mouth open. Somehow deep inside me I realised this was death and for some seconds I remained quietly beside him, my mind saying, 'We have been through so much together – we can take this too'. Then I ran for Richard, crying, 'Come quickly, something has happened to Daddy'. On seeing his father, Richard immediately telephoned the doctor and then I rang Courtfield for a priest. Both arrived within fifteen minutes and the priest administered the last rites while Joe was still alive though deeply unconscious.

He had suffered a colossal cerebral haemorrhage and died in about thirty-five minutes. Richard, Dr McMinn, Father Hurley and myself watched his spirit depart. This was on Monday 14 August 1972, the eve of the feast of the Assumption. His funeral service took place at Courtfield on Thursday 17 August, our four sons carrying his coffin up to the Hermitage where he was buried beside his father and sister. I had a granite Celtic cross erected and, after his name and dates, the words 'Loving and greatly Loved' inscribed. On his memorial card were St Thomas More's lovely words from his last letter to his daughter Meg, 'Pray for me and I will pray for you and all your friends that we may merrily meet in Heaven'.

On the reverse side I put a seventeenth-century poem by George Wither (1588–1667), 'A Widow's Hymn':

> How near me came the hand of Death,
> When at my side he struck my dear,
> And took away the precious breath
> Which quicken'd my belovèd peer!
> How helpless am I thereby made!
> By day how grieved, by night how sad!
> And now my life's delight is gone,
> – Alas! how am I left alone!
>
> The voice which I did more esteem
> Than music in her sweetest key,
> Those eyes which unto me did seem
> More comfortable than the day;
> Those now by me, as they have been,
> Shall never more be heard or seen;

But what I once enjoy'd in them
Shall seem hereafter as a dream.

Lord! keep me faithful to the trust
Which my dear spouse reposed in me:
To him now dead preserve me just
In all that should perform'd be!
For though our being man and wife
Extendeth only to this life,
Yet neither life nor death should end
The being of a faithful friend.

I also wrote some verse, describing my feelings at Joe's death:

You left us when the leaf was green
early upon a summer day
unexpected, unforeseen
folded your wings and slipped away.

My darling friend of thirty years
my own, my sweet, my only Joe,
in agony too deep for tears
I held your hand and watched you go.

And now you rest in God's good care
but leave me lonely here below:
O comfort me against despair
until we meet in Heaven my Joe.

And wander in that garden fair
with myriad golden souls aglow
till God's own Son shall greet us there
and show us perfect love to know.

THE PRESENT GENERATION

Patrick joined Knight Frank & Rutley in their Hereford office after leaving school and remained there for several years before going to London and working in their country house department. Later he left the firm and set up on his own as a property developer, and did well until the property market crashed in 1974.

His father made the estate over to Patrick on his marriage in 1971, thereby hoping to escape some death duty, but alas this did not work out as Joe died suddenly a year later. (The requisite interval being seven years, full death duty had to be paid.) Patrick married Lorna Findlay, daughter of John Findlay, a Hertfordshire farmer, on 5 February 1971 at St Mary's, Cadogan Street. They have three sons and two daughters. He recently sold Waterscross Farm on the other side of the river and used the money to rebuild The Green, a romantic old stone-built farmhouse, where they spend weekends and holidays. Their other house is in Paultons Square, Chelsea. Making the most of these two homes occasions a lot of motoring up and down.

Richard went to Cirencester Agricultural College in 1967 and took his National Diploma in Agriculture in 1969 and now farms at Huntsham Court, a 400-acre farm which has been in the family since 1650. He married on 30 October 1981, at Courtfield, Susan Kania, eldest daughter of Mr T. J. Kania. They now have two darling little daughters, Clementine Mary and Alice Louise. Oliver went into Lloyds but soon got bored with such a sedentary life and left after a year to start his own discotheque. We thought this a chancy way of life, but Joe, more optimistic than I was about it, told him to work hard and make a success. He also lent him £1,000 with which he bought an old van and equipment and toured the country playing at private parties and dances.

That was in 1966. From such small beginnings his enterprise and hard work have certainly succeeded. Today Oliver and his brother Thomas, who joined him in 1967, run Juliana's Discotheques, a worldwide concern. A further and exciting chapter was added to the family history when, in May 1983, Oliver and Thomas Vaughan brought their company to the stock market with Morgan Grenfell underwriting a sale by tender of 1.35 million new shares at a minimum price of 225p, thus valuing Juliana's at £12.4 million with a total of 5.5 million shares then in issue. The shares, which went on sale on 1 June (Derby Day), caught the imagination of the City and were five-times over-subscribed. Hard work and staying power have brought them where they are today, though they always had imagination and vision and were cheerfully prepared to work that little bit extra hard. It's all a far cry from their small but enthusiastic beginning in 1966, playing at friends' dances themselves and driving their old van and equipment all over the country. They now run discotheques in over a hundred of the world's great international hotels – Hilton, Hyatt, Sheraton, Four Seasons, etc. Their firm that started with a 'one-man band' now employs around 180 people. The original Travelling Discotheque is carried on by a young man, William Bartholomew, who appears to give satisfaction wherever he goes.

Courtfield and the Vaughans

Tommy married, on 15 September 1979, Sarah Harding-Rolls, only daughter of Squadron Leader Michael Harding-Rolls – and distantly related, for in 1830 John Francis Vaughan had married Eliza Rolls, Sarah's great-great-aunt. They had a charming country wedding at St Cenedlon's church, Rockfield, Monmouth. Their first child, a daughter, Sophia Henrietta, was born in New York on 14 March 1983 – so now we have an American Vaughan again.

On 26 October 1983 Oliver announced his engagement to Diana (Boo) Martineau, youngest daughter of Commander and Mrs Philip Martineau of Moses Hill Farm, Haslemere, Surrey and they were married on 16 June 1984 in the beautiful old church of St Margaret's, Fernhurst, Sussex by the Rev. Clifford Hankins, assisted by Father Richard Incledon. Oliver's brother Richard was best man and Patrick's little daughter Blanche one of the bridesmaids. This most happy occasion took place in glorious weather and all the family and about 250 guests attended. The reception in the beautiful gardens of Moses Hill could not have been more enjoyable. This was – of course – followed by a really delightful Juliana's dance which went on till 3 a.m. The marquee was decorated with beautiful flowers, helium balloons with Olly and Boo on them festooned the ceiling, and champagne flowed. I danced with each of my four sons and thoroughly enjoyed the occasion.

The bridal couple went off on the Orient Express to honeymoon in Venice and Florence, before settling in Hong Kong and Singapore amid their many Juliana's interests. Oliver looks after his 'empire' for all of South-East Asia and Australia; Tommy lives in New York and deals with America and Canada, while the London end of the business is in the capable hands of Nick Irens who joined them in 1969. There has even been a book written about them. They bring to my mind great-great-uncle Bernard, who once said that if he were only a street-crossing sweeper his crossing would be so beautifully kept that people would exclaim 'see Vaughan's crossing!' The present generation appear to be as active and enthusiastic in their chosen professions, and just as fond of travelling, as their splendid nineteenth-century forebears were in their work for the Catholic Church.

Courtfield itself, transformed from our family home into the Mill Hill ecclesiastical establishment, which gives retreats, conferences, marriage guidance, missionary vocations, etc., to a large number of people, is carrying on the family love of Christ and His Church which so many generations of Vaughans have implanted in the unique atmosphere here. The church, often full to overflowing, where parents bring their children and often small babies, must rejoice Eliza's heart as she and all the good and holy Vaughans look on from Heaven.

Epilogue

As funerals go, the author of this book, Mary Vaughan (1910–89) was given a relatively happy one. Having led a very active, full life that was not always easy – and one that ended with considerable suffering – she had not wanted people to be unduly sad at her departure. She had apparently died in complete faith and with some anticipation of the unknown excitements in store for her in the next world.

Bishop Mahon, Father Paul Crowley (Rector at Courtfield) and six other priests from the Mill Hill Missionary Society officiated at a family funeral mass, held in the Chapel at Courtfield, which was full to overflowing with family and friends.

As they had at their father's funeral (but this time also assisted by her eldest grandson, Jerome) her four sons bore the coffin from the Chapel up the hill to the Hermitage, where she was buried beside the body of her husband, exactly seventeen years to the day after his own burial. Both graves are now marked by a simple, shared, Celtic cross.

In introducing today's generation of grandchildren and the current whereabouts of the four continuing branches of the Vaughan family, I begin with further references to the author's four sons and their respective families, in descending order.

Patrick and Lorna Vaughan, the author's eldest son and daughter-in-law, have five children – three boys and two girls. Their principal family residence is The Green, a wonderful, rambling, former Herefordshire farmhouse, with an abundance of detached, tile-roofed, stone-built barns. It is set in the most beautiful and tranquil corner of the Courtfield Estate, overlooking a secluded and private reach of the River Wye. They also have a London home in Chelsea.

In age order, Patrick and Lorna's children start with Theresa (17), who attended Amanda Hanbury's Kindergarten school in London, followed by New Hall boarding school. She is currently in her final year at Francis Holland in London.

Jerome (16) attended Westminster Cathedral Choir School and is currently at Ampleforth.

Charles (14) also attended Westminster Cathedral Choir School and is currently at Ampleforth.

John (12) attended Cameron House (then called The Learning Tree) followed by Gilling Castle, in preparation for Ampleforth.

Blanche (9) also attended Cameron House and is currently scheduled to start at St Mary's, Ascot.

Oliver and Boo (Diana) Vaughan, the author's second son and daughter-in-law, have two children – both boys. Their principal residence is a London house in Kensington. They will also be using the author's former home, Glen Wye, in something of a caretaker capacity, pending the majority of Jerome (or later agreed date) to whom Glen Wye will one day belong, following its reversion to the Courtfield Estate at the time of the author's death. (It brought considerable happiness and comfort to our mother in her declining months to know that Oliver and Boo would be taking over her much loved home and garden.)

Oliver and Boo's eldest boy, Jamie, is three and their second son, Jeremy, is one.

Oliver and Boo also have a daughter, Joanna Eu (19), by informal adoption, who, athough she does not carry the Vaughan name, is and has always been treated and considered as a daughter in all other respects.

Richard and Sue Vaughan, the author's third son and daughter-in-law, are the only Vaughans of their generation to have been married in the Chapel at Courtfield. They have three children – two girls and a boy. Their historic and romantic residence is Huntsham Court Farm – the principal farm of the Courtfield Estate, that occupies an enviable position in a horseshoe of the River Wye, immediately below Symonds Yat Rock – a famous beauty spot, commanding spectacular views into five counties.

Between them, Richard and Sue have developed their farm to include a much visited and immensely interesting 'Open Farm' that preserves and shows rare breeds of numerous domestic farm animals and birds, plus the history of old Herefordshire cider-making – all in an exceptionally beautiful rural environment, offering extensive woodland and riverside walks.

Richard and Sue's children are Clemmie (7), followed by Alice (6), both of whom are currently attending St Joseph's Convent School in Ross. Their third child, Charlie or Joseph (1), is often called just 'the boy' in order to avoid the confusion of apparently having two names – depending on which parent you talk to!

Tommy and Sarah Vaughan, the author's fourth son (a twin with Richard) and daughter-in-law, have two daughters. They have two homes, one a London house in Kensington, and the other Morgan's Run, in New Hampshire, USA. The latter residence is a rambling confusion of traditional and contemporary New England architecture, set in its own land, in an elevated south-facing position, with expansive views over rolling New Hampshire forest to Mt Kearsarge and Mt Sunapee. The author had twice been to stay at Morgan's Run and on her last visit gave Tommy and Sarah a native Copper Maple tree to mark their sixth wedding anniversary. She also participated in and personally supervised its careful planting in the sloping field immediately below the house, circumscribed by the driveway.

It is now known as 'The Granny Tree', having thus been christened by Sophia (6), the eldest of Tommy and Sarah's two daughters, who has so far attended Brick Church School in New York; Buckingham, Browne and Nichols in Cambridge, Massachussets; and currently Cameron House in London.

Their youngest daughter, Georgianna, is three. Both girls were born in New York and have dual American/British citizenship.

Although our mother may yet have further – at this moment unthought of – grandchildren (and hopefully, in time, a host of great-grandchildren!) whom she will never know, thanks to the scholarly book she has left behind, they at least will have a chance to know something of her and their family history.

It will be the work of some future generation Vaughan to update and continue this history, if the family merit it and if they so desire.

Thomas Vaughan

The Vaughan Descent

I **Adam ap Herbert** (according to the Heralds) **Lord of Llanllywel**. He *m.* Christian. dau. of L. of Gwaryn Ddn, Lord of Wern-ddn.

II **Jenkin ap Adam of Werb-ddn**. He *m.* Gwenllian, dau. of Sir Aron ap Rhys of Bledri, Knight of Rhodes, Lord of Cilsand.

III **Gwilyn ap Jenkin of Wern-ddn** (jure ixoris) of Cefn-ddyglwyd, eldest son, Master Sergeant of Abergavenny, 1345–77. He *m.* Gwenllian, dau. of Howel Veyhan ap Howel ap Torwerth of Cefnddyglwyd.

IV **Thomas ap Gwllym of Perthir**. Mon. Fourth son of Gwilym ap Jenkins, alias Herbert of Gwardinee. He *m.* Maud, dau. of Sir John Morley of Llansantffrid. Mon. and died in 1483 leaving issue, of whom the fourth son,

V **Howell ap Thomas ap Gwillam ap Perthyr** *m.* Catherine, dau. of Grono ap Ivor and had issue, of whom the third son,

VI **William Vychan**, or William the yr. resided at Llanrothal not far from Perthyr. He *m.* Maud, dau. of John Pye of the Mynd Park, Hereford and had issue, three sons and three daughters, of whom the second son,

VII **Thomas Vaughan**, *m.* Ann, dau. of Lewis John Gwilyn and had issue of three sons, of whom the eldest,

VIII **James Vaughan of Llangattock-veibron-Abel**, *m.* Sibille (Sybil) dau. and heiress of John Gwilym of Gillow, Hereford, Lord of Welsh Bicknor, 1563. By his wife Catherine, dau. of Richard Mytton, he had issue of three sons of whom the second son,

IX **William Vaughan of Courtfield** and of Clifford Park, Lord of Welsh Bicknor, *m.* in 1570 Jane, dau. and heiress of Richard Clarke of Wellington, Hereford and *d.* 1601 having had issue five sons and three daughters, of whom the eldest son,

X **John Vaughan of Courtfield** and of Clifford Park, Hereford, Lord of Welsh Bicknor, *b.* 1575, *m.* Anne, dau. of Richard Lingen of Hereford and *d.* 1639, leaving with other issue an eldest son. He *m.* 2ndly Elizabeth Powell of Whitchurch.

XI **Richard Vaughan of Courtfield, Lord of Welsh Bicknor**, 1600–97, *m.* 1st in 1631 Bridget Wigmore of Lucton, dau. of William Wigmore, and had issue two sons and three daughters. Richard the eldest son relinquished his inheritance to his brother John. Theresa *m.* Joseph Griffin and Mary and Anne died unmarried. Richard *m.* 2ndly in 1675 Agatha, dau. of John Berrington of Cowarne Court, Hereford, later of Little Malvern; they had issue, one son, two daughters. This son John, *b.* 24 April 1676, inherited frrom his half-brother John Vaughan of Huntsham, who was childless. This John of Huntsham *m.* 7 September 1659 Mary Vaughan, dau. and heiress of John Vaughan of Over Ross by his wife Dame Mary Cholke, widow of Sir Alexander Cholke and of John Rudhall of Rudhall, Hereford and dau. of Sir William Pitt of Strathfield. Vaughan of Over Ross was a different family descended from a twelfth-century chieftain Moreiddig Warwina and bore his arms: sable, three Saxon's head proper. Mary brought her husband the manors of Ruardean and of Cleiro with other estates in Gloucestershire and Radnorshire, greatly augmenting the property and as there was no issue of this marriage it all passed to her husband's younger half-brother and heir. John Vaughan of Huntsham *d.* 27 March 1721.

XII **John Vaughan of Courtfield, Lord of the manors of Welsh Bicknor and Ruardean.** He was *b.* 24 April 1676, and *m.* 1stly in 1698 Catherine, dau. of Sir John Curzon of Waterperry, Oxon. Marriage settlement 18 June 1698, issue one dau. Mary, *b.* 6 October 1699. She *m.* Rowland Bartlett of Hill End, Wares on 23 Nov. 1723 and died 11 May 1727. Not recorded when Catherine died, but John married 2ndly on 24 July 1705 his kinswoman in the paternal line, Elizabeth, dau. of Philip Jones of Llanarth Court, Mon. and had issue, four sons and one daughter: John (*b.* 1707), Richard (*b.* 1708), Philip (*b.* 1715, *d.* 1734), William (*b.* 8 Dec. 1716), Theresa (*b.* 1713 and *m.* Edward Weld of Lulworth on 15 Oct. 1740). Richard and William fought for Bonnie Prince Charlie in the Duke of Perthshire division at Culloden (1746), were subsequently outlawed and had the distinction of being excluded from the General Pardon of 1747. Richard *d.* 27 Nov. 1754.

XIII **John Vaughan Junr. of Courtfield**, *b.* 1707, *m.* 10 Aug. 1749 Catherine, dau. of James Cornewall of Buckland, Hereford, *d.* 21 Jan. 1780. Catherine *d.* 26 June 1778. They had no issue and were succeeded by his nephew William Vaughan, eldest son of Richard Vaughan and his Spanish wife Donna Francesca, dau. of Don Guillermo Fort-y-Magueire and Catalina Marquerez-y-Onel.

XIV **William Vaughan of Courtfield, Lord of the Manors of Welsh Bicknor and Ruardean**, *b.* 1738, *m.* 1768 Frances, dau. of John Turner of Hampstead, and *d.* 18 April 1796, aged 56, leaving issue one son, and one daughter who *m.* Thomas Watkins Davies, Major in the Royal Monmouthshire Militia and had an only child Cordelia Mary who *d.* unmarried *c.* 1867.

XV **William Michael Vaughan, Lord of the Manors of Welsh Bicknor and Ruardean**, DL, JP, High Sheriff of Monmouthshire 1833, *b.* 25 September 1781 *m.* 1stly, 22 Aug. 1803 Teresa Maria, dau. of Thomas Weld of Lulworth Castle, Dorset (sister of Cardinal Weld) and had issue four sons and three daughters: the eldest son John Francis, *b.* 2 July 1808, *m.* 1830 Eliza Rolls, *d.* 1880. William *b.* 10 Feb. 1807, *d.* on Palm Sunday 26 March 1809, William, Catholic Bishop of Plymouth *b.* 12 Feb. 1814 *d.* 25 Oct. 1902; Richard Joseph, a Jesuit, *b.* at Courtfield Nov. 1826, *d.* 19 March 1899; Edmund, Provincial of the Redemptorists, *b.* at Courtfield 26 Nov. 1827; Frances Angela, a Visitation nun, *b.* 22 April 1810, *d.* 7 April 1841; Teresa Mary, *b.* 22 March 1818 *m.* 1839 Thomas Weld Blundell of Ince Blundell. William Michael, *m.* 2ndly Lady Mary Anne, widow of Sir Thomas Gage, dau. of Valentine, 1st Earl of Kenmare. They *m.* in Rome in 1835. She *d.* 13 June 1840, aged 53, without issue. He *d.* 18 Oct. 1861.

XVI **John Francis Vaughan of Courtfield, Lord of the Manors of Welsh Bicknor and Ruardean**, DL Mon., JP Glos., Mon., Herefordshire, Radnorshire and County Mayo. Lt.-Col. of the Royal Monmouthshire Militia, *b.* 2 July 1808, *m.* 1stly 12 July 1830 Eliza Louise, dau. of John Rolls of The Hendry, Mon. at St Mary's, Bryanston Square, London and had issue nine sons and five daughters: Herbert *b.* at Gloucester 15 April 1832, *Cr.* Cardinal Vaughan 1893, *d.* 1903; Roger William *b.* 9 Jan. 1834, 2nd Archbishop of Sydney, Australia *d.* 1883; Kenelm, a priest *b.* 12 Aug. 1840, *d.* 1909; Joseph, a priest, OSB, Prior and founder of St Benedict's Abbey, Fort Augustus, *b.* 24 Sept. 1841, *d.* 1896; Francis Baynham of Courtfield, *b.* 18 March 1844, *d.* 1919; Bernard, priest and preacher, *b.* 20 Sept. 1847, *d.* 1922; Reginald of Glen Trothy *b.* 15 June 1849, *d.* 18—; John (Rt Rev.) Bishop of Sebastopol, DD, Rector of St Bedes, *b.* 24 Jan. 1853, *d.* 1925. Gwladys, a Visitation nun, *b.* 27 Feb. 1838, *d.* 1880; Helen Teresa, a Sister of Charity *b.* 7 Aug. 1839, *d.* 1861; Clare, a Poor Clare nun, *b.* 22 Feb. 1843, *d.* 1862; Margaret, *b.* 8 May 1851, *d.* unmarried 1936; John Francis *m.* 2ndly 15 Feb. 1860 Mary, dau. of Joseph Weld of Lulworth Castle, Dorset and had issue: Charles, *b.* 1860 *d.* an infant; Eliza, *d.* an infant; Mary *d.* 7 Dec. 1880. He *d.* 17 Dec. 1880.

XVII **Frances Baynham of Courtfield, Lord of the Manors of Welsh Bicknor and Ruardean**, DL, JP Hereford and Mon. Colonel of the Royal Monmouthshire Militia, Privy Chamberlain to His Holiness Pope Leo XIII and HH Pope Pius, Knight Commander of the Order of Pius, *b*. 18 March 1844, *m*. 16 Aug. 1871 Caroline Ruth, dau. of Dr Charles Alexander Pope of St Louis, USA. She *d*. 6 Nov. 1922, he *d*. 9 Sept. 1919, leaving issue three sons and three daughters: Charles Jerome of Courtfield, *b*. 30 Sept. 1873 in London; Herbert Joseph (Rev.) DD, *b*. 19 Nov. 1874. Francis John (Rt Rev.), *b*. 5 May 1877, Bishop of Menevia 1925–35; Clare, *b*. 1872, *m*. Leonard Colin Lindsay, FAS, of Deer Park, Devon; Mary, *b*. 1878, a nun BSB *d*. 9 April 1936; Alice, *m*. 2 July 1913 Wolstan Berkely of Spetchley, *d*. 1959.

XVIII **Charles Jerome Vaughan of Courtfield, Lord of the Manors of Welsh Bicknor and Ruardean**, OBE, FZS, DL 1933, JP Mon., JP Herefordshire 1923. High Sheriff of Herefordshire 1933. Chamberlain to HH Pope Pius XI, formerly Popes Benedict XV and Pius X. Major Royal Monmouthshire Engineers, formerly Lt 7th Dragoon Guards. Served in South African war and in World War I; *b*. 30 Sept. 1873, *m*. 3 March 1908 Florence Christine, dau. of Sir Cecil Edmund Lister-Kaye of Danby Grange, Yorkshire. She *d*. 19 Oct. 1961. He *d*. 30 Jan. 1948, leaving issue one son and one daughter: Joseph Herbert, *b*. 15 March 1910, *d*. 14 Aug. 1972. Henrietta Mary Christine, *b*. 24 Dec. 1908, d. Oct. 1918.

XIX **Joseph Herbert Vaughan of Courtfield, Lord of the Manors of Welsh Bicknor and Ruardean,** Major RE (M) SR. Served in World War II, ret. 1950. Barrister-at-Law, Inner Temple 1936, *b*. 15 March 1910, *edu*. Downside and Christ Church, Oxford, *m*. 15 July 1942 Mary Lavender, only dau. of Capt. Rowland Henry Tyssen Holroyd-Smyth of Ballynatray, Co Cork. He *d*. 14 Aug. 1972 leaving issue four sons: Patrick Charles More, *b*. 31 May 1943; Oliver John, *b*. 28 July 1946; Richard Herbert and Thomas Francis (twins), *b*. 28 May 1948.

THE VAUGHAN COAT OF ARMS

The Vaughan coat of arms, Party per pale azure and gules, three lions rampant argent, is the same as the Herberts (formally Jones) Proger of Wrnddu (extinct 1780) and Powel of Perthir (extinct 1750), all of the same illustrious tribe. The Vaughan Crest is a boy's head with a snake entwined round the neck, and their mottoes: 'Duw a Digon' is Welsh for 'God is enough', and 'simplices sient pueri, sagaces sient serpentes' may be translated 'guileless as children, wise as serpents'.

I am often asked the significance of the boy's head with the snake; there are several versions of this, but the story I like best is of the nurse leaving baby Vaughan on the grass on a fine summer's day while she goes to the house for a moment to collect something – imagine her horror on her return to see this large snake entwined around the infant's neck, and both apparently quite happy. Being a resourceful woman she did not panic but ran back to the house for a bowl of bread and milk which she placed close by and with indescribable relief watched the snake glide down to eat it. The butler, whom she had called to bring a poker, quickly put paid to it.

The Vaughans came from one of the oldest Roman Catholic families in England, said to be descendents of the Count of Vermandois who came over with William the Conqueror. Throughout their history they have fought for their Church and the State.

INDEX

Acland, Sarah, letter from
  husband, 121
  letter to son, 121
Acland, Wentworth Dyke, 121
  letter to wife, 121
Argentina, visit by Kenelm
  Vaughan, 97
Australian connections, 53–4,
  85–91

Barker, Bishop, 86
Bartlett, Mary (1699–1727),
  daughter of John Vaughan, 25
Bayneham, George, lessee of
  Welsh Bicknor Manor, 2
Baynham, Dame Joan, 23–4
  married John Vaughan of Cleiro
  and Kinnersley, 23
Baynham family connection, 23–4
Berrington, Agatha, married
  Richard Vaughan, 16
Blundell, Thomas Weld, married
  Teresa Vaughan, 42
Bodenham, Charles, 34, 35
  letter from William Vaughan, 37
Bolivia, visit by Kenelm Vaughan,
  98
Bookings, R. S., 138
Brazil, Herbert Vaughan's visit,
  70–1
Bristol Bridge rebuilt by John
  Vaughan, 32
Brydges, Margaret (c. 1600),
  married William Vaughan, 10

Catholic faith, atrocities during
  1600–1700, 19

help by Protestants, 15
lands confiscated, 15
severe trials (c. 1600), 11–12
Chile, Herbert Vaughan's visit,
  69–70
  Kenelm Vaughan's visit, 98
Clarke, Jane, married William
  Vaughan 1570, 10
Clobe, Mr, 139–40
Cooper, Bernard, 121
Coppit Hill road rebuilt, 35, 37, 38
Cornewall, Catherine, died 1778,
  married John Vaughan, 32
Cotton, George, lessee of Welsh
  Bicknor manor, 2
Courtfield
  dilapidated state, 36
  home of Vaughan family since
  1563, 1
  in 1796, 16–19
  sold to Mill Hill Missionary
  Society, 39
Crimean War, 50
Culloden, 27
Curzon, Catherine, married John
  Vaughan 1698, 18

de Vere, Aubrey, 64
Dent, Vernon, letter to Joe
  Vaughan, 174
Dublin Review, 73

Findlay, Lorna, married Patrick
  Vaughan, 176
Fingall, Lord, 51
Fitzherbert, Mrs, 37
Flaneford Priory, 8

189

196